White-Collar Power

Christopher Wheeler

WHITE-COLLAR POWER

Changing Patterns of Interest Group Behavior in Sweden

UNIVERSITY OF ILLINOIS PRESS
Urbana Chicago London

LIBRARY OF CONGRESS CATALOGING IN PUBLICATION DATA

Wheeler, Christopher, 1940–
  White-collar power.

  Includes bibliographical references.
  1. Tjänstemännens centralorganisation.   2. Trade-
unions—Sweden—Political activity—Case studies.
I.   Title.
HD8572.T5W53   329′.03′09485   75–15541
ISBN 0–252–00431–0

To Penny

Acknowledgments

I am indebted to a large number of people for their thoughtful and valuable assistance during the progress of this study. At Columbia University, Professor Lewis Edinger proved to be a model dissertation adviser, providing that essential blend of encouragement, insight, criticism, and discipline for which graduate students are grateful. Other members of my committee, Professors Dankwart Rustow, Mark Kesselman, and Harold Barger contributed in important ways to improving the manuscript.

M. Donald Hancock of the University of Texas at Austin, Thomas J. Anton of the University of Michigan, and Roy Adams of Hamilton University carefully read all or parts of the manuscript and thereby saved me from numerous errors.

Without the encouragement and support of a number of Swedish scholars, this study would have been impossible to execute. In particular I wish to thank Professor Olof Ruin of the University of Stockholm. He has followed this study from its inception, offering advice, encouragement, and criticism tempered by wit and charm. Hans Meijer, formerly chairman of the department at the University of Stockholm and now Rector of the University of Linköping, made a number of helpful suggestions at the initiation of the study. I am also grateful to Dr. Magnus Isberg, who took me under his wing during my years in Stockholm and taught me where to go in the Swedish bureaucracy to find what I wanted.

At the Central Organization of Salaried Employees, my debts are particularly numerous. Dr. Lennart Bodström, TCO's Director (whose Ph.D. is in political science), supported my work from the outset. In addition to reading and commenting on different drafts of the manuscript, he saw to it that doors often closed to scholars were opened. Åke Isling, head of TCO's educational division during my period of field work and now with the National Board of Education, provided invaluable assistance. His kindness toward an inexperienced researcher and his knowledge of the political process in Sweden were imposed upon far too often. I only hope the results of this study justify in some respect those demands.

Others at TCO who kindly read and commented upon the manuscript at various stages include: Ivar Asp, Christer Asplund, May-Britt Carlsson, Hans Engman, Lennart Forsebäck, Yngve Hjalmarsson, and Jan-Erik Nyberg.

I am also grateful to a number of interviewees in the case studies who took additional time from their own work to read and comment on the study. In several instances, their contributions were indeed substantial. A promise of anonymity prevents me from directly naming these people.

Credit for much of the merit of this book lies with these people; responsibility for the faults and errors which remain belong to me.

Financial assistance from the Fulbright Commission, the American-Scandinavian Foundation, and the Sverige-Amerika Stiftelsen supported my doctoral research. For postgraduate research I received support from the Cullister Funds of Beloit College and the Central Organization of Salaried Employees. A grant from the Social and Behavioral Science Research Committee of Beloit College helped defray part of the publishing costs of this study.

Thanks are also due to Mrs. Margaretha Svegander of the Central Organization of Salaried Employees, who demonstrated an uncanny ability to rapidly type in English one flawless draft after another, while maintaining her good humor.

Finally, let me thank my wife, Penny. Her editorial skill immeasurably improved the manuscript. Her patience and support made the book a reality.

Contents

Key to Abbreviations

AMS or Arbetsmarknadsstyrelsen—The Labor Market Board

CF or Civilingenjörsförbundet—The Swedish Association of Graduate Engineers

DACO or De Anställdas Centralorganisation—The Salaried Employees' Central Organization

FCF or Försvarets Civilförvaltning—The Office of the Comptroller for the Swedish Armed Forces

FOA or Försvarets Forskningsanstalt—The Research Institute of the Swedish National Defense

"gamla TCO" or Tjänstemännens Centralorganisation—The Public Employees' Central Organization

HAF or Handelsanställdas Förbund—The Federation of Swedish Commercial Employees

HTF or Handelstjänstemannaförbundet—The Swedish Union of Commercial Employees

LO or Landsorganisationen—Confederation of Swedish Trade Unions

LR or Lärarnas Riksförbund—Association of Secondary Teachers

SACO or Sveriges Akademikers Centralorganisation—The Swedish Confederation of Professional Associations

SAF or Svenska Arbetsgivareföreningen—The Swedish Employers' Association

SALF or Sveriges Arbetsledareförbund—The Swedish Union of Supervisors and Foremen

SF or Statsanställdas Förbund—State Employees Union

SI or Statsverkens Ingenjörsförbund—The Association of State-Employed Engineers of Sweden

SIF or Svenska Industritjänstemannaförbundet—The Swedish Union of Clerical and Technical Employees in Industry

SIFO or Svenska Institutet för Opinionsundersökningar—The Swedish Institute for Public Opinion Research

SK or Statstjänarkartellen—Civil Servants' Cartel (affiliated with the LO)

SN or Sveriges Statstjänstemannanämnd—The Swedish Civil Servants Association

SNAU or Statens Nämnd för Arbetstagares Uppfinningar—The National Board for Employees' Inventions

SÖ   or Skolöverstyrelsen—The National Board of Education
SR   or Statstjänstemännens Riksförbund—The National Confederation of
         Civil Servants
ST   or Statstjänstemannaförbundet—The Federation of Civil Servants
SUF   or Svenska Uppfinnareföreningen—The Association of Swedish In-
         ventors
TCO   or Tjänstemännens Centralorganisation—Central Organization of Sal-
         aried Employees
TR   or Trafiktjänstemännens Riksförbund—The Federation of Civil Ser-
         vants in Traffic Communications

Introduction

This study investigates the political activities of the Central Organization of Salaried Employees (Tjänstemännens Centralorganisation or TCO), a Swedish white-collar national trade union confederation.

My decision to study an interest group does not imply that I endorse the claim of some group theorists that the group approach tells us all there is to know about the politics of a particular system.[1] On the contrary, it is my opinion that the efforts to define, for example, governmental institutions as "official groups,"[2] or individuals as nothing more than combinations of group identifications, in fact reduce the utility of this approach to the study of politics. To define everything as group action is to define nothing. One has only stated in group language what could be stated just as well in other terms. As Harry Eckstein notes:

> Used by its more extravagant exponents, group theory tends indeed to become nothing more than a language, based on the plausible but arbitrary metaphysic that in politics the ultimately "real," the component alike of individuals and institutions, the unit which really "acts," and underlies ideas, is the group—not individuals, interactions, institutions, or the larger political system. Nothing can escape the clutches of this metaphysics if only one stretches it far enough, but precisely because of this nothing is illuminated by it either.[3]

In brief, it is my contention that the utility of the group approach to the study of politics is still great provided more modest claims are made on its

[1] As Arthur Bentley put it: "The great task in the study of any form of social life is the analysis of these groups; when the groups are adequately stated, everything is stated. When I say everything, I mean everything." *The Process of Government* (Evanston, Ill.: Principia Press, 1949), pp. 208–209. For Truman's adherence to these remarks see *The Governmental Process: Political Interests and Public Opinion* (New York: Knopf, 1960), especially pp. 48 and 51.

[2] Earl Latham, *The Group Basis of Politics* (Ithaca, N.Y: Cornell University Press, 1952), pp. 33–53.

[3] Harry Eckstein, *Pressure Group Politics: The Case of the British Medical Association* (London: Allen & Unwin, 1960), p. 153.

behalf. Thus when attempting to answer certain questions about the political process, I find the group approach a useful tool. Let me give several examples of how I will use it.

First of all, I will seek to determine the scope and limits of a particular group's ability to influence public policy in a particular political system. Second, to the limited extent it is possible from the study of a single interest group, I will discuss the implications of my findings for the democratic process in Sweden. Third, I will relate the question of system stability to the study of interest groups. (Harry Eckstein's provocative attempt to suggest reasons for system stability or instability by studying the relationship between authority patterns prevailing in nongovernmental organizations and those in governmental institutions is one important example of this fruitful use of the group approach.)[4] From my material I will suggest certain tentative conclusions in this regard which might profitably serve as starting points for additional research on the Swedish political system.

In the Swedish context the study of interest groups is particularly justified, owing to the thoroughgoing organization of the society. A staggering 79 percent of the population between the ages of eighteen and eighty, for example, belongs to one or more organizations.[5] This makes Sweden the most organized Western democratic society.[6] In choosing to study the Central Organization of Salaried Employees, a white-collar national trade union confederation, I was motivated by an interest in following the activities of a group whose importance continues to grow as the service sector of the economy expands. Moreover, this organization is the most highly developed white-collar confederation in the Western world (organizing 80 percent of the potentially organizable in the public sector and 70 percent in the private). One would think that if lessons are to be learned regarding future developments in other countries, the activities of this organization should provide at least some of them.

Having justified the study of an interest group in Swedish politics, let me turn to the major contributions I believe this study makes to political science.

[4] Harry Eckstein, "Appendix B: A Theory of Stable Democracy," in Harry Eckstein, *Division and Cohesion in Democracy: A Study of Norway* (Princeton: Princeton University Press, 1966), pp. 225–288.

[5] Svenska Institutet för Opinionsundersökningar AB, *Svenskt föreningsliv 1971: en tabellrapport indikator serien, S/I* (Stockholm: Svenska Institutet för Opinionsundersökningar, AB, 1971), p. 1.

[6] For data on England, Germany, and Italy, see Gabriel Almond and Sidney Verba, *The Civic Culture: Political Attitudes and Democracy in Five Nations* (Princeton: Princeton University Press, 1963), p. 302. For France, see Henry W. Ehrmann, *Politics in France* (Boston: Little, Brown, 1968), p. 173.

An examination of three examples of attempts by the Central Organization of Salaried Employees (TCO) to influence public policy suggests the following theses:

> TCO's influence over policy outcomes is greatest when political partisanship is least. TCO's leadership seeks to keep issues from being politicized, that is to say from becoming the subject of partisan conflict among the political parties. To the degree its leadership is successful, the influence TCO brings to bear during the early stages of the decisionmaking process can often become crucial in determining the final outcome. To the degree TCO fails, its leadership may still influence the final outcome but such influence, if it occurs at all, is dependent on the outcome of a conflict among the political parties. Such a conflict is likely to seriously divide and weaken TCO.

As one of the major established interest groups in Swedish society, TCO actively participates in a variety of ways in the policy-making process. Its weak cohesion, however, forces its leadership to select certain strategies for influence over others. Given the heterogeneity of political party sympathies which permeates its membership (a heterogeneity which in turn reflects the economic diversity of its membership), TCO concentrates its efforts on gaining access to the early stages of the decision-making process. As the example of the supplementary pensions dispute will demonstrate, when an issue becomes the subject of partisan conflict among the political parties to the point where elections and the Riksdag become the effective points of decision-making, TCO's cohesion disintegrates and the organization's influence on the final outcome becomes marginal at best.

An examination of two other attempts to influence public policy will show happier endings, at least from TCO's point of view. In the case of inventors' rights, TCO's leaders successfully convinced political party representatives not to pursue the issue. Success in this instance meant that TCO's influence in the deliberative stage of policy-making (Royal Commission and *remiss*)[7] became crucial in determining the final outcome of the issue.

In the case of the revision of the Comprehensive School's curriculum, TCO's skillful use of its staff of educational "experts" led to important changes in the proposed curriculum which were favored by TCO organizations. Then the unanimous agreement on these proposed changes by the members of the executive board of the National Board of Education reduced the likelihood that the political parties would take up the commission's results and make them a partisan issue. Thus here again TCO's

[7] The different stages of the Swedish political process are discussed in greater detail in Chapter 3.

influence during the early stages of the decision-making process played a major role in determining the final outcome.

Having once reached these conclusions about TCO's ability to affect public policy, I will suggest some tentative generalizations about the democratic nature of the contemporary Swedish political process. In particular the emerging subsystem of interest group—agency policy-making will be examined as it affects opposition party attempts to present constructive alternatives to government programs and as it affects the ability of the government to give direction to the policy-making process.

Except for the summer of 1936, the Social Democrats have formed the government, either alone or in coalition since 1932. To the right, the Liberal, Center, and Conservative parties have normally formed the opposition. To the left, the Left-Communists, while formally opposing many Social Democratic initiatives, have never voted against the party on any issue which could have brought about the government's downfall. Thus while technically a part of the opposition, their role is more that of critic than opponent.

My use of the terms government and opposition, however, has less to do with identifying those particular parties which now formally occupy these positions (as the 1973 election suggests, the long reign of the Social Democrats may soon be over) and more to do with the roles themselves and the ability of those who occupy them to play them effectively.

As for my remaining area of research interest, the question of system stability and instability, I will use the results of my case study to suggest some tentative conclusions regarding the rapid proliferation in Sweden of single-issue–oriented ad hoc groups working outside the established group structure. Here I will argue that the rise of such groups reflects in part a reaction against the general passive style of participation which presently prevails within the institutions and nongovernmental groups in Swedish democracy. Moreover, I will suggest that the rise of such groups stems in part from a tension which exists not only in Sweden, but also in other Western industrialized political systems as well: the tension between participation and effectiveness.

The effects of such ad hoc group action for the political system are potentially profound. For interest groups such as TCO which seek a depoliticized atmosphere in order to maximize cohesion and thereby influence, such developments may well hamper their efforts to affect public policy.

But more than the effectiveness of a single interest group may be at stake. As new patterns of authority emphasizing active political participation by the average Swede replace the old passive form of deference toward expertise, the central problem for all established groups and parties becomes one of how to maintain organizational effectiveness while allowing greater membership participation. Both interest groups and political parties may well have to decentralize authority over certain policy issues if they are to continue to effectively protect the interests of their membership.

The disposition of the essay is as follows: after introductory chapters on the definition of "white-collar" in the Swedish context and the reasons for the rise of Sweden's well-organized trade union movement, I present in Chapters 3 and 4 the Swedish decision-making process, and the general importance of interest groups in the Swedish political system, orienting the reader to the political system and laying the groundwork for an analysis of specific TCO activity in the political arena. Chapters 5 through 8 then present examples of TCO's influence in the political system. In Chapter 9 conclusions are drawn regarding the scope and limits of TCO's ability to influence public policy and some tentative generalizations are suggested regarding the democratic process in Sweden. In Chapter 10 the relationship between interest group activity and the growing instability which characterizes the Swedish political system is examined.

Data Collection

Finally a word is in order regarding the data presented in this study. Initial field research was carried out between June, 1965, and December, 1967. During the months of September through December, 1971, this material was updated and supplementary data collected. Between May and December, 1972, several chapters were revised and the material in Chapter 10 was considerably expanded.

TCO provided an ideal setting for serious scholarship. The organization gave me full access to their archives for materials concerning the case studies and for minutes from executive board meetings, general council meetings, and congresses.

TCO kindly gave me the opportunity to witness first-hand the workings of the organization by inviting me to five conferences organized by its headquarters for local TCO representatives. In addition I had the opportunity to attend meetings where *remiss* reply drafts were discussed, as well as two general council meetings and one congress. Finally, officials at TCO were always willing to take time from their busy schedules for interviews, in some cases not just once but on a number of occasions.

In this context it is important to note the manner in which I have cited data from the ninety-four interviews, which were carried out in Swedish, for this project. In interviewing TCO officials, leaders of other interest groups, political party representatives, and public officials, I made it a practice to guarantee anonymity for each reply. In order to fulfill this promise I have cited interview information in the footnotes simply as "interview" or "interviews." Where the source was still relatively obvious, I have checked with the person to insure he feels adequately protected. In every case where important information came to light through an interview, I tried to verify its authenticity during other interviews. When such was the case the footnote will indicate the plural, "interviews."[8]

[8] For those especially interested in the interview process, I offer the following additional information. The sessions were open-ended, but were based on specific sets of questions. Each interview ran between one-half hour and two hours. Thirty-seven were taped directly and transcribed in whole or in part. In ten cases notes were taken during the interview, recorded on tape immediately after the session, and trancribed later. In forty-seven cases notes were taken during the interview and then written up within two hours.

Since anonymity was guaranteed to all respondents only the organizations which they represented are listed below:

Interest Groups: Total 62

1. The Central Organization of Salaried Employees
   (Tjänstemännens Centralorganisation or TCO)—44
   (a) Headquarters—17
   (b) Federations—12[x]
   (c) TCO representatives to regional and local public bodies—15
2. The Swedish Confederation of Professional Associations
   (Sveriges Akademikers Centralorganisation or SACO)—3
   (a) Headquarters—2
   (b) The Swedish Association of Graduate Engineers
       (Civilingenjörsförbundet or CF)—1
3. Confederation of Swedish Trade Unions
   (Landsorganisationen or LO)—3
4. The Swedish Employees Association
   (Svenska Arbetsgivareföreningen or SAF)—3
5. The Association of State-Employed Engineers of Sweden
   (Statsverkens Ingenjörsförbund or SI)—1
6. The Association of Swedish Inventors
   (Svenska Uppfinnareföreningen or SUF)—1
7. Ad hoc groups—7

(x) These people were interviewed in their capacities as federation representatives. TCO representatives to regional and local public bodies come from federations as well. Questions for this latter group centered on their activities in public bodies and on the channels of information between themselves and the central headquarters.

Government Departments and Agencies: Total 16
1. Department level officials—4
2. Agencies—12
   (a) National Board of Education—8
   (b) Other agencies, including public firms—4

Political Party Representatives—Total 6

Private Individuals—Total 6

Private Firms—Total 4

Chapter One

Definitions and Background

What do Swedes mean by "white-collar"? What are the major white-collar national trade union confederations in Sweden? How do they differ in terms of the kinds of members they recruit? What distinguishes white-collar workers from blue? What are some of the major reasons for the steady increase in the number of white-collar workers in the Swedish work force? Answers to these questions form the subject of this chapter.

"White-Collar" in the Swedish Context

Official statistics in Sweden classify the following groups of employees, among others, as white-collar workers.:[1]

Office clerks
Receptionists, telephone operators
Technical personnel (ranging from technicians to engineers)
Foremen and supervisors in all industries (including transportation, commerce, etc.)
Retail clerks
Bank and insurance employees
Civil servants
Police and firemen
Commissioned, warrant, and noncommissioned officers in the armed forces
Doctors, dentists, and nurses
Teachers of all categories

It need hardly be said that any classification system which lumps doctors and office workers, high-ranking civil servants and grocery store clerks, into a common pot called "white-collar" encompasses a wide variety of occupations indeed.

Organizational life among white-collar workers recognizes this diver-

[1] Arne H. Nilstein, "Sweden," in *White-Collar Trade Unions*, ed. Adolf Sturmthal (Urbana: University of Illinois Press, 1966), pp. 264–265.

sity. Let us first look briefly at the national trade union confederations in this area before any attempt is made to generalize about characteristics which distinguish white-collar from blue-collar employees.

White-Collar National Trade Union Confederations

White-collar employees in Sweden are organized into four national trade union confederations. The confederations differ from one another in that some are confined solely to organizing public employees, while others represent private workers as well; in addition, some are industrial while others are occupational. Industrial unionism in this sense means the affiliates belonging to the confederation seek to organize all white-collar workers, from the lowest to the highest salaried, who work for the same employer or for employers represented in negotiations by the same employers' association. The term occupational applies to federations seeking to organize white-collar workers who perform a certain kind of work or have the same kind of education.

The smallest of the four Swedish national confederations, the National Confederation of Civil Servants (Statstjänstemännens Riksförbund or SR), has affiliates that organize according to the occupational principle and consists mainly of high-ranking civil servants and military officers. Formed in 1946 by a merger of two earlier existing organizations,[2] it has always been confined solely to the public sector.

Within the primarily blue-collar Confederation of Swedish Trade Unions (Landsorganisationen or LO) a special cartel was formed in 1937 (Statstjänarkartellen or SK, now called the State Employees Union, Statsanställdas Förbund or SF). Primarily based on the industrial principle, it organizes lower-ranking employees chiefly in the central government. Its heaviest concentration of members lies in government-owned and operated utilities and enterprises, for example, railroads, telecommunications, and the post office.[3]

[2] The Swedish Civil Servants Association (Sveriges Stätstjänstemannanämnd or SN) formed in 1917 and the Federation of Civil Servants in Traffic Communication (Trafiktjänstemännens Riksförbund or TR) formed in 1918.

[3] The Swedish Municipal Workers Union (Svenska Kommunalarbetareförbundet) organizes a handful of white-collar workers at the municipal level. The Swedish Insurance Workers Union (Svenska Försäkringsarbetareförbundet) also organizes some 10,000 white-collar employees at the state, county, and municipal levels. In the private sector the Swedish Commercial Employees' Union (Handelsanställdas Förbund) has nearly all the organized clerks in the field of commerce (in 1971 approximately 100,000). Each of these organizations is affiliated with the LO and in every case the overwhelming majority of its membership is blue-collar. Moreover, none enjoy as independent a position within the LO as the SF.

The Swedish Confederation of Professional Associations (Sveriges Akademikers Centralorganisation or SACO), formed in 1947, also draws its membership largely from the public sector. It is organized on an occupational basis, requiring that all its members be graduates of a school of higher learning: law, medicine, liberal arts (for example, secondary school teachers), and so on. Since the early sixties, it has progressively lowered its admission standards (from requiring a university or college degree to demanding advanced education beyond the comprehensive school), a move that has brought it into a state of open warfare with the largest of the white-collar organizations, the Central Organization of Salaried Employees (Tjänstemännens Centralorganisation or TCO).

The Central Organization of Salaried Employees (TCO) was formed in 1944 by a union of the Salaried Employees' Central Organization (De Anställdas Centralorganisation or DACO) in the private sector and the Public Employees' Central Organization (Tjänstemännens Centralorganisation or "gamla TCO")[4] in the public sector. TCO rapidly grew to become the largest of the four national trade union confederations and includes federations organized on both the industrial and the occupational principles. For example, in 1971 eight were industrial and fourteen occupational.[5] Moreover, as shown in Table 1, its membership is almost evenly divided between the private and public sectors.

TABLE 1

WHITE-COLLAR UNIONS IN TCO IN 1971 ACCORDING TO TYPES OF EMPLOYERS[a]

Employers	Number of TCO Affiliates	Number of Members in 1,000	Percent of Total TCO Actual Membership
Private employers	11	401	56
Public employees	11	308	44
Total	22	709	100

[a]The unions are classified according to the field in which the majority of their members are employed. For instance, some of the unions shown as organizing white-collar workers in private employment also have members employed by central and local government.

SOURCE: *TCO Årsberättelse 1971*, pp. 306–307, 311.

Over the years, jurisdictional lines with the organizations have been drawn as follows (see Table 2): in the public sector, TCO's members come from the range between the lower-ranking members of the SF and

---

[4] I use "gamla TCO" to distinguish it from the new organization, TCO, which resulted from the 1944 merger.

[5] Tjänstemännens Centralorganisation, *Årsberättelse 1971* (Stockholm: Tjänstemännens Centralorganisation, 1971), pp. 9–10.

SACO's college-educated and the SR's very high-ranking civil servants and military officials. In the private sector, TCO's members come from the range between the LO's blue-collar organizations and SACO's professionals. Graph I shows the relative strengths of the confederations.

TABLE 2

MEMBERSHIP IN WHITE-COLLAR ORGANIZATIONS, 1971

	Private Sector		Public Sector	
	Numbers in 1,000	Percent of Total Membership	Numbers in 1,000	Percent of Total Membership
SR	—	—	19	3
SACO	16	4	69	13
TCO	401	96	308	57
SF[a]	—	—	147	27
Total	417	100	544	100

[a]These figures do not include 98,000 white-collar workers who belong to the LO-affiliated Swedish Commercial Employees Union (Handelsanställdas Förbund or HAF), in the private sector and 12,000 and 10,000 white-collar workers who respectively belong to the Swedish Municipal Workers Union (Svenska Kommunalarbetareförbundet) and the Swedish Insurance Workers Union (Svenska Försäkringsarbetareförbundet). The figures are for 1971. For a further discussion of this point, see footnote 3.

SOURCE: *SR Styrelse- och Revisionsberättelsen 1971*, p. 6.
SACO Tjugofem år, p. 94.
TCO Årsberättelse 1971, pp. 306–307.
SF Verksamheten 1971, p. 33.

GRAPH I

MEMBERSHIP IN WHITE-COLLAR ORGANIZATIONS, 1971

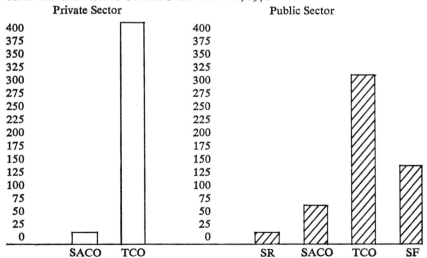

SOURCE: My computations from Table 2.

In terms of occupations the four national trade union confederations for white-collar workers look like this:

SACO (five largest federations)	*TCO*
Doctors	Middle-range civil servants
Dentists	Nurses
Gymnasium and university teachers (also last years of Comprehensive School)	Teachers up to last years of Comprehensive School
	Foremen
Engineers	Office clerks
Lawyers	Retail clerks
	Bank and insurance employees
	Police
	Warrant and noncommissioned
SR	officers
Top civil servants	Technical personnel (ranging from
High-ranking military officers	technicians to engineers with certain degrees)
	SF
	Low-ranking civil servants (primarily in railroads, telecommunications, and post office)

From the foregoing I shall argue that we are in fact dealing with three different but related subgroups within a common category called white-collar. Members of TCO, the largest group by far, come closest to fitting the definition of white-collar devised by the German sociologist, Fritz Croner: employees who perform certain work functions (supervision, construction or analytical, administrative and mercantile) delegated to them by their employers. "White-collar employees' four functions originally were part of the general work done by the employer. Developments in industry have led increasingly to the *delegation* [Croner's emphasis] of tasks involving supervision, construction, etc. from the owner himself to the employee who takes on these 'functions.' "[6] This "delegation" concept means that historically an entrepreneur (a craftsman) at first performed all the work himself. As his operation expanded and the demands on his time increased he was forced to relinquish first the shaping of the material and then the transporting of the finished products. Gradually his role evolved further to that of supervisor; he planned and experimented,

[6] Fritz Croner, *Tjänstemannakåren i det moderna samhället* (Uppsala: Gebers, 1951), p. 33.

received orders and sold the finished products. In time these functions too were delegated, often to members of the entrepreneur's family, and as such became positions of trust. As hired personnel took over these tasks, they remained in close contact with the entrepreneur and came to identify closely with his way of thinking. As the enterprise grew in size, the functions were divided among ever larger groups of employees whose social position was still characterized by the fact that they were performing managerial functions.[7] A similar explanation applies to the origins of white-collar workers in public service.

At both ends of its organizational sphere, however, TCO member federations take on characteristics which blend into those of federations belonging to the SF and to SACO (for example, lower middle-range civil servants on the one hand and teachers and nurses on the other).

Members of the SF come closer to fitting the German sociologist Theodor Geiger's view of white-collar workers. "From the point of view of class structure in Marx's sense a salaried employee is undoubtedly closer to the worker than to any other figure of modern society."[8] This approach is based on the similarities in actual work done by the blue- and white-collar workers. Whether or not such white-collar workers see themselves as performing jobs similar to those of blue-collar workers, the fact remains that the LO-affiliated SF has enjoyed great success in its organizational efforts among just such groups. For example, selling stamps in the post office differs only slightly from the manual work involved in distributing letters to offices and homes. Clerking in a department store is another good example of an occupation which now differs little from what is ordinarily considered manual labor. Thus it is not surprising that on several occasions bitter jurisdictional disputes have arisen between LO-affiliated federations and TCO-affiliated federations for organizational rights to these groups.

Finally at the upper end of the scale we find the professional groups in SACO: doctors, dentists, lawyers, engineers, gymnasium and university teachers, and so on. The origins of these groupings have no connection with any delegation process. Rather, their heritage lies more in the crafts and guilds which have played such an important role throughout Swedish history. As state intervention into different sectors of social and economic life has progressively increased, however, most of the members of these occupations have become parts of the civil service and as such have come

[7] *Ibid.*, pp. 31–136; Nilstein, "Sweden," p. 263.
[8] Theodore Geiger, *Die Klassengesellschaft im Schmelztiegel* (Cologne and Hagen, 1949), p. 167.

to champion interests common also to middle- and low-ranking public employees: advancing up the wage scale system and securing a wide range of social benefits. Moreover, those remaining in the private sector have wasted no time in seeking gains commensurate with those granted their counterparts in public service.

Thus there are several different categories of white-collar workers. Each has its own national trade union confederation, and as shall be observed later, each confederation goes its own way to some degree.

Are there any ties at all, then, which unite white-collar employees differentiating them clearly from blue-collar? No. The most that can be said is that certain characteristics have tended to distinguish the two groups but that these distinctions increasingly have become blurred.

Given this qualification, two characteristics can be mentioned: white-collar identification with management and the social benefits, that is the more favorable terms of employment white-collar workers enjoy. Given the principal functions the majority of white-collar workers perform, it is not surprising that those belonging to the white-collar occupational groups listed above generally see themselves as being more similar to management than to manual workers, and generally are regarded by manual workers as one of "them" rather than one of "us." Similarly employer-managers view them as part of the "staff" rather than part of the "works."[9] Bain's comments on white-collar workers in England are directly relevant to the Swedish case. He writes:

> Regardless of the white-collar workers' position in society or in the authority structure of the enterprise, they are linked with employer-managers by being associated with that part of the productive process where authority is exercised and decisions are taken. Even in nonindustrial sectors of the economy such as the distributive trades and national and local government, the white-collar worker is the person who takes your money in shops and gives you orders in offices; in Lockwood's words, the person "on the other side of the desk who is somehow associated with authority."[10]

Second, the terms of employment in Sweden also serve to differentiate blue- from white-collar. White-collar workers enjoy monthly salaries instead of hourly rates, longer job tenure, better old-age pensions, better health insurance benefits, better promotion possibilities, shorter working hours, and pleasanter working conditions.[11]

[9] George Sayers Bain, *The Growth of White-Collar Unionism* (London: Oxford University Press, 1970), p. 4.
[10] *Ibid.*, pp. 4–5.
[11] See Valter Åman's speech, *Minutes from TCO Congress May 13–15, 1955*

During the postwar years reforms concerning terms of employment have blurred previously sharp distinctions between blue-collar and white-collar occupations. Moreover, the routinization of tasks which previously were much more closely related to those of management, as per Croner's delegation theory, has reduced significantly the differences in fact between the work done by blue-collar and white-collar workers and correspondingly has weakened the authority previously invested in white-collar occupations. Thus in no sense do white-collar employees form a completely separate group in Swedish society.

Here is one concrete example of how the differences in the terms of employment, which at one time were quite great, have been reduced in scope, although not eliminated, by such reforms. Prior to the introduction in 1951 of a legislated three-week vacation, blue-collar workers had at best only two weeks free a year whereas white-collar workers in all the national trade union confederations discussed above enjoyed benefits which exceeded the existing two-week minimum. For example, SF-affiliated members had between fifteen and eighteen days. Also TCO clerks in private industry enjoyed fifteen to eighteen days, as did its bank tellers, employees in insurance companies, dental nurses, journalists, and so on. And for TCO, SACO, and SR-affiliated members in public service the figures ranged between twenty and forty-five days![12] After the reform, blue-collar employees came to enjoy the same benefits as many low- and middle-ranking white-collar employees. Thus while differences remained, they were reduced in scope.

The area of overlap does not mean that all differences have vanished, but rather that the farther one travels down the economic scale, the less significant the differences between blue- and white-collar workers become. Conversely, the differences increase as one moves up the economic scale within TCO and on into the ranks of SACO and the SR.

The Numerical Growth of White-Collar Workers

The number of white-collar workers in Sweden's total work force has risen rapidly in this century, as Table 3 indicates. Industrialization, commercialization, the expansion of the public sector, and rationalization have all contributed to this rapid growth.

(Stockholm: Tjänstemännens Centralorganisation, 1955), pp. 40–43. See also Croner, *Tjänstemannakåren*, pp. 283–286; Per Sandberg, *Tjänstemannarörelsen: uppkomst och utveckling* (Stockholm: Tiden, 1969), pp. 20–21.

[12] "PM: Tjänstemännen i samhället," TCO's Research Division Memorandum Series, 1964, TCO Archives, Stockholm, p. 9 (mimeographed).

TABLE 3
DISTRIBUTION OF LABOR FORCE BY OCCUPATION IN PERCENT, 1900–1960

	1900	1910	1920	1930	1940	1950	1960
Agriculture	31.4	28.8	23.4	21.0	18.2	13.0	8.7
Employer	5.7	6.2	5.4	7.3	8.2	7.8	6.6
Salaried employee	6.1	8.8	11.8	13.5	20.4	27.6	34.9
Blue-collar worker	56.9	56.2	59.4	58.2	53.2	51.6	49.8
Total	100.0	100.0	100.0	100.0	100.0	100.0	100.0

SOURCE: Stig Hadenius, Hans Wieslander, Björn Molin, *Sverige efter 1900* (Stockholm: Aldus/Bonniers, 1967), Appendix, Table 6a, p. 288.

The process of industrialization fostered structural changes that reduced the role of agriculture and increased the importance of various city trades in which the number and scope of white-collar functions are great. Examining the distribution of the population among the main fields of economic activity since 1870, Table 4 illustrates this point. Data presented in

TABLE 4
DISTRIBUTION OF POPULATION ACCORDING TO ECONOMIC ACTIVITIES, IN PERCENT OF TOTAL POPULATION

Year	Total Population in 1,000	Agriculture, Forestry, Fishing	Mining, Manufacturing, Construction, etc.	Commerce, Transport, Communications	General Administration Professions	*Total*
1870	4,169	72.4	14.6	5.2	7.8	100
1880	4,566	67.9	17.4	7.3	7.4	100
1890	4,785	62.1	21.7	8.7	7.5	100
1900	5,136	55.1	27.8	10.4	6.7	100
1910	5,522	48.8	32.0	13.4	5.8	100
1920	5,904	44.0	35.0	15.2	5.8	100
1930	6,142	39.4	35.7	18.2	6.7	100
1940	6,371	33.9	37.9	19.7	8.5	100
1950	7,042	24.6	42.7	22.6	10.1	100

SOURCE: Statistiska Centralbyrån, *Historisk statistik för Sverige, 1720–1967, Del. I., Befolkning* (2nd ed.; Stockholm: Allmänna Förlaget, 1969), p. 83.

Table 5 on the economically active population by industry demonstrates even more clearly this shift to urban occupations where the number and scope of white-collar functions are great.[13]

As the output of industrialized society increased, greater demands were

[13] Owing to a major revision in 1940 in the method of computing census data, information for earlier years on the economically active population by industry is unavailable. See Statistiska Centralbyrån, *Historisk statistik för Sverige, 1720–1967, Del I., Befolkning* (2nd ed.; Stockholm: Allmänna förlaget, 1969), p. 24.

TABLE 5
ECONOMICALLY ACTIVE POPULATION BY INDUSTRY IN PERCENT

Year	Agriculture, Forestry, Fishing	Mining, Manufacturing, Construction, ect.	Commerce, Transport, Communications	General Administration, Professions	Total
1940	28.8	35.5	17.7	18.0	100
1945	24.5	38.0	19.3	18.3	100
1950	20.2	40.6	21.5	17.7	100
1960	13.5	45.2	21.1	20.2	100
1965	10.2	43.8	23.1	22.9	100
1970	8.1	40.3	26.7	24.9	100

SOURCE: Statistiska Centralbyrån, *Historisk statistik*, p. 84. Statistiska Centralbyrån, *Statistisk årsbok 1973* (Stockholm: Kungl. Boktryckeriet Norstedt, 1973), p. 30.

placed on the distribution, communication, and transportation systems, which in turn led to their expansion. The growth of other commercial service sectors (banking and insurance, for example) was stimulated in part because of this rise in production and in part because of the increased purchasing power of the population.

Moreover, as the state laid claim to an ever greater share of society's total resources in an effort to satisfy certain collective needs, public services were expanded (for example, education, social insurance, and public welfare). Table 6 shows that the percentage of white-collar functions is considerably higher in these urban sectors than in agricultural occupations.[14]

TABLE 6
WHITE-COLLAR WORKERS AS A PERCENT OF LABOR FORCE, BY ECONOMIC SECTIONS

Year	Agriculture, Horticulture, Forestry, Fishing	Industry, Crafts	Commerce, Communications, Transportation	Public Administration, Professions	Total
1930	2	9	36	29	13
1940	3	11	41	42	20
1950	4	15	48	59	27
1960	5	23	59	58	35

SOURCE: Arne H. Nilstein, "Sweden" in *White-Collar Trade Unions*, Adolf Sturmthal (Urbana: University of Illinois Press, 1966), p. 267.

[14] Information in Tables 3 and 6 is available only through 1960. The difficulty involved in distinguishing clearly between blue- and white-collar employees (a point

In this connection it is important to note that as a result of rationalization, the percentage of white-collar workers in all fields of economic activity has gradually increased. Systematizing and standardizing work processes has caused blue-collar occupational functions to be replaced by machine operation and white-collar functions. Thus Table 6 figures showing the growth of the proportion of white-collar workers in different fields also constitutes a measure of the structural changes which have occurred within each field. Finally, there has occurred a shift from fields of employment with low percentages of white-collar workers to fields with high percentages, as well as a shift from small to large enterprises (where the percentage of white-collar workers is usually greater).[15] The overall effect of these changes has been a rapid rise in the number of white-collar workers in the total work force, as Table 3 indicated.

In summary it can be said that in the Swedish context white-collar employees in general terms can be distinguished from blue in at least two respects: their identification with management and the social benefits they enjoy. However, these differences have become considerably reduced in scope, especially since 1945.

White-collar workers in Sweden do not make up a homogeneous class, for important differences exist within their ranks, especially in terms of the nature of the work they do. Group organization among white-collar workers has come to mirror these differences, with the LO-affiliated SF organizing those whose work most resembles that performed by blue-collar workers, SACO and the SR organizing those whose work bears the least resemblance, and TCO organizing those in between. This middle position affects the strategies its leaders use in efforts to influence public policy, as shall be noted in greater detail later.

Finally, it was shown that four developments have been important in contributing to the rapid numerical growth of white-collar workers in Sweden: industrialization, commercialization, the expansion of the public sector, and rationalization. While these developments have served to expand the pool of potentially organizable white-collar workers, they do not explain why organizational efforts in Sweden have been so successful. This is the subject of the next chapter.

---

discussed above) led the Census Bureau to discontinue such a division after 1960, replacing it with the categories "employer" and "employee." The data presented in Table 5, however, shows that the structural trends which have led to an increase in white-collar occupations have continued unabated. Thus the general conclusion which can be drawn from Tables 3 and 6 still stands, namely, that the number of white-collar employees has continued to steadily expand.

[15] Nilstein, "Sweden," p. 267.

Chapter Two

Origins and Development

Over 70 percent of all white-collar employees in Sweden are organized into highly centralized national trade union confederations which enjoy an existence separate from the blue-collar confederation, the LO. The reasons for this can be summarized.

Aggregate growth of white-collar trade unionism in Sweden can be explained by reference to attitudes, policy (public and private), and employment concentration (including increased levels of bureaucratization).

National trade union confederations developed out of white-collar federation cooperation on questions of pensions, unemployment, poor promotion possibilities, and the right to negotiate collective contracts with employers.

Finally, it was status considerations, the impact of personalities, and the ability of white-collar unions to deliver for their members (at the bargaining table and in the political arena) which helped white-collar unions to develop and later maintain their independence from blue-collar organizations.

Aggregate Growth of White-Collar Trade Unionism

For the average white-collar worker in contemporary Sweden, membership in a white-collar trade union is a legitimate, natural expression of his interest in improving both his wages and his general working conditions. At most firms, in fact, it has become standard operating practice to make sure a new employee meets the trade union representative during the introductory rounds at the office.

This positive milieu does much to explain the remarkable success of white-collar unionism in Sweden, where density percentages in the private sector, for example, rose from a mere 16 percent in 1930 to 70 percent by the late 1960s.[1] Certainly study after study of efforts to organize salaried workers has commented on the importance of an environment in which trade union activity is regarded as legitimate. Indeed, often the greatest hurdle the organizer has to overcome is the disdain salaried employees hold for trade union activity.[2]

In part this milieu reflects an underlying general acceptance by Swedes of the legitimacy of group activity. Gunnar Heckscher in his classic study of interest groups in Swedish politics completed in the late 1940s argues that the Swedish system is best characterized by the term "free corporatism." As part of a "completely organized society,"[3] each group bargains to protect the interests of its members. Such a collective effort at problem-solving has its roots deep in the Swedish past. The four-estate system, for example, made a strong impact on Swedish life. In fact, the estate system formed the basis for representation in the Riksdag until the reform of 1866.

Moreover, throughout Swedish history group participation in government has been seen as legitimate and even necessary for sound public policy.[4] For example, the Constitution (adopted in 1809) has come to be interpreted as requiring that groups affected by a proposed policy have the opportunity to comment on such proposals before they are submitted to the Riksdag.[5]

This heritage of group rather than individual action has probably made

[1] Nils Elvander, *Intresseorganisationerna i dagens Sverige* (2nd ed.; Lund: Gleerup, 1969), pp. 48–50.

[2] For two recent books which discuss this problem, see Adolf Sturmthal, ed., *White-Collar Trade Unions* (Urbana: University of Illinois Press, 1966), and Albert A. Blum, *et al.*, *White-Collar Workers* (New York: Random House, 1971). While the milieu has been particularly favorable since the passage in 1936 of the Act on the Right of Association and Collective Bargaining which forced employers to negotiate collective contracts with white-collar associations (a point which is discussed in greater detail below) and hence comes close to being a certain "climate of the period," to use Bain's term, it is more than that, as the next two paragraphs in the text indicate. See George Sayers Bain, *The Growth of White-Collar Unionism* (Oxford: Oxford University Press, 1970), pp. 60, 142.

[3] The term, *det genomorganiserade samhället*, is Professor Gunnar Heckscher's. See Gunnar Heckscher, *Staten och organisationerna* (Stockholm: Kooperativa Förbundets Bokförlag, 1946), pp. 22, 215, and 249.

[4] See Chapter 3 for a fuller discussion of these points.

[5] See, for example, Article 10 of the Constitution, which reads: "Before matters are submitted to the King-in-Council, they shall be prepared by the member submitting them, who shall collect for this purpose the necessary information from the competent administrative officers." Regeringsformen para. 10 in Robert Malmgren, Halvar G. F. Sundberg, and Gustaf Petrén, *Sveriges grundlagar och tillhörande författningar* (11th ed.; Stockholm: Norstedt, 1971), p. 17. For a fuller treatment of this paragraph and the entire *remiss* system, see Chapter 3.

it easier for organizers in Sweden to convince salaried employees to band together to protect their interests than in countries where this ethic has not been so strong (for example, the United States and France).

Moreover, Sweden's homogeneity of religion, ethnic composition, and language has no doubt helped create the environment in which economic matters such as wages could push their way to the center of the stage. Certainly such homogeneity has enabled the trade union movement to avoid the internecine wars over religion and race that have often divided and weakened labor movements elsewhere.

Despite these generally favorable value orientations, however, both blue- and white-collar unions did have certain barriers to overcome in the early decades of this century before their rights to association and negotiation were finally recognized. An examination at this point of the blue-collar breakthrough is important, for their success helped pave the way for white-collar workers.

As the doctrine of free trade swept through Sweden between 1830 and 1890, it utterly destroyed the prevailing system of mercantilism with its emphasis on state regulation of labor market conditions. So, too, the death knell sounded for the guild system which controlled so many of the activities of the craftsmen. The success of this doctrine was so complete, in fact, that by the 1880s a blue-collar worker enjoyed a position of complete legal independence from his employer, his guild, and from the state.[6] No regulations existed to circumscribe his right to strike (these had been lifted by reforms in 1864 and 1885, especially the latter); nor did the state place any significant barriers in the way of union organization.[7] From a comparative perspective this last point is especially remarkable. In most other countries the success of the doctrine of free trade meant in reality removing restrictions on the new trading class. Would-be union organizers thus constantly faced legal hurdles with the result that the first, and often the most vicious, battles came to center on the question of whether a worker had the legal right to join a union at all. In Sweden this battle was comparatively easy to win, which helps to explain much of its later peaceful development toward a mature labor market system.[8]

---

[6] Guilds, while formally abolished by the requirement that association be made voluntary, in fact managed to live on. This development is discussed in greater detail in Chapter 11.

[7] Jörgen Westerståhl, *Svensk fackföreningsrörelse: organisationsproblem, verksamhetsformer, förhållande till staten* (Stockholm: Tiden, 1945), pp. 11–13.

[8] Laws outlawing membership in trade unions were never passed. A vagrancy law (försvarslöshetsstadgan) proved a minor barrier to labor mobility but was eliminated in 1885. On at least one occasion, the Sundsvall Strike in 1879, government troops

Yet the absence of major state regulations on blue-collar trade unions did not mean that private industry welcomed organization with open arms. While significant legal barriers were never put in the way, there did exist many practical obstacles. "Yellow-dog" contracts stipulating as a condition of employment that signers would not join a trade union, and "blacklisting," employer collusion to refuse employment to trade union members and organizers, were among the tactics used. It was not until 1906 that employers first formally recognized the right of their employees to union membership. And then it was only in return for agreement that they would have the final say as to the hiring and firing of employees.[9] Moreover, it was not until 1909, in the wake of the "Great Strike," that employer associations finally accepted union activity.[10]

Accepting blue-collar union activity meant confirming as well collective contracts as a means of regulating labor-management relations. Collective contracts were seen to be potentially advantageous for both labor and management. For labor such contracts meant a written guarantee that oral concessions granted at the bargaining table would in fact be forthcoming during the period covered by the agreement. For the employer, the contracts meant that he was protected against additional requests for salary increases during the time of the agreement, a guarantee which considerably aided planning efforts.[11] While many smaller firms had agreed to collective bargaining as early as 1899, the major turning point for larger industries came in 1905 when the engineering industry (verkstadsindustrin) negoti-

---

were used to break up a strike. The Åkarp Act of 1899 protected strikebreakers by providing penal sanctions against persons who attempted to coerce anyone to take part in a stoppage of work or who prevented anyone from returning to work or from accepting a job that was offered. The act was never vigorously enforced. It was modified in 1914 and then repealed in 1938. See *ibid.* and T. L. Johnston, *Collective Bargaining in Sweden* (Cambridge: Harvard University Press, 1962), p. 163.

[9] This was the famous "December Compromise," named after the month in which it was reached in 1906. Article 23 (now clause 32) read "The employer is entitled to direct and distribute the work of his enterprise, to engage and dismiss workers at his own discretion, and to employ organized or unorganized workers as he sees fit." Johnston, *Collective Bargaining*, pp. 78–79.

[10] Employer asssociations, particularly SAF, had been moving steadily in that direction since 1903, but as Westerståhl notes, the final decision came only after the "Great Strike" in 1909. SAF succeeded in rolling a number of small disputes into a major clash with the LO, which SAF won, leaving the LO in feeble shape. The "Great Strike" had the effect of encouraging moderation within the trade union movement and of convincing the "hard-liners" in SAF that the costs outweighed the gains of any attempt to completely crush the labor movement. Westerståhl, *Svensk fackföreningsrörelse*, pp. 145–150, 170. See also Johnston, *Collective Bargaining*, p. 77.

[11] Westerståhl, *Svensk fackföreningsrörelse*, p. 160.

ated its first collective contract.[12] In 1909 the "Great Strike" had the same effect on the emerging system of collective contracts as it had had for union recognition, as employers decided finally that it was the route they wished to go.[13]

For white-collar organizations the blue-collar struggle had the "spill-over" effect of settling the issue of the right to belong to an association. The two major challenges to this principle (one in 1930 and the other in 1931, affecting foremen and clerks in private industry) resulted in such favorable publicity for the employees that they served to further benefit organizational efforts.[14]

The right for white-collar associations to negotiate wage and employment conditions, however, was harder to come by. In the public sector, a civil service position was considered a form of public service. Associations might present their ideas, but the thought of their negotiating was out of the question. As for the private sector, until forced by legislation in 1936 (a law which is discussed in greater detail below), the vast majority of employers simply refused to negotiate with white-collar associations over these issues.[15] Denial of these rights can be traced directly to negative employer attitudes. Employers resisted the implications of the erosion in their patriarchal relationship with white-collar employees and they resented sharing their power with yet another group.

Such resistance posed a serious problem for budding white-collar associations, for it meant that either more militant tactics would have to be used or that relief would have to be sought through legislation by the state. It was this latter strategy which finally proved successful after the Social Democrats came to power in 1932.

[12] *Ibid.*

[13] *Ibid.*, p. 161.

[14] In the case of the Swedish Union of Clerical and Technical Employees in Industry (SIF) several leading members of the organization were called in by their employers and told to leave the "radical" federation. In short order the press learned of the incidents and the stories made front-page headlines. See C. Gösta Malmström, *Svensk Industritjänstemannaforbundet 1920–1945* (Stockholm: Svenska Industritjänstemannaförbundet, 1945), pp. 65–68. For a discussion of both incidents, see Finn Bergstrand, "DACO: fackligt samarbete mellan de privatanställda tjänstemännen" (Ph.D. dissertation, University of Lund, 1962), p. 46.

[15] As the next section will make clear, with few exceptions, white-collar associations were not interested in economic questions until the second decade of this century. The shift in goal-orientations came especially during the 1920s. See Bergstrand, "DACO," pp. 1–35, 67. For an example of resistance experienced by the Federation of Bank Employees (Svenska Bankmannaförbundet) when it began to raise economic issues after 1919, see Gunnar Palmquist, *Segrande samverkan: historik till svenska bankmannaförbundets 75-årsjubileum* (Stockholm: Svenska Bankmannaförbundet, 1962), pp. 82–87.

It is a truism in labor organization that politics influences the growth of union membership. In the United States, for example, it has been argued that the New Deal and to an even greater extent the Wagner Act contributed to the rapid growth in blue-collar unionization during the 1930s. And those unions trying currently to reach white-collar workers argue that a favorable administration in Washington and a sympathetic National Labor Relations Board could help their efforts considerably.[16]

In Sweden, too, official government actions played a crucial role in spurring trade union organization among white-collar employees. Passage in 1936 of a law guaranteeing the right to union membership and the right to sign collective contracts for both blue- and white-collar workers ended employer resistance to negotiating with white-collar associations.[17] In 1937 a government decree extended similar rights to employees in state employment, and in 1940 coverage was extended to local employees in public service. The law and these decrees provided a strong stimulus for the growth of white-collar unionism in Sweden,[18] helping create a consensus now taken for granted: that membership in a white-collar union is fully legitimate.

Social Democratic rule in the 1930s also led to increased pressure on the labor market parties to resolve the issue of neutral third parties, a question which had increasingly gained attention during the late 1920s and early 1930s owing to the rising number of strikes and lockouts. Beginning in 1936 and continuing through 1938, continuous talks were held between representatives of labor and management at the seaside resort town of Saltsjöbaden, roughly an hour's drive from Stockholm. In December, 1938, it was announced that agreement had been reached on the basic rules of procedure governing relations between labor and management. The basic agreement, still in effect in amended form, resembles a treaty of mutual nonaggression, making mandatory the negotiation of disputes and setting out in detail the procedures to be followed.

In many ways this was a remarkable document. Instead of stepping in itself to regulate an important sphere of economic life, the government

---

[16] Albert A. Blum, "The Office Employee," in *White-Collar Workers* by Blum, *et al.*, p. 14.

[17] The law is called: 1936 Act on the Right of Association and Collective Bargaining.

[18] This was particularly true for the private sector. For example, in the wake of the reform, membership rolls in the Swedish Union of Clerical and Technical Employees in Industry (SIF) began a take-off which now has resulted in a density of over 75 percent. In 1935, membership figures were 5,640, in 1936, 7,176, in 1937, 9,206, in 1940, 16,358, and so on. See Malmström, *SIF*, pp. 97, 108.

encouraged the interest groups directly involved to reach agreement on the procedures to be used. Their success resulted in a reduction of state interference in the labor negotiation system, with government officials now only participating prior to actual wage round negotiations in informal discussions regarding the state of the economy. Only parties of comparable strength could have entered into such negotiations. They thus signified the coming of age of the labor movement in Sweden. Moreover, the ability of the two sides to reach agreement, coupled with the recognition given such an accord by the government, did much to underscore the legitimacy of trade union organization.

The "spirit of Saltsjöbaden" has resulted in a kind of ritual surrounding the collective bargaining process. In the September prior to the February or March when contracts expire, bargaining between the LO and SAF begins.[19] They may at any time request the aid of a government-appointed mediator, but if talks should break off, the government is automatically required to place a mediator at their disposal.[20] As the deadline approaches, the talks lengthen into what is popularly labeled "night-mangling." When the final agreement is reached the resulting contract, known as the "frame agreement," sets the general increases for the LO's affiliates and their locals, which then negotiate specific contracts for their own members within these general limits.

White-collar organizations have consciously modeled their own negotiating procedures after those established by the LO and SAF in their basic agreement. The stable system of wage negotiations which has resulted has proved valuable in strengthening the aura of legitimacy around white-collar trade union organization, as well as blue.

Attitudes and policy (public and private) have thus been important factors determining white-collar trade union growth in Sweden. A third variable has been the changing relationship between employers and salaried workers brought about by the rise of larger industrial firms. As can be seen in Table 1, the decade between 1910 and 1920 marks the take-off point for the numerical expansion of white-collar workers in Sweden.

Not only concentration, but also the resulting bureaucratization, served to stimulate white-collar trade union growth. Attention has already been focused on Sweden's general evolution from an agrarian to an industrial and then a service society. As the number of white-collar employees with-

---

[19] Joseph B. Board, Jr., *The Government and Politics of Sweden* (Boston: Houghton-Mifflin, 1970), pp. 52–55.
[20] The best the mediator can do is offer his services; he cannot force the parties to negotiate.

TABLE I
INCREASE IN WHITE-COLLAR OCCUPATIONS, 1910–1930

	1910	1920	Increases in Percent	1930	Increases in Percent
Office personnel in industry	4,800	29,000	600	37,000	130
Engineers and foremen in industry	11,000	21,000	190	23,000	110
Clerks in retail trades	59,000	98,000	165	120,000	123
Bank employees	7,000	16,000	230	18,000	113
Industrial workers	43,500	68,800	158	756,500	110

SOURCE: Finn Bergstrand, "DACO: fackligt samarbete mellan de privatanställda tjänstemännen" (Ph.D. dissertation, University of Lund, 1962), p. 27.

in a given firm grew, delegated functions were increasingly parceled out into smaller and smaller bits, a development which served to erode the old relationship between salaried worker and employer. Moreover, when a large firm brought together employees performing similar tasks, similar demands against the employer could easily arise, a characteristic common to the origins of all trade unions.

In the public sector an additional factor came into play as well. The prevailing wage-grade system served to encourage the growth of a wide network of self-help organizations prior to the turn of the century. Since 1870 there had existed a scale of wage gradations in the state sector that had imposed on the different levels of bureaucracy a homogeneity which they might otherwise not have had. Thus for all employees in the state sector there existed a common hierarchy of salary steps. Each occupation fit in at a certain point and, along with his entire occupational group, an employee could attain only a certain fixed level. Rather quickly employees saw the advantages of working together to push their entire group upward. As the basic salary scale had not been adjusted since 1870, the move for a general revision had gained considerable ground within the rank-and-file by 1900, a factor which contributed significantly during the first decades of this century toward forcing a shift in the goal-orientations of the organizations in this sector of employment, as the next section will show.[21]

These variables, then, help to explain white-collar trade union growth in Sweden. Particular events and specific grievances served to crystallize

[21] Karl-Wilhelm Samuelsson, "Fackliga organisationssträvanden bland statstjänstemännen" (Ph.D. dissertation, University of Stockholm, 1963), pp. 6–51. Such a structural factor has played a similar role in stimulating white-collar trade union growth in England; see Bain, *White-Collar Unionism*, pp. 72–82.

latent groups into manifest organizations. A study of these provides a means of understanding the rise of the four national confederations which represent salaried employees in Sweden today. Special attention will be given to the rise of TCO.

From Mutual Aid Societies to Trade Unions

Trade union activity by white-collar workers in Sweden is a development of this century. The roots of white-collar organization, however, stretch back into nineteenth-century Swedish history. In the public sector, for example, the Swedish Medical Society (Svenska Läkarsällskapet) had its founding in 1807, while in the small town of Vekerum, the Swedish Society of Secondary School Teachers followed suit in 1838.[22] Within the private sector, the same developments could be observed. In 1848, for example, the governor of Stockholm authorized the constitution of the Marine Engineers' Society.[23]

Conspicuously absent from the bylaws of these organizations was any mandate for the organization to support the economic interests of its members. In fact, in some cases such activity was expressly prohibited.[24] Instead social service was the order of the day. Thus from such mutual aid societies, as they might be labeled, help came in times of sickness, birth, or death; savings plans were established to help their members adjust to new market mechanisms; in short, social relief activities provided the central justification for their existence.

Between 1900 and 1920 internal pressures led many of the existing mutual aid societies in both the public and private sectors to shift their goal orientations away from the social service philosophies discussed above. In their place came the view that the real task at hand was a need to defend the economic interests of the groups' members. Also during this period, newly formed organizations clearly were setting economic priorities first.[25]

In the public sector where the wage-gradation system had not been adjusted since 1870, discontent had reached the point by 1900 that most organizations were in the process of upgrading economic issues.

Employees in the private sector began the same internal metamorphosis

[22] Samuelsson, "Fackliga organisationssträvanden," p. 28.
[23] Arne H. Nilstein, "Sweden," in *White-Collar Trade Unions*, ed. Sturmthal, p. 268. See also Johnston, *Collective Bargaining*, p. 96.
[24] Bergstrand, "DACO," p. 31.
[25] *Ibid.*, pp. 1–25; Samuelsson, "Fackliga organisationssträvanden," pp. 1–51.

from 1910 to 1920. It has already been pointed out that these years were a time of rapid growth in the number of white-collar employees in private industry. At the same time their salaries were falling progressively behind those earned by the blue-collar worker, as indicated in Table 2. This con-

TABLE 2
CHANGES IN REAL WAGES IN PRIVATE SECTOR, 1914–1930

	Technical Personnel	Clerical Workers	Manual Workers
1914[a]	100	100	100
1915	80	91	93
1916	87	87	92
1917	80	81	89
1918	73	74	91
1919	72	77	100
1920	78	85	110
1921	88	95	114
1922	100	105	108
1923	102	108	115
1924	103	108	122
1925	102	107	123
1926	104	104	129
1927	103	104	132
1928	104	103	129
1929	105	103	136
1930	107	104	142

[a] Base year.
SOURCE: Adapted from Bergstrand, "DACO," Table 1, p. 26.

cern over the narrowing of the differences in reward, and hence status, between the two groups, accelerated the process whereby budding white-collar organizations came to take up economic issues.[26]

*From Many to One: The Movement to Create a National
Confederation among Employees in the Private Sector*

During the 1920s three issues served to focus attention in the private sector on the need for cooperation among white-collar organizations: pensions, unemployment, and the right to negotiate collective contracts with employees. The lessons learned from cooperation on these questions led directly to the creation in 1931 of the first national confederation for sala-

[26] Per Sandberg, *Tjänstemannarörelsen: uppkomst och utveckling* (Stockholm: Tiden, 1969), pp. 46–47.

ried workers in the private sector, the Salaried Employees Central Organization (DACO).

Pensions were an early source of friction owing to the employer practice of not allowing a salaried worker, if he changed jobs, to transfer to his new firm the pension funds he had accrued at the old. Only coordinated action could rectify this state of affairs. By 1917 unions representing clerks, custodians, and office workers had banded together to create the Swedish Private Employees' Pension Fund (Sveriges Privatanställdas Pensionskassa, or SPP) which secured the right of transferability. Members of these unions, and others as time went on, joined with employers in administering this new common fund, an act which also served to underscore the importance of cooperation among white-collar unions.

During the economically difficult years following the end of World War I, the pension question again became the subject of considerable discussion. In an effort to secure badly needed capital funds, a number of industries began to dip into their employees' pension funds. This practice spelled economic disaster for elderly workers employed by those firms, which in spite of such drastic action still could not survive. Not unexpectedly white-collar unions reacted strongly, lobbying vigorously in the highest circles of government for legislation to prevent such actions. By 1927 unions representing clerks, foremen, and bank employees, among others, had formed a committee specifically to protect the interests of white-collar workers in this area. Their actions bore fruit by the end of the year and in December, 1927, the government formally introduced legislation to correct these abuses.[27]

Unemployment proved to be the second rallying point for the white-collar movement in the 1920s when, as a consequence of the rapid increase in the number of salaried workers during the decade 1910 to 1920 and the sharp recession that hit Sweden in 1920, a large number of white-collar workers faced the threat of joblessness, some for the first time. While the numbers actually let go never matched predictions (except for foremen),[28] the psychological trauma among all white-collar workers served the same effect. No longer could a white collar guarantee security during hard times. From such anxiety sprang yet another committee, the Salaried Workers Unemployment Compensation Committee (Tjänstemannaorganisationernas Arbetslöshetskommitté or TAK) in April, 1926. The fourteen organizations that founded this committee sought to improve

[27] Bergstrand, "DACO," pp. 11–17, 175.
[28] *Ibid.*, pp. 28–29.

placement procedures and to jointly establish a rudimentary system of unemployment compensation.[29]

Finally, during these years it also became increasingly clear to the leadership of the budding white-collar trade union movement that if they were to achieve a real breakthrough in recruitment, they would have to coordinate efforts aimed at forcing the employer to bargain in good faith once he consented to come to the negotiating table. Hence the decision was made to pressure jointly for legislation guaranteeing to all trade unions, blue-collar and white-collar, the right to negotiate collective contracts.

From the mid-twenties until success was finally achieved in 1936, efforts to achieve legislation in this area represented the single most important force bringing the many different existing white-collar unions together. Moreover, once DACO was formed in 1931, the issue represented the single most important force in holding this new organization together during its first years.[30]

From Many to One: The Movement to Create a National Confederation among Employees in the Public Sector

Only in 1937 was a national confederation created for the vast bulk of salaried workers in the middle salary range of the state sector. Prior to this, however, national confederations had been created for those at the lowest and the highest ends of the salary scale.

The decline in the value of the Swedish crown between 1914 and 1920 was such that the cost of living (using 1905 as a base year) rose from 116 to 306.[31] Even with the reforms in the state wage-grade system during the first decade of the twentieth century, the salaries of state employees continued to fall behind those paid to salaried workers in the private sector and even more behind those paid to blue-collar workers.[32] In the face of such inflation, solidarity stemming from the attempts to reform the 1870 wage-grade system which had united salaried workers of all wage groups dissolved. In its place developed a solidarity among those lowest on the salary scale and a separate solidarity among those highest. Each group proposed different solutions to rectify its plight. Those lower down on the salary scale argued that the same increase in crowns should be made for

[29] *Ibid.*, p. 176.
[30] *Ibid.*, p. 183.
[31] Samuelsson, "Fackliga organisationssträvanden," p. 61.
[32] *Ibid.*

all salaried workers in public service. In contrast to this, those higher on the scale argued that equal percentage increases should be made for all and that compensation should be given for the rise in the cost of living. Obviously each group was out for its own good alone. In 1915 the fore-runner of the LO's cartel (itself created in 1937) came into existence (Statstjänarnas Centralorganisation) for those at the lower end of the salary scale. In 1917 and 1918 two organizations (which eventually merged in 1946 to create the SR) held their founding conventions: Sveriges Statstjänstemannanämnd (SN) and Trafiktjänstemännens Riksförbund (TR). But the vast middle of salaried workers in public service thus still remained organized only in trade union federations. Three developments led to the successful creation in 1937 of a national confederation for these employees.

By 1930 the worldwide economic crisis had come to Sweden. Reflecting that period's economic conventional wisdom, the bourgeois government moved quickly to cut back state services, which meant among other things a shelving of promised salary increases for civil servants. The same fate befell proposed increases in their pension plans. Meanwhile with considerable fanfare their counterparts in the private sector were launching a national confederation specifically with the intent of protecting the economic interests of their members. Under the leadership of unions representing secondary school teachers, police, and communal employees, the first steps toward the creation of the Public Employees' Central Organization (Tjänstemännens Centralorganisation or "gamla TCO") were taken.[33] By 1937 the goal had been accomplished.

Merging National Confederations

Between 1937 and the summer of 1943 little real progress was made toward merging DACO from the private sector with "gamla TCO" from the public. First the leaders of "gamla TCO" felt they had to expand their membership base in order to achieve parity in size with DACO before risking any merger. By 1941 fifteen new unions had joined and this goal had been achieved.[34]

Second, in an effort to prevent possible disintegration resulting from a two-front war with the LO's cartel on the lower end of the salary scale and the SN and TR at the upper, the leaders of "gamla TCO" decided to make an all-out campaign to woo the latter two national confederations

[33] *Ibid.*, pp. 112–131.
[34] *Ibid.*, p. 139.

into joining them. Merging with DACO before this was accomplished, it was felt, would hinder such efforts. However, when attempts in this direction consistently met with failure, "gamla TCO's" leadership decided in 1943 to go ahead with the merger with DACO in any event, and to form a new national confederation, to be called the Central Organization of Salaried Employees (Tjänstemännens Centralorganisation or TCO).[35] On June 11, 1944, TCO came into being.

The Last to Organize: SACO

Conditions facing young university graduates during the 1930s and 1940s were grim. Few jobs were to be had and those that existed offered long working hours, little pay, and few opportunities for advancement. In the early 1940s a number of associations sprang up and by the mid-1940s a committee had been established to coordinate efforts on behalf of the new graduates. The next step toward creation of a national confederation of professionals was taken in 1947 with the creation of the Swedish Confederation of Professional Associations (Sveriges Akademikers Centralorganisation or SACO).

Publicly TCO expressed considerable regret over this action, arguing that its organization was the logical home even for professionals. Privately, however, TCO's leaders were quite willing to admit they had failed completely to attend to the needs of this group. In any case, much of TCO's activity during the next twenty years centered around moves and countermoves to try to force a merger between the two national confederations.

White-Collar Trade Unionism: Its Separate Existence from the LO

White-collar national confederations in Sweden in contrast to their counterparts in Germany, England, and the United States (to name only a few) have succeeded in organizing nearly all white-collar workers into organizations independent from the blue-collar LO.[36]

Status considerations, personalities, and the ability of white-collar organizations to deliver at the bargaining table and in the political arena are all major factors explaining this accomplishment.

---

[35] The SN and the TR created in 1946 their own national confederation, the SR.

[36] The only major exception in this regard is the State Employees Union (SF) which has a limited field of recruitment among public employees and in fact enjoys such an independent position within the LO that it can be viewed as a national confederation in its own right. In the private sector there is the HAF.

In theory the LO has been open to white-collar workers for membership from its inception in 1898. However, status considerations on the part of white-collar employees kept them from wanting to join blue-collar federations. And conversely, the general view that white-collar employees were "one of them," instead of "one of us," kept blue-collar federations from expressing much interest in actively recruiting such members.

Until the twentieth century rather clear lines existed between the two groups. The nature of their jobs differed significantly, with white-collar workers enjoying considerably more responsibility, especially in giving orders to other employees, than blue-collar workers. Finally, the patriarchal relationship which prevailed between the firm's top leadership and white-collar employees led to an identification by the latter with the goals of management, reinforcing their sense of natural distance from the manual workers. Even when times changed and the differences between manual and white-collar working conditions eroded, they still felt that they were different from blue-collar workers, that their position, their status, demanded a separate form of union organization.

The clearest form of this difference in attitude was expressed in white-collar distaste for the fighting (kamp) methods of the LO affiliates, particularly their use of the strike weapon. For many employees in state service this tactic was illegal; for those in private employment, the nineteenth-century notion that one could sit down and reason with the boss was long in dying out.

Status considerations and conflicting views over the use of the strike weapon were only two of the significant values helping white-collar organizations evolve independently from the LO. A third was their desire to avoid commitment to a single political party. The bourgeois background of many members of the white-collar social clubs which sprang up in the latter half of the nineteenth century led them to disavow affiliation with any union organization that had intimate ties with the Social Democratic party, such as the LO had had from its inception.

The major exception in the private sector has been the Federation of Swedish Commercial Employees (Handelsanställdas Förbund or HAF), which has successfully organized almost all the clerks in the field of commerce. But even this example calls for an important footnote, one which helps to clarify why breakthroughs in the private sector have in fact been limited almost completely to HAF.

When the LO in 1906 formally recognized the industrial unionism principle as an alternative to the occupational,[37] HAF requested permis-

[37] Johnston, *Collective Bargaining*, p. 62.

sion to move beyond the field of commerce and begin recruiting clerks in industry as well. This permission was denied. HAF's request had stemmed from its frustration over the consistent refusal of the Swedish Metalworkers Union (Svenska Metallindustriarbetareförbundet) to recruit such employees, owing to their feeling that white-collar employees were "one of them" rather than "one of us."[38] By denying HAF's request, the LO left open the emerging group of clerks in industry for later harvest by the Swedish Union of Clerical and Technical Employees in Industry (Svenska Industritjänstemannaförbundet), a TCO federation.

In the public sector, the major exception proved to be the State Employees Union (SF), which successfully organized lower-ranking employees primarily in government-owned and -operated utilities and enterprises.[39] Similarity of job tasks and salary interests did not extend very far up the ladder of responsibility and income, however, so that the vast middle-range of civil servants came to find their organizational home in TCO. Moreover, the independent position within the LO which the SF has traditionally enjoyed again supports the thesis that white- and blue-collar employees have until recently not felt entirely at home in one another's company.

While attitudes and values thus played a significant role in determining the direction of white-collar unionism in Sweden, the importance of personalities cannot be overlooked, particularly in the case of Sigfrid Hansson, the chairman of the Swedish Federation of Journalists and editor of the LO's periodical *Fackföreningsrörelsen* during the 1920s.

Hansson became in effect the patron saint of the budding white-collar movement in the private sector. Throughout his career, he acted to defend the interests of DACO. He wrote favorable articles about DACO's activities in the LO's major periodical, *Fackföreningsrörelsen*, in an effort to dispel concerns by some factions that DACO's creation posed a threat to the LO's future. He saw to it, in his capacity as a member of the Riksdag, that DACO's voice was heard on a number of legislative issues. He championed DACO's interests in the Royal Commissions to which he was appointed. In short, at every turn he sought to support DACO and to justify its existence to those in power at the national level and in the LO.[40]

Valter Åman was also important in this connection, for his decision to leave his position at the LO to become TCO's first director in 1945 signi-

[38] Interview.

[39] Also approximately 10,000 employees classified as white-collar belong to the Swedish Municipal Workers Union (Svenska Kommunalarbetareförbundet) as of 1972.

[40] Bergstrand, "DACO," pp. 112–131.

fied official recognition by the LO in TCO's right to exist. In fact it was with the express permission of the LO's chairman at the time, August Lindberg, that Åman took the job.[41]

Important also in more recent years for the efforts of white-collar national trade union confederations to maintain organizations separate from the LO has been their ability to develop wage programs different from the LO's, to realize many of the goals of these programs, and to protect the interests of salaried employees in the political arena of decision-making.

The LO in the postwar period has followed a policy of wage solidarity. The cornerstone of this policy has been their desire to reduce income differentials by seeking greater percentage increases at each wage round for those lower on the salary scale.[42] This policy of wage solidarity is congruent with the principle of equal pay for equal work while also accepting a certain differentiation of wages. It does not, however, allow for wage differentials according to productivity, for firms that are unproductive and must rely on cheap labor for their survival are to be forced out of the market.

TCO presented in 1963 a report on the wage policy principles followed by its member unions. Basic to these policies is the idea that white-collar workers over time should receive real wage increases commensurate with the nation's rise in productivity.

A second basic principle of the white-collar wage policy is that wages should be based also on the difficulty of the job (arbetsvärdering). Thus greater responsibility stemming from higher position, better education, greater practical experience, uncomfortable working hours, and so on, all should justify greater salary rewards. As a basis for the principle of arbetsvärdering, white-collar unions, with considerable help from TCO's central headquarters, have been active in developing detailed job descriptions and wage statistics. Such efforts make it possible to compare different jobs and to evaluate the difficulty of similar tasks.

The third principle demands that consideration be given to experience (meritvärdering), such as the number of years of employment, and so forth. These principles mean that TCO supports a policy of wage differentiation different from the LO's, a fact that has at times caused mutual irritation.

SACO and the SR as organizations representing the highest paid public

[41] Interview.

[42] In the 1950s this meant singling out specific branches where union members were poorly paid. By the 1960s it became increasingly clear that this policy was not producing the intended results. Thus a shift took place so that special increases now apply only for the poorly paid in each union.

employees (and in SACO's case those possessing academic degrees in the private sector as well) have come to stress similar goals of real wage improvement, compensation for more demanding work, and salary differentials. SACO has added a new wrinkle, however, by charging that tax considerations should be involved in wage demands. Thus net income rather than gross income is the figure SACO would like to see keep up with the rise in the nation's productivity. This has rather drastic effects on the kind of gross salary demands SACO needs to realize, owing to the tax bracket of most of its members. Thus for every 1.5 to 2 percent net increase, a 10 percent increase in gross wages has to be achieved. Not an easy task, nor an argument that is likely to be favorably received by either business or the minister of finance.

Yet approval by other parties of white-collar wage policies is not the issue; rather these policies reflect the perceived interests of the white-collar worker in Sweden. And, what is important in this context, white-collar organizations have been largely successful in realizing many of the goals of their wage programs.

As the Swedish economist Per Holmberg notes, the coming of age of white-collar organizations during the 1950s meant that the reduction in wage differentials between white-collar and blue-collar workers which had been underway in Sweden from 1900 until the middle of the 1940s had ground virtually to a halt (see Table 3). White-collar organizations had proved they could deliver.[43]

TABLE 3
WAGE DIFFERENTIALS IN INDUSTRY BY PERCENT, 1950–1960

Employer group (men)	1950	1960
Blue-collar workers[a]	100	100
Technical personnel	179	168
Foremen	138	135
Office clerks	138	141

[a] Industrial blue-collar workers' wages held constant.
SOURCE: Per Holmberg, *Arbete och löner i Sverige* (Solna: Rabén och Sjögren, 1965), p. 151.

Moreover, white-collar organizations have succeeded in negotiating agreements on behalf of their members which effectively influence such important aspects of the work situation as job security (procedures gov-

[43] Per Holmberg, *Arbetare och löner i Sverige* (Solna: Rabén och Sjögren, 1965), p. 155.

erning dismissals, lay-offs, and re-engagement) and the decision-making process in the firm (works councils).[44]

Finally, the ability of white-collar national confederations to create and maintain organizations independent from the blue-collar LO can be attributed to their ability to defend the social interests of their members in the political process, for both TCO and SACO have avoided limiting their spheres of activity solely to economic matters. They have from the outset understood that social policies affect the pocketbooks of their members, and thus have sought and received representation in administrative agencies and Royal Commissions,[45] as shown in Table 4.

TABLE 4

REPRESENTATION BY NUMBERS IN ADMINISTRATIVE AGENCIES AND ROYAL COMMISSIONS, 1959–1971

	TCO		SACO	
	Admin. Agencies	Royal Comm.	Admin. Agencies	Royal Comm.
1959	19	16	6	8
1960	22	20	7	12
1961	26	28	9	12
1962	30	29	16	14
1963	43	33	22	14
1964	52	32	28	19
1965	50	40	28	26
1966	54	37	36	33
1967	50	25	39	30
1968	56	26	43	27
1969	62	28	51	27
1970	60	43	55	28
1971	70	43	56	30

SOURCE: *TCO Årsberättelser 1959–1971* and *SACO Årsberättelser 1959–1971*.

Having now examined the creation of white-collar national trade union confederations, particularly TCO, in Sweden and the factors which have enabled these organizations to remain independent from the LO, it is time to place trade union activity in the larger framework of Swedish politics.

[44] Johnston, *Collective Bargaining*, pp. 205–232. In recent years the issue of environment in the work place has received considerable attention. There is a movement underway by both white-collar and blue-collar confederations to increase employee influence in this area of policy.

[45] These two important points of access to the political system are discussed in greater detail in Chapter 3.

Chapter Three

Interest Groups and the Governmental Policy-Making Process

Interest groups play an enormously important role in policy-making in Sweden. In addition to influencing legislation during the process of law-making, groups shape policy through an elaborate system of consultations which often results in agreements in lieu of legislation.

The Swedish governmental policy-making process can be divided into four steps: initiation, deliberation, decision, and implementation.

Policy Initiation

An *initiative* can come from many different sources: members of parliament, cabinet officials, administrators, political parties, interest groups, and so forth. Such an initiative usually takes the form of a request that the government establish an ad hoc commission to study a particular problem and make recommendations.[1]

Policy Deliberation

In the normal legislative process the *deliberative stage* consists of two steps: the creation of an ad hoc commission and the circulation (*remiss*) of the commission's report to affected groups in Swedish society. During the decades after the Social Democrats assumed power in 1932,[2] however, the deliberation stage has in most cases become the effective decision-making point in the Swedish political system.

Ad hoc commissions for the study of particular issues are becoming in-

[1] Private member bills presented in the Riksdag are examples of legislative initiatives which are finished products, ready for passage or defeat.

[2] Except during the summer of 1936 when a government crisis caused them to leave office for a brief four months.

creasingly indispensable elements in all Western democratic political systems.[3] Whether they come into being in a time of crisis (as in England or
the United States) or are routinely used as a part of the normal process
of decision-making (as in Sweden), their indisputable purpose is the same:
they serve to "lend an atmosphere of authority and non-partisanship to
investigations which must stand above suspicion of being under the influence of the special interests of a particular party or group."[4]

In Sweden in 1296 a twelve-man commission under the chairmanship
of Birger Pettersson presented for royal approval a revised edition of the
laws governing the province of Uppland.[5] Swedish historians agree, however, that while the roots of the present commission system can be traced
at least as far back as the Pettersson Commission, it was not until the
seventeenth century that the system became an established part of Swedish
political life.[6] The Constitution of 1809 (which is still in effect today)
further legitimized existing practice by commanding, in paragraph ten,
that "before matters are submitted to the King-in-Council, they shall be
prepared by the member submitting them, who shall collect for this
purpose the necessary information from the competent administrative
officers."[7]

The importance of the Royal Commission process in Sweden is under-
scored by its very magnitude. In any given year over 100 commissions are
in operation, each with staff and funds.[8] On the average seventy-five new
commissions are appointed each year.[9] Once appointed, they may take
two, three, five, or even more years to complete their task and present their
findings.[10] These typically are in the form of hefty reports which include

[3] Hans Meijer, "Bureaucracy and Policy Formulation in Sweden," in *Scandinavian
Political Studies*, ed. Olof Ruin, Vol. 4 (New York: Columbia University Press,
1969), p. 103.

[4] *Ibid.*

[5] Gunnar Hesslén, *Det Svenska kommittéväsendet intill år 1905: dess uppkomst,
ställning och betydelse* (Uppsala: Lundequistska Bokhandeln, 1929), p. 13, footnote 1.

[6] *Ibid.*

[7] Robert Malmgren, Halvar G. F. Sundberg, and Gustav Petrén, *Sveriges grundlagar och tillhörande författningar* (11th ed.; Stockholm: Norstedt, 1971), p. 17;
Hesslén, *Svenska kommittéväsendet*, p. 100. As shall be seen, this paragraph also
provides the legal basis for another part of the political process, the *remiss* system,
discussed below.

[8] For example, in 1966, 318 were in progress. For the budget year 1965 to 1966,
5.6 million dollars were allocated for Royal Commission studies. Nils Andrén, *Svensk
statskunskap* (Stockholm: Liber, 1968), p. 344.

[9] Meijer, "Bureaucracy," p. 109.

[10] Hans Meijer, *Kommittépolitik och kommittéarbete: det statliga kommittéväsendets utvecklingslinjer 1905–54 samt nuvarande funktion och arbetsformer*
(Lund: Gleerup, 1956), p. 27.

proposals documented by research, both historical (how the problem developed, how it was handled in the past) and analytical.[11]

From the government's perspective these commissions performed an invaluable service. The breakthrough in the use of commissions came during the seventeenth century when the King's officials felt the need for sources of information beyond those which were then available.[12] In the era of the advanced industrial state characterized by widespread governmental involvement in many areas of social and economic life, the need for advice from the affected producer groups[13] is at least as great.

But advising is not the only function such commissions perform. They also serve as important forums for consensus building. When a common position can be reached with the members of the commission all in agreement, the government can then feel relatively sure of both the acquiescence and the approval[14] of affected groups for its new policy ventures. As one Swedish scholar has observed: "Interest groups (involved in Commission studies) are forced at an early stage to take a stand which can have the effect of morally binding the group in the future to loyally accept state policies to realize measures which they assisted in formulating."[15]

Pressure to achieve agreement in such commissions is great for other reasons as well. It is widely believed by the parties involved that unanimity at this stage of the decision-making process can greatly enhance chances for influencing the contents of the policy which is finally approved. After all, if business, labor, and the different political parties are all able to come to some agreement on a common recommendation from the Royal Commission, there are not a great many more interests which need to be satisfied. In short, decisions may in effect be made at this point and then formally ratified by the Riksdag.

Given this orientation, the atmosphere pervading the work of Royal

[11] Thomas J. Anton, "Policy-Making and Political Culture in Sweden," in *Scandinavian Political Studies*, ed. Olof Ruin, Vol. 4 (New York: Columbia University Press, 1969), p. 93.

[12] Hesslén, *Svenska kommittéväsendet*, pp. 14–15, 43.

[13] For a fuller discussion of the concept of producer groups, see Samuel Beer, *British Politics in the Collectivist Age* (New York: Random House, 1969), pp. 318–339.

[14] The terms are Beer's. See *ibid.*, pp. 325–331.

[15] Sweden, Justitiedepartementet, "Former för kontakt och samverkan mellan organisationerna," by Lars Foyer, in *Författningsutredningen: V organisationerna, beslutsteknik, valsystem*, Statens Offentliga Utredningar 1961:21 (Stockholm: Justitiedepartementet, 1961), p. 11. Note also that the Royal Commission system is a handy tool for delaying consideration of an issue as well as a way to bridge the formal constitutional gap which exists between ministries and central administrative boards, a point which is discussed in greater detail in Chapter 8.

Commissions is one of bargaining. Each party recognizes the importance of reaching consensus; each party has resources (its own expertise, its threat to destroy unity by making a reservation). When standpoints are already clearly defined, the room for compromise is significantly narrowed and discussions may lose some of their usual flavor of friendly give-and-take. This does not mean that attempts to negotiate an agreement cease, however. The chairman, in such cases, often delegates authority to a staff member, usually the commission's secretary, to see if he can elicit some sort of agreement. At other times, he takes an active hand himself through informal contacts to see if unanimity can be reached. Where positions are less clearly defined at the outset, general discussion meetings within the commission actually serve as opportunities for effective bargaining. As a strict rule of secrecy pervades commission meetings until the major decisions have been made, members of the commission feel free to actively participate. On occasion, of course, consensus is impossible to achieve despite all these provisions. In such cases the Royal Commission reports serve to mobilize public opinion as each representative seeks to gain maximum publicity through reservations for his or her position. In the cases which follow in later chapters, examples of each of these points will be given.

Interest groups place a high priority on gaining access to such commissions in their efforts to influence public policy.[16] At this early stage in the decision-making process, when positions are still highly flexible in many cases, groups have great opportunity for influence. Given their large staffs of experts and their ability to "speak with one voice" owing to the centralization which has come to characterize interest group life in Sweden, groups are generally able to take advantage of the opportunities for influence presented them through commission studies.

The government has come to recognize the important contribution interest groups can make to policy-making and so has granted them established positions on Royal Commissions. When the number of their representatives is compared with the numbers from the Riksdag and the opposition political parties, as in Table 1, the considerable importance of interest groups can be clearly seen.

Finally, it is an expression of interest group strength and their generally recognized position in Sweden's political life that they are, as a rule, represented in Royal Commissions that affect their areas of interest, that invitations for their participation are made by ministers at the departmental

[16] Nils Elvander, *Intresseorganisationerna i dagens Sverige* (2nd ed.; Lund: Gleerup, 1969), pp. 253–255.

TABLE I
RECRUITMENT OF COMMISSIONERS

Year	No. of Commissions	No. of Comm.	Percent of Riksdag Members	Percent of Civil Servants	Percent of Interest Group Reps.
1905–14	403	1579	27	51	21
1915–24	504	2083	27	47	26
1925–34	452	1690	32	43	25
1935–44	618	2560	23	47	30
1945–54	752	3306	25	41	34
1955–67	989	3651	19	60	20[a]

[a]This decline in interest group representation, especially during the 1960s, is in part compensated by their participation in studies done within departments and administrative agencies, a practice which has increased rapidly in recent years and is not included in the above statistics. This point will be discussed in another context.
SOURCE: Hans Meijer, "Bureaucracy and Policy Formulation in Sweden," in *Scandinavian Political Studies*, ed. Olof Ruin, Vol. 4 (New York: Columbia University Press, 1969), p. 109.

level, and that interest groups themselves choose the representatives they wish to have serve on such commissions.[17]

After a commission has presented its report, the minister responsible for the creation of the commission, again in response to the charge laid down in paragraph ten of the Constitution,[18] circulates copies to interest groups and public institutions likely to be affected by the proposed policy change. They are requested to submit their views to the minister before the drafting of legislation is to take place.

This *remiss* or circulation stage provides the government with two sources of valuable information. Comments on the *technical* aspects of the proposal serve as important checks on the findings of the Royal Commission. Moreover, it is of equal importance at this stage for the government to get a feeling for the intensity of emotions stimulated by a proposal. This *political* information is important for the government as it tries to determine what concessions, if any, should be made to protesting groups, given its long-run desire to be re-elected.

For interest groups the *remiss* stage offers a chance to make known their criticism both of the general principles and specific details of a proposal.

[17] *Ibid.*, pp. 171–176.
[18] As Lars Foyer points out, this paragraph guarantees access to Royal Commissions for bureaucratic agencies. Through practice interest groups have also come to share in the process. Their participation thus is not technically constitutionally enshrined, but in practice it has become so. See Lars Foyer, "Statsdepartementets remisser till organisationerna och vissa frågor rörande remissväsendet" (Ph.D. dissertation, University of Stockholm, 1962), p. 8.

As the policy is still in the formulating stage, the opportunities for influence are great. Owing to the vast number of *remiss* replies received by the government on any given issue, however, the opportunities for influence, when compared with those of the chosen few who sit on a Royal Commission, must be seen as smaller, particularly when the commission is able to produce a common proposal.

The *remiss* process provides other advantages for interest groups as well, however. Even if the government fails to heed the views of a group at the *remiss* stage, it does experience an indirect pressure eventually, in part because such views are likely to reappear later in the form of motions in the Riksdag. Moreover, these motions often receive coverage by the communications media. Over time such statements become a part of the on-going debate as these issues surface and re-surface. Finally, for the vitality of group life in general, such a system has the important result of continually forcing the groups to take stands, which in turn forces them to continually review the justifications for their own policy positions.

Once the *remiss* replies are in, the minister has to decide whether or not legislation is justified and if so what the specific contents will be. Opportunities for discussions between high officials in the department and affected interest groups are plentiful at this stage, proceeding on an informal basis. Telephone conversations, corridor discussions between meetings, and post-dinner chats following formal addresses to interest group members are accepted procedures. During the final drafting of a proposal, however, groups remain on the outside. The same holds true when the Cabinet is considering legislative proposals.[19]

Some government propositions according to the Constitution must be sent to the Supreme Court before they reach the Riksdag, for example, civil and criminal laws as well as laws governing the relationship between church and state. The court's responsibilities since its creation in 1809 have steadily diminished to the point where it now avoids any comment on contents, dealing instead with the task of ensuring that the legal text squares with that of the Constitution.[20]

Policy Decision

Once the bill (proposition) has reached the Riksdag, the *decision-making stage*, interest groups must depend for their influence on Riksdag members

[19] Elvander, *Intresseorganisationerna*, pp. 185, 187. Exceptions concern negotiated agreements between the state and interest groups, a point discussed on pp. 45–48.

[20] Andrén, *Svensk statskunskap*, p. 469.

who sympathize with their goals and are willing to be their spokesmen. Given the general decline in the significance of the Riksdag and the opposition parties in the policy-making process since the mid-1930s, however (a point which will be discussed in the next chapter), the importance of Riksdag channels for group influence should not be overemphasized. It should also be noted that exchanges between interest group and Riksdag members are initiated from both directions. While interest groups seek avenues for the expression of their views, Riksdag members will often turn to groups for information and advice.[21]

In addition to contacts with individual Riksdag members, interest groups seek to gain access to committee meetings, where they may on occasion be asked to testify at hearings. They may also engage in formal communication with a committee. In less direct attempts at swaying opinions, groups may also seek to gain entrance to strategy meetings of the respective political parties in the Riksdag (through their own representatives).[22] And in the hope of influencing the long-range positions or parties, interest groups send copies of *remiss* replies and arrange conferences where they can air their views on particular policy issues.[23]

For some political parties a particular segment of the electorate constitutes such an important part of their overall support that a special section is created ostensibly for the purpose of championing the views of this group within the party. Minutes from the Liberal party's white-collar section indicate, however, that an even more important function can be to see that white-collar organizations are made aware of stands the party has already taken.[24]

In sum, while groups still seek access to the Riksdag, the era of "majority parliamentarianism" has seen the function of the Riksdag transformed on most issues from one of effective decision-making to one of ratifying decisions made elsewhere.

Policy Implementation

Once a policy has been passed by the Riksdag, signed by the King, and officially promulgated by the Cabinet, interest group attention turns to the administrative arena, the *implementation stage* of policy-making. In ad-

---

[21] Elvander, *Intresseorganisationerna*, pp. 213–231; Foyer, "Former för kontakt," pp. 67–68.

[22] Elvander, *Intresseorganisationerna*, p. 217.

[23] *Ibid.*, pp. 217–218.

[24] Minutes from the Liberal party white-collar section, 1954–1967, Liberal Party Archive, Stockholm (typewritten).

dition to participating in advisory councils, interest groups have gained representation on the decision-making bodies of a number of administrative organs at both the national and local levels.

For example, in 1946 only 28 percent of the administrative agency executive boards (which set policy for the agencies) had representatives from outside the agency. By 1968 the percentage had risen to 64, of which 35 percent came exclusively from interest groups.[25] Moreover, just those agencies responsible for the most important policy areas were the ones to receive interest group representation.

During the 1960s direct representation was expanded to regional administrative organs. Thus regional labor market boards, school boards, and planning councils now each possess more interest group representatives than civil sevants on their respective executive boards.[26]

And, as shall be explained in some detail later, the scope and depth of this kind of interest group representation in the implementation stage creates the preconditions for greater autonomy by agencies and their clientele interest groups from effective political control by elected representatives.

The normal governmental policy-making process is shown in diagram form below. In a very real sense, it can be said that participating in Royal Commissions, responding to *remiss* reply requests, and serving in administrative positions have all served to legitimatize a form of group access to policy-making separate from representation by political parties. In this sense functional representation has firm roots in the Swedish political system.[27]

In addition to interest group access to the normal legislative process through an extensive system of functional representation, a system of consultation between interest groups and policy-makers has evolved to the point where it can be said that a system of extra-Parliamentary rule-making now exists in Sweden. In this connection governments actually negotiate agreements with interest groups outside the halls of the Riksdag and in so doing bypass the normal process of legislation. This system of consultation takes three major forms: negotiated agreements where it is publicly announced that the Riksdag's only role is to ratify rather than to modify; negotiated agreements in lieu of legislation; and understandings

[25] Björn Molin, Lennart Månsson, and Lars Strömberg, *Offentlig förvaltning: stats och kommunalförvaltningens struktur och funktioner* (Stockholm: Bonniers, 1969), p. 357.

[26] Nils Andrén, *et al.*, eds., *Svensk statsförvaltning i omdaning* (4th ed.; Stockholm: Almqvist and Wiksell, 1968), pp. 45–47.

[27] See Beer, *British Politics*, pp. 71–73, for definition; see also p. 166 of this work.

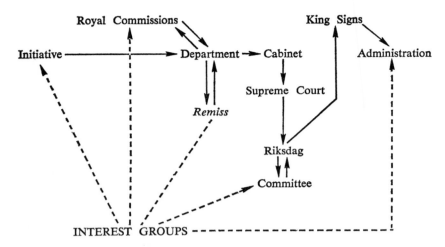

(Solid lines indicate the governmental decision-making process; dotted lines the points where interest groups seek to gain access.)

reached through informal agreements. As in the deliberative stage of policy-making during the normal process of legislation, effective decision-making during such consultations can take place because of the majority position (either alone or at the head of a coalition) which the Social Democrats have enjoyed since the 1930s.

The first major form of consultation, in which the Riksdag only ratifies previously negotiated agreements, developed during World War II. At that time a system of state-employee wage round negotiations patterned after that prevailing in the private sector emerged. In 1950 a permanent negotiating organ, a newly created Ministry for Civil Affairs, took over the task of negotiating salary agreements on a regular basis, and in 1966 civil servants gained the right to strike. A key element in these developments was the declining role for the Riksdag and the opposition political parties in shaping the outcome of these negotiations; by the 1950s such agreements had the character of binding contracts, subject only to Riksdag ratification.

Similar events took place in negotiations between the government and the major farm organizations. Beginning in 1939 a system had emerged whereby commodity prices and subsidies were subjects for regular negotiations.[28] As with wage negotiations in the public sector, these agreements have come to be considered final, subject only to Riksdag ratification.[29]

[28] Elvander, *Intresseorganisationerna*, p. 40.
[29] *Ibid.*, pp. 189–190, 244–249.

The second way agreements can be reached between the government and interest groups lies completely outside Riksdag control. Here the government, instead of proposing legislation, either negotiates an agreement with the appropriate interest group(s) or accepts an agreement negotiated between the interest groups themselves. Assuming the group is truly representative and its members abide by the leadership's directive, such agreements in effect obviate the need for legislation. Organizations which participate in such a procedure expect to have greater opportunities for influence, over both the details and the administration of the proposal, than would be the case if the matter were the subject for legislation.[30] Thus in these instances the government always retains an ultimate sanction, a threat to introduce legislation if the provisions of the agreement are violated.

Decisions in the housing industry provide a good example of this process of "extra-Parliamentary" legislation at work.[31] Between 1953 and 1956 real estate owners under the watchful eye of a government-designated mediator reached an agreement governing the criteria and administration of means tests (behovsprövning) for occupants, an agreement which the government then accepted in lieu of legislation. A similar process led to government acceptance of agreements between the Real Estate Association (Sveriges Fastighetsägareförbund) and the National Tenants Association (Hyresgästernas Riksförbund) regarding the question of compensation for repairs and interest rate increases on mortgages between the years 1957 and 1958. In 1968, after an agreement among all the political parties regarding the scope and timing of the dismantling of rent controls fell through, the Swedish Real Estate Association and the National Tenants Association reached on their own a rent control agreement, which in turn was accepted by the government.[32]

The third major way of reaching agreements, that of informal consultations between interest groups and the government, has caused a considerable stir in Swedish political life, particularly among the opposition political parties who have consistently been left out of such discussions. Research into what actually goes on at these meetings has dispelled the notion that formal agreements are reached on specific policies.[33] Rather

[30] Foyer, "Former för kontakt," p. 35.

[31] An example of direct negotiations between the government and affected interest groups is provided by the National Bank of Sweden, private banks, savings banks, and insurance companies regarding credit policies during the 1950s. On these and other examples, see *ibid.*, pp. 36–42.

[32] Elvander, *Intresseorganisationerna*, pp. 198–199.

[33] *Ibid.*, pp. 201–203.

information is exchanged, complaints are discussed, trial balloons are floated—all toward the end of creating a sense of mutual understanding regarding the intentions of the major power-wielders in Swedish society. As such the flavor of discussions takes on the quality of "ear-stroking," that charming phrase Beer cites in his work on British politics.[34]

Between 1949 and 1955 such discussions were held on Thursdays, hence the name Thursday Club. Primarily such discussions focused on problems created by different regulations carried over from the war. It was not uncommon for such exchanges to lead to follow-up discussions between the Minister of Finance, Per Edvin Sköld, and the complaining industry, resulting eventually in changes.

Between 1955 and 1964 Harpsund, the Prime Minister's official summer residence, became the site of the discussions, and instead of weekly meetings, annual conferences were held. As wartime controls had been eliminated by 1955, these discussions came to focus more on the general state of the economy. Also during these years special meetings were held on occasion to discuss particular problems, for example, Sweden's possible entry into the Common Market. Interest groups as well as government officials did not pass up the chance to use such opportunities for additional lobbying on issues which were not the subject for direct discussions.[35]

Starting in 1962 Harpsund meetings gradually came to be replaced by planning councils which were attached directly to different ministries. By 1968 the Departments of Finance, Education, Interior, Agriculture, and Industry all had such councils.

In summary, these forms of consultations between interest groups and the government—in which the Riksdag only ratifies previously negotiated agreements, negotiated agreements in lieu of legislation, and understandings reached through informal agreements—have created an arena of extra-Parliamentary rule-making in Sweden. Combined with the functional representation of groups during the normal process of law-making, the existence of this arena serves to further underscore the important role interest groups play in the Swedish political system, a topic which will be more thoroughly discussed in the next chapter.

---

[34] D. H. Robertson, the originator of the phrase, uses it in this sense: "encouragements which are not quite promises, frowns which are not quite prohibitions, understandings which are not quite agreements." See Beer, *British Politics*, p. 327.

[35] Elvander, *Intresseorganisationerna*, p. 202.

Chapter Four

The General Role of Interest Groups in the Swedish Policy-Making Process

The important role interest groups play in the Swedish decision-making process cannot be explained solely in terms of institutional factors, such as the rise of the Social Democratic party to a majority position (either alone or in coalition) in the system. Ideological changes in the Social Democratic party, the pattern of policy which has emerged since the 1930s, and certain characteristics of interest groups themselves which have enabled them to take advantage of the new opportunities presented them are important explanatory variables as well. The sum total of these variables has been to dramatically change the balance between parties and groups as channels for public opinion.

In representative democracies parties and interest groups are the two main channels through which citizen views are communicated to decision-makers. In this connection, S. E. Finer provides a useful, straightforward definition of each when he writes that interest groups are those organizations which are "occupied at any point of time in trying to influence the policy of public bodies in their own chosen direction; though (unlike political parties) never themselves prepared to undertake the direct government of the country."[1]

This distinction between parties and interest groups can become blurred in a multiparty system. Cooperation may become so intimate that a particular party may be essentially representing no more than one particular interest group, as Duverger has demonstrated. Certainly in Sweden during different periods of its history the Farmers party (now the Center party) has acted more as a pressure group in a party's clothing than a political party according to the above definition. Nevertheless, such a distinction

[1] S. E. Finer, *Anonymous Empire* (2nd ed.; London: Pall Mall Press, 1966), pp. 2–3.

between parties and interest groups can still be usefully made in Sweden. One indication of this is the result of a 1968 post-election survey, presented in Table 1. Responses suggested that while each party has a core of supporters from a particular social or economic group, none is dependent solely on the support of one group alone.

TABLE 1
DISTRIBUTION OF VOTES FOR PARTIES BY OCCUPATIONAL GROUPS IN PERCENT, 1968

Occupational strata	Party					
	Cons.	Lib.	Center	Social Dems.	Did not vote	*Total*
Big enterprisers, professionals, salaried employees in higher positions	24	13	6	2	2	6
Small businessmen and enterprisers (excl. farmers)	12	13	11	4	7	8
Salaried employees in lower positions (excl. foremen, etc.)	28	35	17	16	24	20
Foremen, shop assistants	4	6	3	10	6	8
Workers (excl. farm and lumbering workers)	12	21	26	61	44	44
Farm and lumbering workers	2	3	7	5	6	4
Farmers	15	5	29	1	8	8
Students and others not included in any occupational category	3	4	1	1	3	2
Total percent	100	100	100	100	100	100
Number of cases	286	370	469	1,458	214	2,943

NOTE: The total column includes all interviewed respondents in the sample, that is, also minor party voters and the "not ascertained" category.
SOURCE: Bo Särlvik, "Voting Behavior in Shifting Election Winds," in *Scandinavian Political Studies*, ed. Olof Ruin, Vol. 5 (New York: Columbia University Press, 1970), Reference Table II.B., p. 279.

Between 1921 and 1935 political parties were the dominant channel for inputs into the political system. The giant national trade union confederations and other national confederations (such as trade associations, farmer organizations, and so on) which were soon to form the core of the group infrastructure of modern Sweden were still in the process of consolidating. Such groups were nearly completely excluded from the national political arena during the period 1870 to 1910. While many gained access to local and municipal levels of policy-making during these years, their entry onto the national stage did not come until the 1930s. Instead only groups which shared close personal and ideological ties with the ruling privileged classes enjoyed such access.[2]

Pressure for democratization of the political system reached its zenith during the three decades between 1890 and 1920. In 1909 the suffrage was extended to half a million new voters, most of them from the working class, and proportional representation was introduced. By 1917 the King had come to accept the Riksdag as the final source of legitimate authority, and by 1921 universal suffrage had been achieved. In the process, a mature party system had been created. Thus by 1920 every major element of Swedish society had at least one national political party vying for its support, as the Conservative, Liberal, Farmer, Social Democratic, and Communist parties all had representatives in the Riksdag. By 1911 party discipline had become established, a development which sharply reduced the number of small blocs of Riksdag representatives who sought to go their own way. During the same period parliamentary party groups in the Riksdag progressively established a position of leadership even within parties which originated as mass-based organizations outside the hall of Parliament.[3]

As no party approached a majority position in the electorate during the 1920s, political parties made policy in the committees of the Riksdag or in Royal Commissions, whose party strength was carefully balanced according to the proportion of support enjoyed by each party in the Riksdag.[4] Groups, during those years, sought to influence the normal process of policy-making through the parties, primarily in the Riksdag. The system of direct contact between the government and interest groups was

[2] Pär-Erik Back, *Sammanslutningarnas roll i politiken 1870–1910* (Lund: Studentlitteratur, 1967), pp. 215–220.
[3] Edvard Thermaenius, *Sveriges politiska partier* (Stockholm: Gebers, 1933). See also Pär-Erik Back, "Det svenska partiväsendet," in *Samhälle och riksdag* (5 vols.; Stockholm: Almqvist and Wiksell, 1966), II, pp. 6–12.
[4] Hans Meijer, *Kommittépolitik och kommittéarbete; det statliga kommittéväsendets utvecklingslinjer 1905–54 samt nuvarande funktion och arbetsformer* (Lund: Gleerup, 1956), pp. 69–73. See also Hans Wieslander, *I nedrustningens tecken: intressen och aktiviteter kring försvarsfrågor 1918–1925* (Lund: Gleerup, 1966), pp. 245–310.

used extensively only during the war years and thereafter progressively reduced in scope.[5]

But the 1930s came to mark a watershed in Swedish politics. The era of "minority parliamentarianism," characterized by weak governments dependent for their survival on their ability to create "hopping majorities,"[6] gave way to the era of "majority parliamentarianism," as the Social Democratic party passed the 40 percent mark for the first time in the 1932 election, and succeeded a year later in forming a coalition with the Farmers party, a coalition which for the first time guaranteed a solid majority for a particular policy orientation over a period of years.[7]

As effective decisions were no longer made in the Riksdag, a shift in emphasis by interest groups took place. From the 1930s on, Royal Commissions, the *remiss* stage, and the administration of policy became the important points of access. The pattern of policy which emerged during those years served both to reinforce the importance of these new access points and to increase the need for direct contact between the government and interest groups.

While groups previously had enjoyed influence over policy-making separate from their position in the system of parliamentary representation and party government, this access from the 1930s on underwent a qualitative change—both in scope and depth—and with it came a change in the balance between parties and groups as channels for public opinion. Extension of government control over the economy, regulation of agricultural production, and the introduction of wide-sweeping welfare programs formed the cornerstone of this "revolution."

Between 1880 and 1920 Swedish Social Democracy faced the same tensions as its counterparts in other Western democracies. These tensions derived from the simple fact that Marxist theory provided little guidance for everyday political life.[8]

It was in the late 1920s that the Social Democrats resolved the problem, at least to their own satisfaction. Ernst Wigforss, one of the party's leading theoreticians and strategists, succeeded in winning the party over to an expansionist economic program,[9] arguing that the government should

[5] Gunnar Heckscher, *Staten och organisationerna* (Stockholm: Kooperativa Förbundets Bokförlag, 1946), pp. 145–146, 229–231.

[6] Neil C. M. Elder, "The Parliamentary Role of Joint Standing Committees in Sweden," *American Political Science Review*, 45 (June, 1951), pp. 464–473.

[7] In 1936 the working coalition became a coalition ministry.

[8] Herbert Tingsten, *Den svenska socialdemokratins idéutveckling* (2 vols.; Stockholm: Tiden, 1941). See particularly volume I.

[9] There seems to be a general consensus among observers of the Swedish scene

appropriate large sums of money for public works and thereby promote employment by increasing purchasing power. Through the multiplier effect, this would create additional outlets for manufactured products, which in turn would further stimulate production and end the economic downturn.

In 1930 the Social Democrats presented a motion to the Riksdag calling for 20 million crowns (roughly 4 million dollars in today's currency) to be spent on employment programs. This sum contrasted sharply with the 8 million crowns the party had proposed in each of the three previous years, to say nothing of the dramatic difference between this sum and the 2.8 million crowns actually approved by the Riksdag in 1929.[10] When the Social Democrats then assumed power in 1932 they took the first steps to act on Wigforss's program.[11]

For the Swedish Social Democrats, such a remedy presupposed considerable state intervention. For example, when the private sector failed to take on the unemployed, the state was to do it, often through public works. Wigforss argued forcefully that nationalization should be avoided in these instances, that what was needed was not ownership per se, but rather influence over the functions which ownership provided.[12] Therefore Wigforss and the Social Democrats sought to achieve influence over prices, capital flow, and economic rationalization in an effort to reduce the effects of downturns and ensure the maximum utilization of resources.[13] Thus was born the Swedish concept of general economic planning.

---

that Wigforss indeed played a leading role in gaining party support for such a program. There is no agreement, however, on the intellectual origins of this program. Some see Wigforss as having developed the program himself, essentially by elaborating concepts originally borrowed from British Liberals, in particular the early writings of Keynes. (See Leif Lewin, *Planhushållningsdebatten* [Stockholm: Almqvist and Wiksell, 1967], pp. 59–66.) Others see Wigforss citing Keynes to provide justification for what in effect was a revitalization of a dormant Social Democratic tradition. According to this view, the program drew heavily on the writings of the early Stockholm School—primarily Knut Wicksell and M. B. Hamilton—which anticipated many of Keynes's concepts. It is outside the scope of this essay to pass judgment on this debate. (See Otto Steiger, *Studien zur Entstehung der Neuen Wirtschaftslehre in Schweden: Eine Anti-Kritik* [Berlin: Duncker & Humblot, 1971]. Also the review of Steiger by M. Donald Hancock in the *Social Science Quarterly*, Vol. 53, No. 2 [September, 1972], pp. 417–418. Also Berndt Öhman, "Krispolitiken 1933," *Dagens Nyheter* [November 5, 1972], p. 2.)

[10] *Ibid.*, p. 63.

[11] *Ibid.*, pp. 59–66.

[12] *Ibid.*, pp. 68–71. For a more contemporary discussion of functional socialism, see Gunnar Adler-Karlsson, *Functional Socialism* (Stockholm: Prisma, 1969), pp. 9–50.

[13] Lewin, *Planhushållningsdebatten*, 68–75.

Whether such a position could be labeled "socialist" or not is another matter. The crucial point is that the policies which flowed from such a perspective demanded a good working relationship between the state and the business world. As Beer notes: "In a free country, as government extends its powers over the economy, it must at the same time so act as to win a substantial degree of consent and cooperation from the groups being regulated."[14]

In Sweden by the mid-1930s the irreconcilable conflict between labor and capital had been replaced by the concept of the "People's Home," where all shared in the rewards of a common effort. Trade unions and trade associations alike gained functional representation on newly established important administrative agencies.[15] By 1938, Wigforss had taken steps which led in 1939 to the first of a series of informal meetings between the government and the business world.[16]

Governmental involvement in agriculture also underwent a considerable expansion. The basis for the 1933 coalition between the Social Democrats and the Farmers party was an agreement that in return for supporting the employment and welfare schemes proposed by the Social Democrats, the Farmers party could expect increased assistance for agriculture.

Such proved to be the case. All across the board government regulation and subsidies were either expanded or introduced for the first time. By the end of the decade there was neither a crop nor a piece of livestock which remained untouched by this quantitative jump in state involvement. To administer the new regulations and subsidies, the government willingly delegated administrative authority to the affected groups. Dairy associations took care of milk products; grain associations, corn and wheat; meat producers, meat products, and so forth.[17] In some cases state enthusiasm outran existing capabilities, in which case the government encouraged the creation of a group and then endowed it with monopolistic rights in that area.[18]

Government extension into new spheres of social life also vastly expanded the importance of interest groups in the policy-making process. Sven Aspling, Sweden's Minister of Social Affairs during the 1960s, summarized the philosophy behind such reforms:

[14] Samuel Beer, *British Politics in the Collectivist Age* (New York: Random House, 1969), p. 321.
[15] Heckscher, *Staten och organisationerna*, pp. 193–199.
[16] *Ibid.*, pp. 197–198.
[17] *Ibid.*, pp. 198–200.
[18] *Ibid.*, pp. 197–198.

Social policy is like a safety net. The point is to weave it as finely as possible to prevent people from falling through. When we're able to provide people with security, to guarantee them a certain material standard, a good education, and a job, we can start to expect them to develop themselves, to be able to use their energy constructively rather than constantly wasting it worrying about protecting themselves against unexpected poverty, unemployment or illness. Only with a feeling of security can people develop their potentialities and contribute to the betterment of society.[19]

While Sweden has had a long history of state involvement in welfare matters, Aspling's comments nevertheless indicate the qualitative change in philosophy which occurred when the Social Democrats assumed power in the 1930s. For example, at the turn of the century, it was not uncommon for the destitute to be farmed out by their parishes on a competitive basis to those willing to pay their subsistence.[20] Further, until the 1930s little assistance was available for the disabled, the feebleminded, the insane, and the sick without means.[21] Thus while the destitute waited patiently and gratefully for social benefits fifty years ago, now Swedes believe that social insurances are not privileges for the needy but the rights of everyone.[22]

Retirement pensions, assistance to the blind, accident insurance, unemployment compensation, health and dental care, compensation for women during pregnancy, rent subsidies, limitation of working hours, child support programs, special assistance for children born out of wedlock—these are areas of social care which underwent fundamental expansion during the 1930s.[23]

Thus the creation of what has popularly become labeled Sweden's "womb to tomb" system of welfare, perhaps the most comprehensive in the Western world, also encouraged intimate cooperation between the

[19] This interview quote appears in Frederic Fleisher, *The New Sweden* (New York: David McKay, 1967), p. 196.

[20] Åke Elmer, *Från fattigsverige till välfärdsstaten* (Stockholm: Aldus, 1963), pp. 46–49, especially p. 47. Harry Martinson, one of Sweden's most prominent authors and now a member of the Swedish Academy, describes in his autobiographical novel, *The Flowering Nettles*, how at the age of six in 1910 he became a public charge when his father died and his mother deserted him to emigrate to the United States. For the next decade he lived on different farms, tolerated only because of the small sum the parish paid for his keep. Harry Martinson, *Nässlorna blomma* (Stockholm: Bonniers, 1944). See also Fleisher, *New Sweden*, pp. 198–199.

[21] Fleisher, *New Sweden*, p. 199.

[22] *Ibid.*, p. 198.

[23] Karl Höjer, *Svensk socialpolitisk historia* (Stockholm: Norstedt, 1952), pp. 188–209.

state and affected groups so that the ambitious programs could in fact become reality.

As the government became increasingly involved in the economy, interest groups began to see the advantages they could gain for their members by exercising their bargaining power. In so doing these groups encouraged the further expansion of government activity, as they sought to bring about controls beneficial to themselves. In the field of social reform, similar developments were taking place, for once the welfare state made its appearance and its basic code was established, its program did much to define further demands on the government during the next thirty years.

The war years also contributed significantly toward institutionalizing this new mutual dependency between interest groups and the state. The cooperation which existed during those years, Heckscher writes, far surpassed that which existed between 1914 to 1918.[24] Groups became intimately involved with all facets of the various controls imposed during World War II: economic preparation, price controls, wage controls, food distribution, press censorship, and so on.[25] Without the administrative assistance of groups, Heckscher concludes, wartime policies[26] would never have gone so smoothly nor have been so effective as they were.[27]

Why was it that group participation by this time had become so crucial for policy-making? Groups possessed the resources needed by the government to make effective policy. First of all, their advice enabled the government to obtain technical information, without which economic regulation would have been impossible. Second, their acquiescence was necessary if government programs were to operate successfully. Thus, for example, a national health plan could only hope to succeed in a climate where most doctors were prepared to support the program. Finally, the approval of groups was essential if particular policies affecting them were to be regarded as legitimate by them and the public at large.[28]

It is not enough to say that these resources derived from governmental expansion into certain areas of policy-making, for groups had to have reached a certain level of development before they could utilize these re-

[24] Heckscher, *Staten och organisationerna*, p. 230.
[25] *Ibid.*, pp. 230–231.
[26] By wartime, I do not mean to imply that Sweden was at war, but rather that the international economic dislocation stemming from the war necessitated far-ranging measures of internal economic coordination in Sweden, as elsewhere, during the war.
[27] Heckscher, *Staten och organisationerna*, p. 243.
[28] See Beer, *British Politics*, pp. 320–331, for a fuller discussion of these resources as they apply to the British case.

sources. It is to certain attributes of the affected groups that I now turn.

One of these, particularly remarkable by standards of international comparison, is the degree of density which has come to characterize organizational life in Sweden. Thus 95 percent of the blue-collar workers belong to the LO, TCO represents 75 percent of the potentially organizable white-collar workers, and SACO includes 90 percent of the professionals. On the employers' side, SAF has nearly 100 percent affiliation from firms which negotiate with federations belonging to the LO.[29]

A second important attribute, amalgamation, the degree to which the organized have been brought together in one body,[30] has proceeded steadily during the twentieth century. What is most clear to the outside observer, of course, is the development of strong national trade union confederations. Thus, for example, in contrast to the TUC in England, the LO in Sweden has had the authority to coordinate the wage policy of its individual federations since 1941.[31] Moreover, it has actively promoted the rationalization of its own union structure. The same trend, while most prominent in the labor market parties, is exhibited all across the board in Swedish group life. Increasingly a group must "speak with one voice" if it is to gain access to the points of influence which are vital to it. Thus for an interest group to fill a spot on a Royal Commission, there must in fact be one group rather than an assortment of smaller entities which can step forward to accept the position. The same holds true for *remiss* replies. Nothing weakens the overall effectiveness of a group more than to have all its various factions express their opinions on a proposed policy change; so too with representation in the bureaucratic arena of policy-making, direct negotiations between interest groups and government, and delegation of administrative authority. Each of these forms of contact requires that the groups be of sizable scope, density, and amalgamation.

Finally there is expertise. For the Swedish system to work, the government is heavily dependent on the expertise of the affected interest groups. That it works so well can be attributed to the ability of national confederations to deliver the goods, in this case the facts. Each one, whether economic or promotional, has its own staff of full-time research experts. Their specific tasks are to draft *remiss* replies, execute studies requested by member federations, and launch investigations of their own which will serve to further the interests of the members they represent. Not an in-

---

[29] Elvander, *Intresseorganisationerna*, pp. 48–50.
[30] Beer, *British Politics*, p. 332.
[31] Elvander, *Intresseorganisationerna*, p. 29.

significant contribution to Social Democratic ideology, in fact, has come from the research staff of the LO.

Thus the forms of contact during the normal legislative process, as well as the practice of policy-making through direct contact between the government and interest groups, underwent a fundamental transformation in the wake of developments during the 1930s and World War II. The most significant result was the reduced importance of political parties in communicating citizen views to policy-makers. Their role, which had been dominant during the 1920s and early part of the 1930s, now declined in the face of the expanding importance of interest groups.

In summary, then, the significance of interest group activity in the policy-making process in Sweden has been the result of a number of interrelated factors, only one of which was the shift from "minority parliamentarianism" to "majority parliamentarianism." The effect of such a change, however, when combined with ideological developments in the Social Democratic party, the pattern of policy which emerged during the 1930s, and certain group characteristics, has led to a system of policy-making in which groups effectively rival parties as channels for public opinion.

Having examined the political process in Sweden and the general importance of interest groups in that process, a detailed analysis of the efforts of the Central Organization of Salaried Employees (Tjänstemännens Centralorganisation or TCO) to influence public policy follows.

Chapter Five

TCO's Resources and the Problem of Cohesion

TCO has a wealth of resources for influencing public policy. As Table I indicates, TCO enjoys excellent access to the three major points of effective decision-making in the contemporary Swedish political system: Royal Commissions, *remiss* replies, and administrative organs. TCO representatives to Royal Commissions and administrative organs come almost exclusively from its central headquarters, and the *remiss* replies are entirely its responsibility.

The staffing available to ensure that TCO's stands are well researched is indeed impressive. In 1971, not counting secretarial help, TCO's headquarters had forty-seven full-time functionaries spending some or all of their time on issues of public policy. Moreover, within TCO's central headquarters a number of special advisory organs have been created, each charged with responsibility for following either developments in a particular policy area or policies as they affect particular groups belonging to TCO. Thus when TCO's leadership needs to supply representatives to Royal Commissions and administrative organs, or see that a *remiss* reply is drafted, it can choose according to the kind of expertise needed from one of a host of different groups of experts.[1]

[1] The Director's staff, the Research Division, TCO's Council for Engineers and Specialists in Natural Science (TCO's Ingenjörs- och naturvetarråd), TCO's Inventors' Rights Committee (TCO's Uppfinnarkommitté), TCO's Advisory Council for Foremen (TCO's Arbetsledarråd), TCO's Advisory Council on Education (TCO's Lärarråd), TCO's Educational Committee (TCO's Utbildningsnämnd), TCO's Committee on Family Problems (TCO's Familjepolitiska Nämnd), TCO's Advisory Council on Archives (TCO's Arkivråd), TCO's Committee on Cultural Affairs (TCO's Kulturkommitté), TCO's Committee to Further Cooperation in the Work Place (SAMKO-Kommittén för Samarbetsfrågor på Arbetsplatsen), TCO's Council for Headmasters and School Superintendents (TCO's Sociala Yrkesråd), TCO's Committee on Statistics (TCO's Statistiknämnd), TCO's Advisory Council for Advanced Trade Union Education (Studierådet för Högre Facklig Utbildning).

TABLE I
TCO'S PARTICIPATION IN DECISION-MAKING PROCESS, 1945–1971

Year	Memberships on Royal Commissions	Submissions of *Remiss* Replies	Memberships on Administrative Organs
1945	12	34	11
1946	10	35	11
1947	6	36	8
1948	12	23	8
1949	9	28	11
1950	7	31	13
1951	8	35	13
1952	8	39	13
1953	9	37	14
1954	11	28	16
1955	12	48	17
1956	10	51	17
1957	17	64	19
1958	14	49	19
1959	16	68	19
1960	20	78	22
1961	28	84	26
1962	29	83	30
1963	33	119	43
1964	32	86	52
1965	40	119	50
1966	37	109	54
1967	25	107	50
1968	26	82	56
1969	28	112	62
1970	43	120	60
1971	43	142	70

SOURCE: *TCO's Årsberättelser 1945–71.*

In addition to such permanent organs, TCO's director on occasion creates temporary committees to tackle particular policy issues, the results of which will then serve as base material for later TCO stands. In 1954 a special committee was created to study how best to coordinate existing TCO federation health plans with the National Health Plan passed that year by the Riksdag. It completed its work that same year. A group to study TCO's position on tax issues was created in 1963. And between 1961 and 1963 a special committee studied the wage policies of TCO federations, compiling the first definitive statement on white-collar aims in wage negotiations. (A second committee, appointed in 1969, is planning to present its findings to the June, 1973, Congress.)

In order to insure that TCO's views receive the attention of both its members and the general public, TCO's information section carries on a wide range of activities. *TCO Tidningen*, published twice a month, reaches nearly 60,000 readers; 100 to 200 articles per year are placed in the national press and trade union publications; fourteen to eighteen new brochures and reports on specific TCO stands are published each year. A wide range of conferences, many in part to help special organs within TCO keep in close touch with their local constituents, are carried out each year. Since 1958 TCO's sixty-six local contact committees for white-collar workers (TCO-kommittéer) organized throughout Sweden have been under the supervision of the information section.

In addition to providing two-way communication (from the grass roots to the leadership and vice-versa), these organs communicate to the local populace TCO's positions on different issues. Press coverage in local newspapers of conferences is standard practice, for example. Finally, weekend and monthly courses for white-collar workers are arranged at TCO's two schools, Gällöfsta and Bergendal.[2] Thus TCO clearly has ample resources for influencing public policy. Its problem lies in developing clear policy stands.

Cohesion

In an attempt to gain an indirect measure of the relative influence of different groups, Nils Elvander, a Swedish political scientist, at one point in his study of interest group activity in Swedish politics, asked leading politicians and interest group leaders to list the three groups they believed to have the best contacts with the government.[3] Of the twenty-nine out of thirty-seven who replied, all named the LO, sixteen named SAF, fifteen the Federation of Swedish Industries (Sveriges Industriförbund or SI), and fourteen TCO. Thereafter the number of times any group was mentioned diminished sharply, with the distribution falling among a number of other national confederations.

However, one does not need to depend on a reputational approach to see that TCO has come to enjoy a recognized position as one of the more influential groups in Swedish society. As indicated earlier, TCO's representation on Royal Commissions and administrative organs has grown rapidly, as has the number of *remiss* replies it is asked to give. Even more significant are the kinds of commission, agency, and *remiss* reply activities

---

[2] In 1965 Gällöfsta was sold to the Ministry of Defense.

[3] Nils Elvander, *Intresseorganisationerna i dagens Sverige* (2nd ed.; Lund: Gleerup, 1969), p. 292. Interviews were carried out during 1964 and 1965, p. 326.

in which TCO is asked to participate. Simply put, there are no important domestic issues in which TCO does not participate. Finally, the case studies which follow will support the contention that TCO is no unimportant group.

All this, however, merely underscores what is most interesting about TCO; namely, that TCO should have come as far as it has, given the difficulties it faces in gathering enough internal support to effectively use the resources it possesses to influence the course of public policy on any given issue. By now it has become a truism in the study of interest groups that resources mean little if a group is unable to muster the cohesion needed to maximize their use. And cohesion is the greatest problem TCO faces.

In this connection, two major causes of division stand out: the diversity of economic position and heterogeneity of political affiliation of TCO's membership.

In 1971, for example, the membership had the following income distribution:

11 percent had a salary under 2,000 Swedish crowns per month (approximately $400.00)

51 percent had a salary between 2,000 and 3,000 Swedish crowns per month (approximately $400.00 and $600.00)

26 percent had a salary between 3,000 and 4,000 Swedish crowns per month (approximately $600.000 and $800.00)

12 percent had a salary over 4,000 Swedish crowns per month (approximately $800.00)[4]

This heterogeneity extends into the political realm as well. As Table 2 indicates, support by salaried workers for different political parties runs across the entire spectrum, creating significant problems for the group's cohesion. While it is true that Sweden is a highly consensual society, ideological differences, particularly regarding the role of the state in the economy, are still the subject of considerable controversy among the political parties.[5] Studies of the voting behavior of the Swedish electorate have demonstrated that the major dividing line runs between the socialist parties (the Communist party and the Social Democratic party) on the one hand

[4] Lönepolitiska Utredningen, "Preliminär rapport från lönepolitiska utredningen (Avsnitt I och II)" (Stockholm: Tjänstemännens Centralorganisation, 1972), p. 21 (mimeographed). Note that the spread within TCO has not diminished during the years. In 1961 the percentages were: 17 under 1,000; 46 between 1,000 and 1,500; 24 between 1,500 and 2,000; 13 over 2,000. Speech by Otto Nordenskiöld, Minutes from TCO General Council Meetings, meeting of November 25, 1961, TCO Archive, Stockholm, p. 8 (mimeographed).

[5] Leif Lewin, *Planhushållningsdebatten* (Stockholm: Almqvist & Wiksell, 1967).

TABLE 2
DISTRIBUTION OF VOTES IN OCCUPATIONAL GROUPS FOR POLITICAL PARTIES BY PERCENT, 1968

Group	Cons.	Lib.	Bourg. Coal.	Christ. Dem.	Center	Soc. Dem.	Comm.	Not Known	Total Percent	No. of Cases
Big enterprisers, professionals, salaried employees in higher positions[a]	39	27	1	1	16	14	0	2	100	175
Small businessmen and enterprisers (excl. farmers)	16	22	—	2	24	31	0	5	100	216
Salaried employees in lower positions (excl. foremen, etc.)[a]	15	24	1	1	14	43	1	1	100	549
Foremen, shop assistants[a]	6	11	—	0	7	71	2	3	100	209
Workers excl. farm and lumbering workers	3	7	0	2	10	75	2	1	100	1186
Farm and lumbering workers	6	8	—	1	27	56	1	1	100	119
Farmers	19	9	0	3	61	6	0	2	100	222
Students and others not included in any occupational category	(13)	(32)	(2)	(—)	(13)	(30)	(6)	(4)	100	53

[a] White-collar workers belonging to TCO are included in these groups.
NOTE: The classification includes all respondents in the sample. Retired persons are classified according to earlier occupation, while other not gainfully employed persons are classified according to the occupation of the head of the household. However, students are put in a separate category that also includes a few unclassifiable cases.
SOURCE: Bo Särlvik, "Voting Behavior in Shifting Election Winds," in *Scandinavian Political Studies*, ed. Olof Ruin, Vol. 5 (New York: Columbia University Press, 1970), Reference Table II.A., p. 278.

and the bourgeois parties on the other (the Liberal party, the Center party, and the Conservative party). While switches may sometimes occur on a large scale within these two blocs, there is little crossover from one bloc to the other.[6] For a group whose membership divides almost evenly, one-half supporting the Social Democratic party and the other supporting the bourgeois parties, such political heterogeneity poses serious problems. It can expect to be charged with favoring one bloc (socialist or bourgeois)[7] or the other, depending on the stand it takes. It can expect to see the different political parties aim their propaganda at the sectors of TCO membership most likely to vote for their party, encouraging further division. Finally, once an issue becomes politicized, TCO can expect to experience difficulty in taking a stand, owing to the cross-pressures on TCO members who also support a particular political party.

In this connection, to make matters worse, once an issue becomes highly charged politically, the potential consequences of any TCO stand become even more disastrous owing to the vagaries of jurisdictional competition among trade unions in Sweden.

The central fact of postwar politics in Sweden has been the dominant position of the Social Democratic party. Given the intimate contacts between the party and the blue-collar employees confederation, the LO, relations with the LO are important if TCO wants to influence the outcome of any given issue. Thus TCO headquarters is often interested to learn where the LO stands on a particular issue, so that it can coordinate TCO's position as much as possible. The LO is also interested in such a relationship, but it has of course become more interested the larger TCO has grown.

In any event, daily contact is maintained between the two organizations. For *remiss* replies on such questions as trade policy, labor market policy, taxes, social welfare reforms, and education, to name only the most important areas, it is standard operating practice for an official in one or the other organization to call his opposite number to learn his views on

---

[6] Bo Särlvik, "Political Stability and Change in the Swedish Electorate," in *Scandinavian Political Studies*, ed. Peritti Pesonen, Vol. 1 (New York: Columbia University Press, 1966), pp. 188–222; especially p. 191. Of course this crossover is important to the political parties because only a small margin is needed for either the Social Democrats or the bourgeois parties to assume the reins of power. It should also be noted that the Särlvik data do not take into account the recent trend toward greater vote crossover. Moreover, one or the other bloc can grow through the recruitment of first-time voters.

[7] The terms, socialist and bourgeois, are accepted for differentiating between the socialist parties on the one hand and the Liberal, Center, and Conservative parties on the other. This distinction, therefore, is used in a neutral sense.

the issue. More formal meetings may develop if it appears that initial differences may lend themselves to modification. Moreover, drafts of *remiss* replies are often exchanged prior to final action by the respective executive boards.[8]

Representatives from the two organizations who sit on administrative organs and advisory councils keep a constant informal dialogue going outside the meetings regarding their respective positions in an effort to harmonize them as much as possible.[9]

Good relations with the LO can pay off on particular policies; it can also help TCO gain access to important points in the decision-making process, as I learned from a high-ranking member of TCO's research division: "We side with the LO on many questions to keep in good with them. . . . TCO will go along (on some issues) with a proposal . . . in part to get money in the bank with the LO when a question of representation on a public body comes up. Earlier the LO wanted two or three representatives in a body before TCO could get one. Now it is more one to one. The LO recognizes also that it is good politics since they often say, 'Since you can have a place on this administrative agency, then perhaps we representatives of the workers can join hands on this issue.' "[10]

Finally, the interest in good relations with the LO stems also from a desire to use such contacts to shut out SACO, TCO's most serious competitor, from important points of access. By minimizing SACO's opportunities for influence and demonstrating that it can do more, TCO hopes to prevent further inroads into its organizational sphere. The LO has not been hostile to such activities, as it has consistently looked with disapproval at SACO's attempts to organize the better paid along craft lines.[11]

The risk TCO runs in seeking to square its position with the LO's is that in so doing it may alienate its better paid members. Given the inroads SACO made in TCO areas of recruitment during the late 1950s and 1960s, it takes an expert in balancing techniques at times to come up with the best position.

In sum, the task for TCO's leadership—pulling all these threads together into a coherent stand on each particular issue, one which enjoys enough support so that TCO can mobilize the resources it has at its disposal—is indeed difficult. That the leadership has succeeded to the degree it has must stand as a remarkable achievement.

[8] Interview.
[9] Interviews.
[10] Interview.
[11] Interview.

Chapter Six

The Supplementary Pensions Dispute

Between 1956 and 1960 the supplementary pensions dispute dominated the Swedish political scene. A national referendum, a governmental crisis, a special election to the lower chamber of the Riksdag, and two regularly scheduled elections all focused on the issue of whether a service pension over and above the basic national pension ought to be the subject for legislation or for negotiation through the labor market system.

In failing to unseat the Social Democratic government, the bourgeois opposition parties lost not only the battle but the war as well, at least for another decade, as the Social Democrats succeeded in reversing their downward trend in electoral fortunes for the first time since 1948. The new string of electoral victories which followed in the wake of the reform permitted them to govern alone from 1958. Given the belief that white-collar votes played a major role in propelling the party to victory, many in the party's top leadership during those hectic years felt justified in asserting that the Social Democratic party could indeed survive in an age where white-collar workers were beginning to overtake the blue as the most numerous element in the work force.

The issue had particularly important consequences for the Central Organization of Salaried Employees (Tjänstemännens Centralorganisation or TCO). A majority of its members had already succeeded in making arrangements with which they were largely satisfied, and so they exerted strong pressure on TCO's leadership to keep the issue out of the political arena, and leave it instead as the subject for negotiations among the major organizations in the labor market arena. A sizable minority within TCO's ranks, whose organizations had not been so successful in negotiations with employers, however, objected to this position and in turn looked more favorably upon legislation, provided certain conditions were met.

For a number of reasons (discussed below), the Social Democratic party leadership decided to push for a legislated solution. Having thus failed to keep the issue out of the arena of political partisanship, TCO then went on to seek and win a number of concessions to the proposals which eventually became law.

Moreover, a segment of its leadership succeeded in preventing the organization from taking a stand in its *remiss* reply which could have been used by the bourgeois opposition parties to their advantage during a national referendum which occurred on the issue. In so doing, this segment of the leadership contributed to Social Democratic fortunes in the national referendum and thus marginally to the final outcome which followed after several national elections.

The organization could remain active only up to this point because of the tremendous fissures which broke out as the issue became the subject of ever increasing polarization among the political parties. Shortly after the national referendum these fissures became so great that a crisis of tremendous proportions erupted within TCO, nearly destroying the organization. The limits of TCO's influence over outcomes of politically controversial issues had been dramatically exposed.

Policy Initiation

Beginning in 1948 Social Democratic electoral fortunes started to decline. This election marked a turning point in Swedish politics. While the Social Democrats managed to cling to power, they did so only by a thread, as their supremacy in the lower house over the three bourgeois opposition parties (gained in the 1944 election) shrank from fifteen to a mere two votes after the 1948 election. Drawing the consequences, the party decided to negotiate with the Farmers party (which changed its name in 1957 to the Center party) for a possible coalition government.

By 1951 the coalition had become a reality. But the benefits the Social Democrats had anticipated failed to materialize and electoral problems continued to plague the party. Between the national elections in the lower chamber in 1952 and 1956, the Social Democratic percentage of the votes fell from 46.1 to 44.6. Most important, however, the 1956 national election saw the nonsocialist percentage (including the Farmers party) climb over the 50 percent mark for the first time since 1928. As the Farmers party, too, suffered a steady erosion of support during those years, it was not surprising that harmony within the coalition steadily began to decline.

As Table I graphically demonstrates, the Social Democrats were in desperate need of an issue which would propel them back into a predominant position in Swedish parliamentary life.

TABLE I
ELECTIONS TO RIKSDAG BY PERCENT, 1944–1956

A. National Elections to the Lower Chamber					
Year	Cons.	Lib.	Farmer	SD	CP	Other
1944	15.9	12.9	13.6	46.7	10.3	.6
1948	12.3	22.8	12.4	46.1	6.3	.1
1952	14.4	24.4	10.7	46.1	4.3	.1
1956	17.1	23.8	9.4	44.6	5.0	.1

B. Local Elections to the Upper Chamber					
Year	Cons.	Lib.	Farmer	SD	CP	Other
1946	14.9	15.8	13.6	44.4	11.2	.3
1950	12.3	21.7	12.3	48.6	4.9	.2
1954	15.7	21.7	10.3	47.4	4.8	.1

SOURCE:Stig Hadenius, Hans Wieslander, Björn Molin, *Sverige efter 1900* (Stockholm: Aldus/Bonniers, 1967), Appendix, adapted from Table IB, pp. 278–279.

Certainly the question of a supplementary pension had the potential for mobilizing strong support from the blue-collar confederation, the LO. The dramatic improvement in real wages for blue-collar workers during the 1950s, shown in Table 2 (nearly a 50 percent increase), meant that the basic national pension no longer prevented a sharp loss of income at retirement. Moreover, by 1951 the LO had become convinced that the technical and economic considerations involved in solutions negotiated

TABLE 2
REAL INCOME INCREASES FOR MALE INDUSTRIAL WORKERS, 1930–1960

Period	Real Wage Increase per Hour
1930–1940	4 percent
1940–1950	31 percent
1950–1960	47 percent

SOURCE: Per Holmberg, *Arbete och löner i Sverige* (Solna: Rabén och Sjögren, 1963), adapted from Table 8, p. 41.

through the labor market were of such magnitude and complexity that this route ought to be bypassed in favor of national legislation. Thus the LO wanted the Social Democratic party to push the issue.

Moreover, there proved to be a certain ideological neatness which served to stir the party's leadership into action. At a meeting in June,

1955, at the Prime Minister's summer residence, Harpsund, of the "inner-circle"[1] of the party's executive board, "Kinna" Ericsson, the Minister of Trade, convinced his colleagues to support a legislated solution on the grounds that an obligatory pension had the advantage of including everyone, whereas one negotiated through the labor market would mean the weakest would go without.

A student of the meeting reports, "Ericsson asked whether this (the legislated solution for all) wasn't of crucial importance for the working-class movement. In his eyes, the Party could not be responsible for leaving some groups without a service pension."[2] After that meeting the Prime Minister, Tage Erlander, decided that the party would pursue the issue.[3]

TABLE 3
DISTRIBUTION OF LABOR FORCE BY PERCENT, 1900–1960

	1900	1910	1920	1930	1940	1950	1960
Agriculture	31.3	28.8	23.4	21.0	18.2	13.0	8.7
Employer	5.7	6.2	5.4	7.3	8.2	7.8	6.6
Salaried employees	6.1	8.8	11.8	13.5	20.4	27.6	34.9
Blue-collar workers	56.9	56.2	59.4	58.2	53.2	51.6	49.8
Total	100.0	100.0	100.0	100.0	100.0	100.0	100.0

SOURCE: Hadenius, *Sverige efter 1900*, Appendix, Table 6, p. 288.

From this date strategic considerations became paramount. Structural trends among occupational groups between 1900 and 1960 appeared as shown in Table 3.

Voter support of the party had steadily declined from the late 1940s on. This fact, when viewed in the light of these structural changes, led to the hypothesis that the continued growth of the white-collar group would soon spell the end of Social Democratic rule. Between 1948 and 1957 the Liberal and Conservative parties expounded this thesis. Interviews with leading Social Democrats who held positions on the party's executive board between 1948 and 1957 indicate that even they were seriously concerned that in fact such interpretations might prove correct.[4]

The problem for the party, of course, was to devise a proposal which would have at least some appeal for a group of employees which basically had little or no interest in a legislated solution. As indicated above, a

[1] The term is Ortmark's. See Åke Ortmark, *Maktspelet i Sverige* (Malmö: Wahlström & Widstrand, 1967), p. 67.
[2] *Ibid.*, p. 69.
[3] *Ibid.*, p. 70.
[4] Interviews.

majority of white-collar workers already enjoyed as part of their remuneration a wide range of social benefits, including medical plans, pension plans, vacation time, and so on, all these having been gained in the labor market arena. Thus only a minority could be considered possible supporters, and even their support depended ultimately on how attractive the proposals became.

The Farmers party, the Social Democrats' coalition partner, faced even grimmer structural prospects as its core supporters shrank from 21 percent of the electorate in 1930 to 10.3 percent by 1954.[5] Thus it, too, was looking for an issue. Its core of support, however, dictated a different solution to the pension problem. Since farmers grew or bartered for most of their basic necessities (such as food), their cash income was lower than that of other occupational groups. Hence any supplementary pension plan based on past income would be of little benefit to them. General improvements in the basic national pension stood as the most concrete way to improve their standard of living after retirement.

The Conservatives, drawing their support primarily from business executives and upper income white-collar workers, opposed any legislated solution, opting for the position that any supplementary pension ought to be the subject for negotiations among organizations in the labor market system.

The Liberals had a more difficult time making up their minds. As they had no firm core of support among any particular occupational group, they experienced considerable internal tension whichever way they leaned. Crucial in determination of the party's strategy to oppose a legislated solution, however, was the intimate cooperation which developed between the party's leader, Bertil Ohlin, and Harald Adamsson, chairman of TCO's largest federation, the Swedish Union of Clerical and Technical Employees in Industry (Svenska Industritjänstemannaförbundet or SIF), during the early stages of party maneuverings on the issue. Advice from Adamsson that white-collar workers would not stand for a legislated solution, an opinion that will be discussed in greater detail in a later section,[6] had a telling impact on Ohlin's decision to work closely with the Conservative party as this issue developed.

Not until the end of 1955 and particularly during 1956 did the political parties begin to formulate stands on concrete proposals. These developments followed in the wake of two Royal Commission reports which served to clarify the major areas of disagreement.

[5] See above, Table 1.
[7] See p. 83.

Policy Deliberation

In 1944, as the result of a motion by an LO-affiliated member of the Riks-dag, the Riksdag had instructed the government to investigate the possi-bilities of introducing a supplementary pension plan over and above the basic national plan. In 1947 the first commission was created. It presented its report in 1950 on the major principles such a reform should realize. Under the same chairman, the second commission presented a more de-tailed proposal in 1955.

At that time, division within the commission had come to focus on the following issues:

1. Whether such a reform should be the subject of national legislation or enacted through negotiations by the labor market parties.
2. Whether the plan should be obligatory for all or whether those who regarded their present pension plans as adequate could have the option of remaining outside the reform.
3. Whether the pension should be computed according to the recipient's entire working career or his most recent, most lucrative years.

Ernst Ahlberg, a general secretary (ombudsman) in TCO's second largest federation, the Swedish Union of Supervisors and Foremen (Sver-iges Arbetsledareförbund, or SALF), and TCO's expert on pension matters, had been a member of both commissions. In the second he made a reservation which called for a labor market solution. If legislation were passed, however, he supported the right of groups to remain outside the reform, if they so chose. Finally, he felt any legislated program ought to compute pension benefits according to the recipient's most recent, most lucrative years. In this reservation he was joined by the representative of the Employers' Association (Svenska Arbetsgivareföreningen or SAF) to the commission, Director Brodén.[7]

TCO, in its *remiss* reply to the second commission, echoed Ahlberg's criticisms, although it did not take a stand in opposition as Ahlberg had done. Moreover, TCO emphasized the importance of grappling with the problem of coordinating any proposed legislated solution with already existing plans before any final action was taken.[8]

In January, 1956, the third and last Royal Commission was appointed. Its formal task was to do final research before legislation was introduced.

[7] In his reservation, Ahlberg actually rejected the supplementary pension idea in favor of modifications in the national pension. Note also that Ahlberg was a mem-ber of the Conservative party. He was elected to the Riksdag in 1953.

[8] Björn Molin, *Tjänstepensionsfrågan: en studie i svensk partipolitik* (Gothen-burg: Akademiförlaget, 1965), pp. 26–27.

Its political task, however, proved to be much more significant. During the year this commission worked, the first steps were taken toward broadening the appeal of a supplementary pension plan to include the interests of white-collar workers organized by TCO.

That the Social Democrats were coming to view white-collar support as potentially important for the outcome of the issue could be seen in the government's decision to invite Otto Nordenskiöld, Åman's assistant director at TCO headquarters and a potential supporter of legislation, to become a member of the commission. Ahlberg, too, became a member, but this time as a representative of the Conservative party.

Nordenskiöld's greatest victory came when he convinced the Social Democrats that a recipient's pension should be computed from two-thirds of his best fifteen years' income instead of his entire working career. This insured that consideration would be given to the later peaking of earning power experienced by white-collar workers when compared with blue. Moreover, it insured that benefits would be differentiated according to income. Those who had earned higher salaries during their productive years could look forward to higher pensions during their retirement.

Nordenskiöld in a report to TCO's general council meeting in March, 1957, remarked that he had asked for even more (two-thirds of one's best ten years), but that what he got nevertheless substantially improved the entire proposal from the point of view of the white-collar worker.[9]

During this same report, Nordenskiöld indicated his major disagreement with the proposed labor market solution presented by SAF's representative to the commission and supported by the Liberal and Conservative parties. The absence of any cost-of-living guarantee (which the Social Democratic proposal contained), he argued, would spell real hardship for white-collar workers given the rise in living costs most economists predicted would continue for the rest of the decade.[10]

Nordenskiöld, finally, was not able to have included in the commission report the recommendation that groups be allowed to remain outside the reform if they so desired. He did, however, succeed in inserting the reservation that "pension plans already in existence for different groups would not be negatively affected by the enactment of an obligatory supplementary pension plan."[11] These concessions led Nordenskiöld to join the LO and the Social Democratic party representatives in the commission to form

[9] Tjänstemännens Centralorganisation, Minutes from TCO General Council Meetings, March 16, 1957, TCO Archive, Stockholm, pp. 17–20 (mimeographed).
[10] *Ibid.*
[11] Sweden, Socialdepartementet, *Förbättrad Pensionering*, Statens Offentliga Utredningar 1957:7 (Stockholm: Socialdepartementet, 1957), p. 108.

a majority (of one) in favor of a legislative solution to the problem. Ahlberg again sided with the opponents.

While the Liberal and Conservative party representatives took clear stands during the early days of this commission, it was not until the last stages of the commission's work that the Farmers party developed a middle position between the Social Democratic and the Liberal-Conservative alternatives. The Farmers party alternative called for an increase in the basic national pension (which would benefit farmers) and a voluntary supplementary pension plan up to 3,000 Swedish crowns, to be negotiated by the labor market organizations (which would appeal to some white-collar workers and could thereby serve to broaden the party's ever diminishing base of support).

While the commission was still in progress, Liberal and Conservative party voices were heard demanding that the entire issue be subjected to a national advisory referendum in October, 1957.

Prior to the period after World War II, the constitutional provision for advisory national referenda had proven to be a near anomaly. Only once before, in 1922, when a referendum had been held on prohibition, had the right been exercised. But during the latter half of the 1940s, as it became increasingly clear that the Social Democratic gains of the 1930s were not going to evaporate, cries were raised from the bourgeois side for its expanded use.

The first advisory referendum in the postwar period came in 1955 over the question of whether to change from left to right-hand traffic. A year later in an effort to embarrass the government the Liberal and Conservative parties raised the question of subjecting the pension issue to a referendum. As was clear to all observers, the two members of the coalition government had differing views on how the issue should be resolved. Ten years later my interviews with executive board members of the Social Democratic party indicated that the party's top leadership was concerned that the initiative at that point had slipped from its hands and that the Liberal-Conservative proposal had a good chance to gain considerable support among the populace. After many hours of debate, the executive board decided on March 26, 1957, that the party would take up the challenge, and announced its intention to support an advisory referendum on the issue to be held in October of that year.[12] At the same time it announced that the Swedish voters would be offered three alternatives, representing the Social Democratic, Farmers party, and Liberal-Conservative viewpoints which had emerged during the 1956 Royal Commission.

[12] Interviews.

In preparation for the referendum in October, the government created a nonpartisan national board to ensure that sufficient information about the alternatives reached the public. Moreover, three national propaganda committees, one for each alternative, were also created.

Each support committee had definite political overtones. Arne Geijer, the chairman of the LO, headed the propaganda committee for the first alternative, which called for a supplementary pension for all employees. Eighty-one of the remaining 120 committee members were either functionaries from different LO federations or active members of the Social Democratic party, and four were members of TCO's leadership (Hellenius from TCO's Section for Public Employees [TCO's statsjänstemannasektion or TCO-S], Nordenskiöld, Lindforss from the Swedish Union of Commercial Employees [Handelstjänstemannaförbundet or HTF], and Ericsson from the Swedish Union of Supervisors and Foremen [Sveriges Arbetsledareförbund or SALF]).[13]

Local committees for this alternative were closely connected in most cases with the local Social Democratic party's electoral organization. In fact, many of the party's full-time functionaries were put at their disposal. Moreover, in an effort to extend its appeal at the local level, the party selected a large percentage of committee members from the ranks of the white-collar world.[14]

The second alternative, advocating an increase in the national basic pension and a limited, voluntary supplementary pension, was connected with the Farmers party, although not as intimately as the first alternative with the LO and the Social Democrats. This reflected the Farmers party desire to begin to broaden their base of support. Their local committees, however, were predominantly drawn from the ranks of the party faithful.

Those supporting the third alternative, calling for collective bargaining rather than legislation on the issue, tried the hardest to play down their political connections (in this case with the Liberal and Conservative parties). In fact, on both national and local committees there were fewer party representatives than either of the other alternatives. At the local level, as was the case with line 1, were included a large number of rank-

---

[13] Ahlberg had resigned his position as general secretary by then. Sune Eriksson had become SALF's Chairman in 1956. The federation repudiated Ahlberg's line on the supplementary pension issue by endorsing the legislative alternative.

[14] I shall return to this point in greater detail later in this chapter. See Finn Bergstrand, "Riks- och Länskommittéernas sammansättning i kampanjen inför pensionsomröstningen den 13 oktober 1957," *Statsvetenskaplig Tidskrift*, No. 2 (1958), p. 196.

and-file white-collar workers. On the national committee, Harald Adamsson from SIF accepted the position of first vice chairman.

For several months prior to the October referendum, interest groups actively sought to influence public opinion: the LO for line 1, agricultural organizations for line 2, and business groups for line 3. White-collar national trade union confederations, however, had a more difficult time deciding what action to take.

The differences between the stands taken by Ahlberg and Nordenskiöld in the 1956 Royal Commission reflected the deep divisions which prevailed within TCO over this issue. TCO eventually abstained from taking a position on the central parts of the commission's proposal. Moreover, these differences left such scars that in January, 1958, TCO was plunged into the greatest internal crisis it had ever faced, when SIF signed a contract with SAF in violation of TCO's constitution.

The professional employees' organization, SACO, found none of the alternatives appealing and urged its membership to vote blank. Thus as an organization it sat out the conflict. As for the SR, it urged its members to reject the legislated solution.[15]

The ultimate results of the October, 1957, referendum for each alternative were as follows:

Line 1	45.8 percent
Line 2	15.0 percent
Line 3	35.3 percent
Blank	3.9 percent

Not surprisingly all the parties claimed victory. The proponents of line 1, which advocated the supplementary pension for all employees, pointed proudly to the fact that their alternative had received the most votes. Supporters of the Farmers party (now the Center party) compared the votes for line 2, the alternative calling for an increase in the national basic pension and a limited voluntary supplementary pension, with the votes the party had received in the national election in 1956, and noted an increase of nearly 6 percentage points. Finally, the supporters of line 3, the collective bargaining alternative, argued that their position had indeed been vindicated as the total votes for lines 2 and 3 (in their eyes both "voluntary lines") had received a majority.

For the Social Democratic party the referendum results were of crucial

[15] Sweden, Socialdepartementet, *Remissyttranden*, Statens Offentliga Utredningar 1957:16 (Stockholm: Socialdepartementet, 1957), pp. 310–316.

importance for determining later strategy. Signs pointed to the conclusion
that the party had found its issue. Compared with the results of the 1956
national election to the lower house, the decline in votes for the socialist
parties (the Communist party supported the Social Democratic alternative) proved to be less than that of the Liberal and Conservative opposition parties (from 50.6 to 45.8, or a loss of 4.8, versus 40.9 to 35.3, or
a loss of 5.6). But more important, as Table 4 indicates, in the greater

TABLE 4
ELECTORAL RESULTS OF LOWER CHAMBER ELECTIONS IN 1956 AND 1958 FOR SOCIAL
DEMOCRATS PLUS COMMUNIST PARTY AND RESULTS FOR LINE 1 IN NATIONAL
REFERENDUM, 1957, DIVIDED ACCORDING TO COUNTRYSIDE, CITIES, AND GREATER
METROPOLITAN CITIES (STOCKHOLM, MALMÖ, AND GOTHENBURG)

	In Percent			Increase-Decrease	
	1956	1957	1958	1956-1957	1956-1958
Countryside	48.3	43.1	46.8	—5.2	—1.5
Cities	52.0	49.4	53.7	—2.6	+1.7
Greater metro- politan cities	46.1	46.5	49.1	+0.4	+3.0

SOURCE: Björn Molin, *Tjänstepensionsfrågan: en studie i svensk partipolitik*
(Gothenburg: Akademiförlaget, 1965), p. 177.

metropolitan cities the socialist parties[16] had actually increased their percentages, compared with the 1956 election, their loss being twice as great
in the countryside. And it was in the greater metropolitan cities that white-
collar workers lived. To those in the highest councils of the party, great
comfort was gained from such statistics. It appeared that the concessions
to the white-collar workers were having the desired result.[17] And at the
same time, of course, the Center party was extremely pleased over the
results, for now it seemed as if the party might indeed survive.

Policy Decision

Given these interpretations of the referendum results, further cooperation
within the coalition government proved now to be impossible. On October
25, 1957, the Center party's executive board unanimously decided to

[16] The Communist party in the postwar period has never voted against a Social
Democratic measure where defeat could result in a Bourgeois government. Thus
while the Social Democrats and the Communists are electoral enemies, Communist
party support on such key votes justifies lumping the two together. Moreover, this
procedure is particularly justified in terms of electoral results, for it gives an overall
picture of the support of the left in Sweden.
[17] Interviews.

leave the government. In response, the Social Democratic Prime Minister, Tage Erlander, announced that the entire government would resign. For the first time in Sweden in twenty-one years a governmental crisis was at hand.

The King called the four party leaders to the castle on October 26, 1957. After initial feelers regarding an all-party coalition failed to elicit support from the Social Democrats, the King asked Ohlin (Liberal party) and Hjalmarsson (Conservative party) to investigate the possibilities of creating a coalition government consisting of the three nonsocialist parties. Because the Social Democrats still retained their plurality in joint votes, the Center party balked at the idea of a nonsocialist coalition. When this initiative failed, Erlander received and accepted the task of building a purely Social Democratic government on October 29, 1957.

With its new mandate, the Social Democratic government could be expected to present to the Riksdag a proposal in line with alternative 1. After negotiations with the opposition parties failed to result in a proposal which could be assured of majority support in both upper and lower chambers, the government decided to push ahead with its own proposition. It passed the upper chamber only to meet defeat in the lower. At this point the government again took the initiative, dissolving the lower chamber and calling for a special election.

Between April 28, the date of dissolution, and June 1, 1958, the election date, a bitter campaign of sizable proportions was carried out. As shown in Table 5, the chief loser proved to be the Liberal party, which

TABLE 5
NUMBER OF LOWER CHAMBER SEATS HELD BY EACH PARTY, 1948–1958

	1948	1952	1956	1958
Conservative	23	31	42	45
Center	30	26	19	32
Liberal	57	50	58	38
Total	110	115	119	115
Social Democratic	112	110	106	111
Communist	8	5	6	5
Total	120	115	112	116

SOURCE: Hadenius, *Sverige efter 1900*, Appendix, adapted from Table 2A, pp. 280–281.

lost twenty of its fifty-eight seats in the lower chamber. Most of these went to the Center party, with the rest split between the Conservatives and the Social Democrats.

Since the speaker of the lower chamber, a Social Democrat, did not enjoy the right to vote, the results of the election failed to reduce the tension or resolve the conflict, leaving instead a deadlock of 115 to 115.

Moreover, all the parties except the Liberals felt the election results had justified the positions they had assumed. Thus the Liberal party plea for a compromise solution by the four parties fell on deaf ears. The Social Democrats in particular were jubilant, for, as shown in Table 6, this

TABLE 6
RESULTS IN LOWER CHAMBER ELECTIONS FOR SOCIAL DEMOCRATIC PARTY BY PERCENT, 1948–1958

Election Year	Percent
1944	46.7
1948	46.1
1952	46.1
1956	44.6
1958[a]	46.2

[a] Special election.
SOURCE: Hadenius, *Sverige efter 1900*, Appendix, adapted from Table 1B, pp. 278–279.

election marked a halt in the vote percentage decline they had seen begin in the 1948 election.

The regularly scheduled local elections in September, 1958, showed the same trends: the Liberal party continued to decline, the others made small gains. Now in an effort to reinforce the gains they had made among white-collar workers, the Social Democratic government included in its proposition to the Riksdag a final concession which would enable groups with previously arranged and satisfactory pension plans to remain outside the new plan.

Thus, after three years of conflict, the pension question was on the way toward resolution. Thanks to the last minute abstention by one member of the Liberal party, the Social Democratic proposal passed on May 14, 1959, by a vote of 115 to 114. The victory was heralded as the greatest for social democracy since 1948.

The 1960 Election

As the September, 1960, election to the second chamber approached, interest rose rapidly, for only a slight change was needed to create a bourgeois majority. Given the views of the opposition, especially those of the Conservative party, this election would prove to be particularly significant.

Immediately after defeat on the supplementary pensions dispute, the Conservative party had announced it refused to capitulate. A bourgeois victory in 1960, it proclaimed, would be interpreted as a mandate to rescind the decision. This stance led them into direct conflict with the Liberal party, which by then had joined in support of the Social Democrats on this issue. The Center party, while accepting the decision, claimed it would work to make the plan more voluntary. Thus the stage was set, not only for bitter battle with the Social Democrats, but also among the opposition.

Unfortunately for the Conservatives, support for their position was now declining. From May, 1959, through April, 1960, negotiations had been underway between white-collar confederations belonging to TCO and the Employers' Association, SAF, in an effort to coordinate existing systems with the new state-administered system. When it became apparent to TCO that no special benefits could be gained by contracting out of the new system, an agreement was reached in 1960 which brought them under the new system. The settlement proved lucrative for the white-collar workers. Not only were pension benefits improved but, as the new system called for the employer to foot the bill, it also eliminated contributions formerly made by the employee. This resulted in considerable salary increases for the employees. Thus a large segment of the white-collar working force now opposed any attempt to abolish the pensions scheme, TCO in fact going so far as to warn directly against it. The Conservatives, however, maintained their stance during the campaign, as did the Liberal party. The Center party, on the other hand, did modify its position, now coming closer to the Liberals.

It was thus not surprising that the electoral results, shown in Table 7, brought a marked decline for the Conservatives. They lost 3 percent compared with the 1958 June election and 4 percent compared with the com-

TABLE 7
ELECTIONS TO LOWER CHAMBER BY PERCENT, 1956–1960

Year	Cons.	Lib.	Center	Soc. Dem.	Comm.	Other
1956	17.1	23.8	9.4	44.6	5.0	.1
1958[a]	19.5	18.2	12.7	46.2	3.4	.0
1960	16.5	17.5	13.6	47.8	4.5	.1

[a] Special election.

SOURCE: Hadenius, *Sverige efter 1900*, Appendix, adapted from Table 1B, pp. 278–279.

munal elections of 1958. For the Liberal party the election proved to be at least a step in the right direction, as they won back two of the twenty seats they had lost in the June, 1958, election. The Center party, too, won a small but clear victory. The significant fact of the election, however, was that the total for the bourgeois parties had fallen under 50 percent. Their upward trend had been broken. They had lost the majority they had gained in 1956. For the Social Democrats the election meant another advance, this time by 1.6 percent. The total vote for the socialist parties in the lower chamber now gave them a clear majority (119 to 113 versus 115 to 115).

In a nutshell, the 1960 election results signified that any thought of undoing the supplementary pensions decision must be put to rest (in fact the Conservative party shortly after the election announced it now accepted the reform). For the Center party it meant a new lease on life. And for social democracy, as Table 8 shows, it was thanks in part to white-collar votes that the party had a renewed mandate for continued rule.[18]

[18] It is important to note that I have said that it was only in part because of white-collar votes that the Social Democrats could continue to rule, for it would be incorrect to say that the sole determining factor in the party's electoral successes during those years was white-collar votes. In fact in light of recent voting behavior studies, white-collar support during those years proved to be of only marginal importance. Bo Särlvik in an article published in 1964 writes: "Nothing in the material [data from elections between 1956 and 1960] indicates, however, that this was a question of a major 'break-through' for the Social Democrats in the middle class groups or that there had been any substantial increase in the number of representatives of the middle class in the party's electorate." Bo Särlvik, "Politisk rörlighet och stabilitet i valmanskåren," *Statsvetenskaplig Tidskrift* (1964), p. 219. Leif Lewin emphasizes the same theme in his work, *The Swedish Electorate 1887–1968* (Stockholm: Almqvist & Wiksell, 1972): "Even . . . [the] assertion that the 'pension elections' of 1958 and 1960 resulted in the Social Democrats gaining considerable ground among the white-collar employees is a popular belief which is not supported by our data. In the 'pension elections' of 1958 and 1960 the Social Democrats mainly succeeded in mobilizing even more of the industrial workers than they had done in 1956, while the increase in Class II was less significant" (p. 170).

He continues: "The Social Democrats' relationship with what are termed the middle class groups can briefly be said to be the following. In recent years, more and more employers and white-collar employees have begun voting for the Social Democrats, but these votes are no more than a drop in the ocean compared to the party's vast mobilization of industrial workers. The latter tendency dominates completely at the expense of the former, if we try to establish in percentages from which occupational classes the Social Democrats recruit their supporters" (p. 171). The salient point, however, is that the political elites believed they needed to attract white-collar support. All my interviews on this point plus the public record of statements by party and interest group leaders support the conclusion that during these years elites felt the outcome of the issue would largely hinge on white-collar reaction to different proposals. Moreover, the evidence presented in this chapter on the strategies used by party leaders to attract white-collar votes suggests strongly that they acted on just such beliefs.

TABLE 8
POLITICAL DIVISION WITHIN SOCIO-ECONOMIC STRATA:
PARLIAMENTARY ELECTIONS IN 1956 AND 1960, AND REFERENDUM IN 1957

Party Preference in 1956 and 1960	Cons. Lib.	Center	SD, CP	Un- known		
Pension Scheme in 1956 Referendum	Line 3	Line 2	Line 1	Blank Vote	*Total* Percent	No. of Resp.
Employers (excl. farmers)						
1956	74	4	17	5	100	96
1957	61	22	11	6	100	90
1960	60	15	20	5	100	156
Farmers						
1956	35	48	14	3	100	133
1957	31	56	7	6	100	106
1960	22	69	8	1	100	162
Salaried employees, etc.						
1956	64	1	32	3	100	245
1957	55	8	32	5	100	245
1960	55	5	37	3	100	340
Workers engaged in manufacturing, con- struction, and mining						
1956	13	0	85	2	100	223
1957	10	6	77	7	100	215
1960	9	3	84	4	100	337
Other workers						
1956	29	4	63	4	100	270
1957	24	15	64	7	100	167
1960	14	9	72	4	100	329
Total sample						
1956	39	9	49	3	100	969
1957	34	17	43	6	100	825
1960	30	15	52	3	100	1,324

Data from the 1956 election survey, the 1957 referendum survey, and the 1960 election survey.
SOURCE: Bo Särlvik, "Political Stability and Change in the Swedish Electorate," *Scandinavian Political Studies*, ed. Peritti Pesonen, Vol. 1 (New York: Columbia University Press, 1966), p. 217.

Interest Group Influence in the Supplementary Pensions Dispute

Political party activity dominated the supplementary pensions dispute. The strategic maneuverings, the attempts at compromise, the confrontations were all part of party efforts to determine the kind of pensions scheme Swedish society would eventually endorse.

If one steps back a moment from the scene of battle, however, it is quite clear that interest groups, at least some of them, played an important role in the controversy.

TCO influenced the course of events during the Royal Commission and the *remiss* stages of the decision-making process. Later, during the 1957 referendum, key members of TCO's headquarters along with several leaders of important TCO federations played active roles in support of line 1. These actions in turn influenced marginally the likelihood that the Social Democratic proposal eventually would emerge victorious.

A sample survey by the Swedish Institute for Public Opinion Research (Svenska Institutet för Opinionsundersökningar or SIFO) taken immediately after the 1957 referendum, and presented here in Table 9, showed that a large majority of white-collar workers then supported the collective bargaining proposal.

TABLE 9
SIFO PUBLIC OPINION SURVEY

Line	LO Members	TCO and SACO Members
1—Social Democrats' supplementary pension plan	85 percent	33 percent
2—Center party's modified collective bargaining proposal	7 percent	0 percent
3—Liberal and Conservative parties' collective bargaining proposal	4 percent	67 percent
Blank	4 percent	0 percent

SOURCE: C. Gösta Malmström, *Samverkan slagkraft* (Stockholm: Grafikon, 1970), p. 218.

But the Social Democrats felt they did not have to convince all TCO white-collar workers to support their proposal, only some of them. Therefore once the party had decided to support its core constituency's demands for legislation, the only problem was to determine what kind of concessions it had to grant the white-collar workers in order to insure victory. Thus, although during his tenure on the first two Royal Commissions Ernst Ahlberg had indicated clearly white-collar workers wanted the option of remaining outside any plan, this was ignored. Moreover, the method by which the final pension was calculated worked to the distinct disadvantage of the white-collar group.

However, Otto Nordenskiöld, during the work of the third and final commission, was able to convince the government these concessions were necessary, thus succeeding where Ahlberg had failed. The method of computing the pension was altered to the benefit of white-collar workers and the Social Democrats announced that no one would have their present pension benefits reduced by the reform. Later, in 1959, when the government presented its final proposal, even this general declaration was made more specific: groups would be given the opportunity to remain outside the reform, if they so desired.

TCO's *remiss* reply became the subject of great attention by the political parties. Given the strategic nature of the white-collar vote on the issue, it was believed that TCO's support either for legislation or for negotiations through the labor market would have had immense propaganda value during election time.

Yet TCO, in its reply dated March 21, 1957, refrained from endorsing either major alternative for resolving the pension dispute. Instead, it concentrated its fire on specific aspects of both alternatives which posed unfavorable consequences for white-collar workers.

Abstention meant formal neutrality. By this time, however, the issue had so polarized the political parties that an abstention, in and of itself, had important consequences—all of them favorable to social democracy.

As mentioned earlier, Adamsson had come to work closely with the Liberal and Conservative parties on this issue. Now private meetings between party leaders and representatives of labor market organizations are not uncommon in political life in Sweden; but the meeting Adamsson held with Liberal Bertil Ohlin and Conservative Jarl Hjalmarsson in January, 1957, proved to have especially important consequences for all concerned.

By that time, Adamsson's belief that white-collar workers would reject a legislated settlement was so strong that he was willing to enter into a close working arrangement with the two party leaders on future strategy. The *remiss* reply the Swedish Union of Clerical and Technical Employees in Industry (SIF) sent to TCO in February, 1957, for example, was written at the request of Adamsson by Yngve Holmberg, then a special assistant (borgarrådssekreterare) to a Conservative party city commissioner in Stockholm and a member of the party's research bureau (Holmberg later served as leader of the Conservative party and is presently governor of Halland province).[19] Moreover, Adamsson's position in turn affected Ohlin's, for during this period Ohlin pushed his party closer to the Conservative position on the upcoming national advisory referendum.[20] As we know, this move proved to be only the first of a series of important miscalculations for the Liberal party.

[19] Interviews.
[20] Interviews.

The commitment to coordinate SIF's actions with those of the Liberal and Conservative parties served to toughen Adamsson's stand as he approached the crucial time when TCO would have to decide whether it would support in its *remiss* reply the legislative position taken by Nordenskiöld in the last Royal Commission. Certainly TCO support of the labor market position would be an important first step in making Adamsson's prediction come true.

The Social Democratic leadership learned from Åman, then a member of the party's executive board, that TCO might come to endorse the labor market alternative. The best the party might hope for, Åman said, was a "compromise stand"—formal abstention—and this he was working on. Such a stand, he said, would at least keep TCO from endorsing the Liberal and Conservative parties' supported alternative.[21]

Prior to the time TCO had to draw up its *remiss* reply, Åman's activities had been confined almost entirely to the higher echelons of the party. Within TCO, it was Otto Nordenskiöld, Åman's assistant director, who assumed the task of representing TCO on the important third Royal Commission. Later Nordenskiöld would also play an active role in the Referendum.

The reasons for Åman's relative passivity, compared with his earlier robust enthusiasm both within the party and TCO for legislated solutions to social questions, are not particularly hard to understand. He knew he could be of little direct assistance to the party, as his membership on the executive board and in the Riksdag had increasingly led to charges of partisanship, weakening his position as director of an avowedly neutral organization; he knew a large percentage of white-collar workers opposed legislation; he knew federations in the public sector still harbored bitter memories of the difficulties they had experienced when coordinating their benefits with the recently passed National Health Plan; he knew that Adamsson was dead set against a legislated solution.

Thus it was only with great reluctance that Åman had come to support the Social Democratic decision in 1955 to push for legislation. In fact, during the important June, 1955, Harpsund meeting, when the "inner-circle" debated the issue at some length, Åman argued in favor of a labor market solution.[22] In later meetings of the party's executive board, he questioned the wisdom of the party's decision.[23] His role within the party, once it had decided on legislation, was that of making it aware of conces-

---

21 Interview.
22 Ortmark, *Maktspelet*, pp. 68–69.
23 Interviews.

sions which would gain white-collar support. Thus, for example, he and Nordenskiöld worked together to gain concessions during the third, and final, Royal Commission—Åman through the executive board and Nordenskiöld through the Royal Commission itself.[24] Within TCO, until the time came for the *remiss* reply, the issue had been entirely handled by Nordenskiöld.

The report of the third commission was presented in January, 1957. The time had now come for TCO to decide its *remiss* reply position. John Östlund, chairman of the Federation of Civil Servants (Statstjänstemannaförbundet or ST), after discussions with Nordenskiöld (who in turn received Åman's approval), got the green light to present a "neutral" position, one that would have TCO abstain on the major issue of whether legislation or a labor market solution was appropriate. Recognizing the division which in fact existed within its ranks, TCO would merely append the federation replies it had received on this point to its reply to the government.[25]

On March 14, 1957, the executive board met to determine TCO's *remiss* reply. After considerable discussion came a first vote as to whether TCO should take a stand or seek some compromise wording. Seven voted in favor of a stand and 2 in favor of a compromise.[26] On the crucial vote determining which alternative to support, the executive board divided 4 to 4 with one abstention (Östlund).[27] As TCO's Constitution required a majority of 5 before a proposal could be ratified by the executive board, there was no choice but to call a special meeting of TCO's general council to see if it could break the deadlock.

Ground work for the general council meeting had already been carefully laid by the supporters of abstention. Nordenskiöld, Östlund, and Lindforss (the Swedish Union of Commercial Employees, HTF), among others, had been actively building a coalition of support, in anticipation of an executive board deadlock. Åman, who was out of the country at the time of the executive board decision (as one of Sweden's representatives

[24] Interviews.

[25] Interviews. Tjänstemännens Centralorganisation, Minutes from TCO General Council Meetings, March 16, 1957, TCO Archive, Stockholm, pp. 12–13 (mimeographed).

[26] Åman was not a voting member of the executive board. Tjänstemännens Centralorganisation, minutes for executive board meetings, March 14, 1957, TCO Archive, Stockholm (mimeographed).

[27] It had been a struggle to get even a deadlock. Nordenskiöld, Östlund, and others had worked behind the scenes to get one member of the executive board to vote in opposition to his own federation executive board so that the issue could get to the General Council. Interviews.

to the United Nations), flew in at the last moment to put the final touches on the coalition.[28]

At TCO's special general council meeting on March 16, 1957, it was Östlund's resolution which ultimately prevailed, but not before deep, long-lasting scars had been made. Adamsson led the forces favoring the labor market alternative. He argued that pensions were no more than salaries postponed to a later date and thus, like salaries, belonged in the arena of labor market negotiations. Second, as a majority of TCO's membership supported such a solution, the democratic ethic demanded that the entire body follow suit.[29] He was quite willing for the minority to state its own position as an appendix, but he felt that TCO as an organization had to take a stand on the issue.

Proponents of legislation, led by Lindforss from the Swedish Union of Commercial Employees (HTF) and Ericsson from the Swedish Union of Supervisors and Foremen (SALF), charged Adamsson with the narrow-minded pursuit of SIF's interests to the detriment of other white-collar workers belonging to TCO. Negotiations, from their experience, had not resulted in anything like a satisfactory arrangement.[30] They felt that even though SIF had been able to solve its own pension problems through negotiations, it should show solidarity with those who had not by urging TCO to support legislation.

Those who supported Östlund's abstention position argued that the majority principle, when exercised against a minority which felt strongly about an issue, hardly represented the essence of democracy but rather more a suppression of views. If Adamsson really believed in the democratic ethic, he would let everyone have his say without committing the organization to any one particular viewpoint.[31]

[28] Interviews.

[29] *Ibid.*, pp. 24, 45. Later, when TCO's *remiss* reply was filed, complete with individual replies from member federations, the breakdown for and against a legislated solution appeared thus:

	No. of Federations	No. of Members	Percent of Entire TCO Membership
Approve legislation	15	108,205	30.5
Disapprove legislation	13	163,910	46.2
No stand	7	79,992	22.6
No reply	3	2,407	0.7

SOURCE: Molin, *Tjänstepensionsfrågan*, p. 65.

[30] Tjänstemännens Centralorganisation, minutes from TCO General Council meetings, March 16, 1957, TCO Archive, Stockholm, pp. 16–17 (mimeographed).

[31] *Ibid.*, pp. 11–13.

After further recriminations back and forth, it was time for Åman to take the stage. His attack on Adamsson indicated the tremendous gulf which now separated TCO's two leaders. Certainly there is nothing in any of the minutes of TCO meetings to which I have had access which compares with the bitterness expressed at that time. Later Adamsson returned the insults in kind, but not before the direction of the meeting had been turned. Åman, demonstrating his flair for public speaking, had made an eloquent statement in favor of endorsing Östlund's proposal, and after his speech most of the discussion centered on the merits or demerits of this strategy.

When the time came for voting, Adamsson's line defeated the legislative alternative, 50 to 35. On the crucial vote between Adamsson's proposal and Östlund's "neutral" stand, the latter emerged victorious, 48 to 40.[32] Adamsson was furious.

Adamsson's keen disappointment carried over into the executive board meeting where TCO formally adopted the position recommended by the general council. By making a reservation to the board's decision Adamsson indicated in effect that he did not intend to be bound by TCO's abstention. His reservation read:

> I hereby declare my reservation against the executive board's decision not to take a stand on the central issue of whether a supplementary pension plan ought to be the subject for legislation or left to the parties directly affected to negotiate through the labor market system.
> While it is true that a special general council meeting recommended, by a narrow majority, that TCO abstain on this issue, it is also true that a majority of federations belonging to TCO representing an overwhelming majority of TCO's members have endorsed the labor market alternative.[33]

As Adamsson left TCO's headquarters with Lindforss that day, he sounded an ominous warning: "Don't think it's ended here."[34] Indeed, as events later showed, it was just beginning.

TCO's general council had dictated that the organization refrain from endorsing either alternative for solving the problem of a supplementary pension plan. Thus the Liberal and Conservative parties were without TCO's support. Moreover, TCO's publicity apparatus was stilled. Hence while TCO's newspaper continued to give factual coverage to develop-

---

[32] *Ibid.*, p. 53. See also Rudolf Lindforss, *Av en slump* . . . (Stockholm: Pistolförlaget, 1970), p. 287.

[33] Tjänstemännens Centralorganisation, minutes from TCO executive board meetings, Appendix, March 21, 1957, TCO Archive, Stockholm (mimeographed).

[34] Lindforss, *Av en slump* . . . , p. 288.

ments, no calls were issued for white-collar workers to rally to one side
or the other.

Although no party had the right to claim official TCO endorsement of
its position, this did not prevent individual members of leading TCO federations from publicly endorsing either line 1 or line 3 in the battle over
the upcoming referendum. Similarly in their capacity as private citizens
several leading members from TCO headquarters threw themselves into
the fray. The effect on the average white-collar worker belonging to a TCO
federation was that he no longer could know where TCO stood on the
issue. As Table 10 indicates, complete confusion prevailed by the time the
referendum rolled around.

TABLE 10

INFORMATION REGARDING PARTY AND INTEREST GROUP STANDS ON DIFFERENT AL-
TERNATIVES FOR NATIONAL REFERENDUM IN PERCENT

Party or Interest Group	Percent of all interviewed who think that the party or organization supports:							
	Line 1	Line 2	Line 3	Lines 2–3	Blank	Group Neu-tral	Don't Know	*Total*
Conservative party	3	7	73	1	—	—	16	100
Farmers party	4	71	6	1	—	0	18	100
Liberal party	4	16	56	2	—	0	22	100
Soc. Dem. party	85	1	2	—	—	—	12	100
Communist party	49	2	2	—	—	1	46	100
Employers' Fed. (SAF)	7	6	56	1	—	0	30	100
Cent. Org. of Sal. Workers (TCO)	17	6	28	1	0	7	41	100
Confed. of Trade Unions (LO)	65	5	3	0	—	—	27	100
National Farmers' Union	5	56	5	3	—	1	30	100

SOURCE: Sweden, Justitiedepartementet, Bo Särlvik, "Opinionsbildningen vid
Folkomröstningen 1957," in *Författningsutredning: IV*, Statens Offentliga Utredningar 1959:10 (Stockholm: Justitiedepartementet, 1959), Appendix, Table 18, p.
106.

Thus not only had the Liberal and Conservative parties been denied
TCO's endorsement, but a sizable percentage of TCO's members now believed that TCO actually supported line 1! These efforts on behalf of line
1 would not be forgotten, either by the Social Democrats or by Adamsson.

A month later, in November, 1957, a confidential memorandum was
circulated among a select few at SIF's headquarters. In it Adamsson detailed his criticisms of developments within TCO as they affected SIF. In

another month, Adamsson would take the initiative by signing a contract with the Employers' Association (SAF) in a manner which violated TCO's Constitution. In so doing he plunged the organization into a second, even graver internal crisis.[35]

Developments during the first ten months of 1957 had in effect broken apart TCO from the top. In the end there was no stand TCO could take which would not have consequences in the battle for votes being waged among the political parties. By its participation in the Royal Commission stage it had influenced the content of what would become the final legislation at several key points. By taking a neutral position in its *remiss* reply, TCO affected the outcome of the national referendum. At this point, however, the influence of TCO as an organization came to an end.[36] For the next several years TCO was so involved in its second internal crisis that all the time of its top leaders was fully occupied.

It was during the national referendum that white-collar workers as voters became important. One indication of the great significance all the political parties attached to their votes was their appointments, as shown in Table 11, to the various local committees in support of the three lines of the national referendum. On the average more than one-third of each committee was made up of white-collar workers. For lines 1 and 3, the

[35] Bitterness over TCO's ultimate abstention from endorsing either alternative led to a decision by the chairman of SIF's executive board, Harald Adamsson (who was also the chairman of TCO's executive board) to attempt to halt the growing centralization of authority into the hands of TCO's central headquarters, for this had in part caused SIF's defeat.

On December 11, 1957, SIF signed an agreement with SAF governing severance procedures for white collar workers. TCO's executive board, however, had decided earlier in May of that year that the issue was of such importance for all TCO members that it had invoked paragraph eighteen of TCO's Constitution. This action meant that no individual federation could sign an agreement without executive board approval. SIF's action, thus, clearly violated TCO's Constitution and, not surprisingly, provoked a confrontation of major proportions. In a secret memo, later made public at the height of the crisis, SIF indicated that its displeasure with the trend of developments within TCO was not confined solely to the issue of wage negotiations but included public policy and attempts to mediate jurisdictional disputes as well. While a series of concessions by TCO prevented SIF's immediate exit, Adamsson continued to push SIF toward independence from TCO in all these areas during the years which immediately followed. Not until Adamsson and Åman, TCO's director since 1944, left their respective positions in 1961, did the opportunity present itself for a rapprochement. Under the leadership of Otto Nordenskiöld, TCO's new director, this was achieved. For a more complete discussion of this crisis, see Sven Erik Strand, "Orsaker till schism mellan TCO och SIF" (unpublished seminar paper, University of Lund, 1950).

[36] In 1960 TCO issued a warning to the opposition political parties that it opposed any attempt to undo the supplementary pension reform now that salaried employees had succeeded in coordinating their old pension plans with the new.

TABLE 11
WHITE-COLLAR WORKERS ON LOCAL COMMITTEES.
NUMBER OF WHITE-COLLAR WORKERS AS PERCENT OF TOTAL NUMBER OF MEMBERS

	Total White-Collar Workers		Total Blue-Collar Workers	
	Numbers	Percent	Numbers	Percent
Line 1	616	43.5	392	27.7
Line 2	316	23.7	90	6.7
Line 3	485	42.2	121	10.5
Total	1,417	36.2	603	15.4

SOURCE: Molin, *Tjänstepensionsfrågan*, adapted from Table 12, p. 136.

figures were more than 40 percent. In every case the percentage of white-collar workers far surpassed that of blue-collar.

In comparing these figures with a study done on the social basis of re-cruitment for party electoral lists in the 1952 election, both lines 1 and 2 had nearly 10 percent more white-collar workers than either the Social Democratic party or the Farmers party electoral lists. For the Liberal and Conservative parties the story was nearly the same.[37] Finally, the per-centage of white-collar workers on local committees was greater than the percentage of white-collar workers in the population at large, while the reverse was true for blue-collar workers, as shown in Table 12.

TABLE 12
TOTAL POPULATION'S DIVISION BY EMPLOYMENT ACCORDING TO ELECTION SUR-VEY'S SAMPLE IN PERCENT

	Employer	White-Collar Worker	Blue-Collar Worker
1956	22.5	28.6	48.9
1958	20.2	30.1	49.7

SOURCE: Molin, *Tjänstepensionsfrågan*, p. 136.

Interest in white-collar workers as voters, if anything, grew during the next few years. Moreover, the terminology used, especially by the Social Democrats, shifted from references to "blue-collar" to "wage-earner," as the party sought to identify its program with all workers, rather than a certain segment, as shown in Table 13. In the end these tactics were suc-cessful, for as indicated earlier, enough white-collar workers responded during the years 1957 to 1960 to help ensure the Social Democrats a con-tinued mandate to rule.

[37] Sweden, Justitiedepartementet, *Kandidatnominering vid andrakammarval* by Lars Sköld, Statens Offentliga Utredningar 1958:6 (Stockholm: Justitiedeparte-mentet, 1958), p. 301.

TABLE 13
REFERENCES TO WHITE-COLLAR WORKERS AND REFERENCES TO BLUE-COLLAR
WORKERS, FARMERS, AND WAGE-EARNERS IN PRESS, 1957–1958, AND IN RADIO, 1954–
1960

Reference Group	Press 1957	Press 1958:I	Radio 1954	Radio 1956	Radio 1957	Radio 1958:I	Radio 1960
White-collar	20.6	30.9	1.9	20.8	37.3	29.2	9.4
Blue-collar	14.8	17.1	7.1	24.2	15.5	6.5	34.1
Farmer	3.0	6.3	62.4	28.6	6.2	33.4	47.1
Wage-earner	61.6	45.7	28.6	26.4	41.0	35.9	9.4
Total	100.0	100.0	100.0	100.0	100.0	100.0	100.0
Absolute numbers	528	215	213	178	161	248	170

SOURCE: Molin, *Tjänstepensionsfrågan*, p. 136.

Summary

The supplementary pensions dispute was an example of a most dangerous kind of experience for TCO. While TCO succeeded in gaining a number of significant concessions in the proposals which eventually became law, the organization contributed only marginally to the basic decision of whether there would be a legislated solution at all. Moreover, the internal disruption by which even this limited influence was achieved nearly spelled the end of the organization.

The initial failure of TCO's director, Valter Åman, to keep the issue from getting into the hands of the political parties eventually led to difficulties for TCO. Once the issue became the subject of partisan conflict among the political parties, the Riksdag and eventually the electorate became the crucial points for effective decision-making. As the tensions created by the heterogeneous political party support among TCO's membership, which in turn reflected economic cleavages within the organization, became manifest, there was no position which TCO could take which would not offend one or another important segment of its membership. Worse yet, the willingness of some of TCO's most important leaders to try to use the organization to influence white-collar voters created the preconditions for a total breakdown in organizational cohesion.

In the next two cases, we shall see TCO's representatives succeed in keeping issues from becoming politicized, with the result that TCO's influence during the early stages of the decision-making process helped determine the final outcome of each policy.

Chapter Seven

The Case of the Uncommon Man

Between 1957 and 1965 TCO's legal adviser, Dr. Lennart Geijer, sought to prevent the enactment of legislation which would qualitatively change the position of inventors vis-à-vis their employers on the basic questions of patent rights and remuneration. By successfully preventing the issue from becoming the subject of partisan conflict among the political parties, TCO's influence during the early stages of the decision-making process affected the outcome of the decision in a way which benefited an important segment of its membership.

Inventor Rights—Inventor Obligations

In the eyes of many, the inventor is typically a lonely eccentric who works late at night in the cramped quarters of his basement on a fantastic contraption which only this peculiar man and a patent agency can ever hope to understand.

In the modern industrialized societies of today, however, the inventor usually works in entirely different surroundings. While his creative talents still qualify him as an uncommon if not necessarily eccentric individual, he is usually a white-collar worker employed in the research division of a large firm. His fully equipped laboratory, moreover, is well suited for his educational background, for he often has earned an engineering degree. Thus while the myth may live on, reality is something quite different: the inventor works in a milieu increasingly similar to that enjoyed by other professionally trained groups in advanced industrialized societies.

With this shift from discoveries made in the home to those made in the firm arose the question of the employer's rights to such inventions. It was argued that without the expensive equipment provided the employee by the firm, many inventions would not see the light of day. Yet in Sweden until 1949 when a new law revised the relationship between inventors and their employers, firms were legally, at least, at a distinct disadvantage in dealing with their inventors. Unless an inventor willingly agreed to negotiate a contract with his employer, pre-1949 law held that there was no way for the employer to gain the use of the invention.

However, in practice this legal provision often did not benefit those employed in the *private* sector of the economy. By requiring that, at the beginning of their association with a firm, engineers sign a contract which had the effect of granting the company legal rights to all inventions stemming from such employment, private firms evaded the problem entirely. Naturally inventors were anxious to change this. Moreover, this system allowed little if any special compensation for inventions, an added incentive for seeking change.

In the *public* sector civil service laws prevented the state from concluding contracts regulating employment conditions with employees enjoying civil service status. On the closely related question of whether contract agreements could be negotiated on products resulting from such employment (that is, inventions) legal opinion was at best ambiguous. On the whole, state agencies refrained from attempting to enter into contracts with their employees on this point.[1] The result was that public employees enjoyed a very strong position vis-à-vis their employers. Not surprisingly this meant that state agencies were very much interested in gaining legal rights to inventors' products.

The position of inventors in the public sector was not completely rosy, however. As did their counterparts in private industry, they often felt their efforts went all too often unrewarded. Thus they, too, were interested in seeing the legal establishment of their right to compensation for creative achievements.

From these various pressures came the 1949 law on inventors' rights. The two most important sections were paragraphs three and six. The law under paragraph three attempted to establish standards of legal claim to an invention by an employer by relating the specific terms of the employee's contract to the results of his job. The closer the connection, the firmer the claim of the employer to the fruits of the inventor's efforts. The paragraph, in three sections, provided that certain guidelines must be observed if an employer wished to assume legal rights to his employee's invention. These guidelines can be summarized as follows:

[1] "Rätten att träffa avtal med ämbetsmän," *Statsverksingenjören*, Vol. 8, No. 5 (November, 1958), p. 5.

Paragraph Three

(1) If a person were *hired for a particular research purpose* and if an *invention resulted directly from such an activity,* then the company had a legal right to the entire device or to any part of it, as it chose. The same was true in the case where an invention resulted from the direct assignment of a problem by the employer.

(2) If a person *hired for a particular research purpose* developed during this particular research an *invention unrelated to this purpose,* but which could still be used by the firm, then the employer had the right to use the invention in the operation of the firm. However, an agreement had to be negotiated with the employee before the invention could be used outside the firm by other companies (provided the invention was not the result of a problem directly assigned by the employer).

(3) If an *invention were totally unrelated to the terms of employment* but could still be used by the firm, the employer had to negotiate with the inventor for its use within four months from the time the employee reported his find. The employee was not obligated, as he was in section two, to enter into negotiations with the employer.

Of course if an invention were not the result of employment conditions at the firm and furthermore had no connection with the firm's activity, the employer had no legal claim at all.[2] Paragraph six stated that the employee was entitled to reasonable compensation for his invention but did not specify in detail how this was to be determined.

The law was constructed in such a way that paragraph three was operative only if no other agreement had been reached between employer and employee stipulating different ground rules. Under all circumstances the employee was entitled to reasonable compensation under paragraph six for his invention.

Policy Initiation

In the private sector from 1950 to 1957, the practical workings of the 1949 law improved inventor benefits. While the Employers' Association (SAF) continued to negotiate contracts with inventors (who were assisted in such negotiations by their trade unions), the rights employers gained to inventions were not as far reaching as had been the case prior to the 1949 law. Moreover, through the efforts of their trade unions, employees succeeded in establishing a fixed procedure for securing compensation. A special tribunal was set up comprised of equal membership from

[2] Sweden, Justitiedepartementet, *Rätten till arbetstagares uppfinningar,* Statens Offentliga Utredningar 1964:49 (Stockholm: Justitiedepartementet, 1964), pp. 12–13.

employer and employee groups and was given the specific function of negotiating agreements compensating individual inventors for their creative achievements.

In 1958 the situation underwent a dramatic change. In the spring of that year TCO's largest federation, the Union of Technical and Clerical Employees in Industry (SIF), negotiated with the Employers' Association (SAF) a new contract which significantly altered this relationship, weakening the position of inventors. Under this 1958 agreement employers gained a considerable expansion of their rights to the inventions of their employees. Whereas the law limited the complete access to inventions to those covered under section one of paragraph three and the earlier 1950 agreement between SIF and SAF had only expanded this to include those inventions also covered under section two of the law, the 1958 agreement gave employers full legal rights to inventions falling under all three categories.[3] This meant that the employer owned rights to inventions stemming from (1) the efforts of those hired to research a particular project, (2) the efforts of those hired to research a particular project who in the process discovered something unrelated to the specific project, and (3) the efforts of those who worked in the plant, no matter what their original terms of employment.

Why did SIF agree to such terms? It certainly could not have been in the interest of the federation to bargain away the advantages which its membership already enjoyed.

Negotiations on this particular question had become entangled in the major political controversy of the time, the supplementary pensions dispute. A major split had developed within TCO between TCO headquarters and SIF over the position white-collar unions should take on the issue. It will be remembered (see Chapter 6) that SIF, in an attempt to punish TCO headquarters for its strong support of the Social Democratic position on the issue, had signed a wage agreement with the Employers' Association (SAF) which proved detrimental to many other federations belonging to TCO.

As another part of its campaign to emphasize independence from TCO, SIF refused to comply with TCO headquarters' requests for coordinated negotiations on the issue of inventors' rights. Harald Adamsson, the leader of SIF's strong line against TCO, went so far as to directly take over negotiations on this question, as he had previously done in the wage negotiations, and to push his negotiating team to reach agreement on this

[3] Lennart Geijer, "Partiellt arbetsföra, uppfinnare och sjöbefäl," *TCO Tidningen*, Vol. 12, No. 7 (1958), p. 3.

issue. Because SIF had lost its top legal adviser, Lennart Geijer, to TCO headquarters owing to his personal support of TCO's position on the pensions dispute, SIF's negotiating team was operating under a severe disadvantage. Thus, leadership pressure to quickly sign a contract plus the inexperience of the bargainers led to an unfortunate result, as far as inventors were concerned. The rank and file in the private sector were not happy with the results.

For SIF's long-range interests, as well as TCO's, the agreement came at a particularly inopportune time, as jurisdictional relations between TCO and SACO (which also organized engineers) had been steadily deteriorating. SACO of course did not hesitate to point out the weaknesses of the agreement. Thus it was to be expected that TCO headquarters and later SIF came to be increasingly interested in seeking a revision.

In the public sector, also, discontent was brewing. In terms of the provisions of paragraph three there was no problem, for inventors had maintained their previously strong position from 1950 to 1956. That is, for legal reasons discussed earlier, state agencies refrained from any attempt to negotiate agreements with civil servants, giving inventors in public service much greater latitude in disposing of their creations than was the case in the private sector.

Regarding the terms of compensation, however, from the inventors' point of view, developments were clearly in a negative direction. Paragraph six of the 1949 law (that paragraph which simply stated that reasonable compensation ought to be given) provided no formal machinery from which a binding decision could be handed down determining how much an inventor would receive for a particular creation. The main legal tribunal in this area, the National Board for Employees' Inventions (Statens Nämnd för Arbetstagares Uppfinningar or SNAU) was empowered by this 1949 law only to give advisory opinions, in contrast to its counterpart in the private sector, which had been established by negotiated agreement and which could reach decisions binding on each party. Since there was no way to force an agency to abide by SNAU's recommendation, the board had no real clout. Moreover, the conflicts which resulted when an agency chose not to follow SNAU's recommendation and the inordinate length of time it took to get any compensation at all in the state sector had led to considerable ill will between inventor associations and state negotiators. Thus by the mid-fifties employees in the state sector as well were anxious to see improvements made in the law.

In 1956 developments in the public sector came to a head when employers attempted to reduce the rights inventors had over their handiwork according to paragraph three. This attempt led to a sharp reaction by affected engineers and a serious deterioration in relations. The story behind this action by employers follows.

In an effort to keep pace with international developments in the field of communications, one of the largest state-owned industries, the National Telecommunications Administration (Televerket), signed agreements in 1956 with Western Electric and the Swedish concern, L. M. Ericsson, expanding considerably their cooperative research efforts. One problem became immediately apparent, however: the agreements stipulated that inventions made in one firm would automatically be made available to the other two. But, as was pointed out above, prevailing legal opinion was skeptical as to whether in fact state agencies were free to negotiate contracts with their employees regarding the products of their employment. Since private concerns in Sweden had succeeded through negotiations in achieving much greater legal claim to inventions than that stipulated in paragraph three of the 1949 law, managers of state firms such as the Televerket felt themselves to be at a distinct disadvantage. They felt, indeed, that if they could not enter into such agreements, their whole future in the field of international cooperation would be jeopardized.

Because the law was ambiguous on this point, the Televerket's leaders decided to go ahead and send out in May, 1956, a new set of contracts to their engineers, giving the Televerket rights equivalent to those enjoyed by firms in private industry.

A number of engineers went immediately to their trade unions to seek advice. One federation in particular reacted strongly to the Televerket's actions. The Association of State-Employed Engineers of Sweden (Statsverkens Ingenjörsförbund or SI) called immediately for negotiations. Moreover, it sought to coordinate the actions of other affected unions.

The SI was not affiliated with any national trade union confederation, such as the TCO. It had come into existence in 1941 simply to promote the interests of state-employed engineers. When the large national confederations, TCO and SACO, had been formed in 1944 and 1947, the SI experienced a rapid decline in membership (from over 90 percent of the state-employed engineers to less than 15 percent by 1959).[4] No longer the major wage-negotiating organization for engineers, SI activities underwent considerable transformation. It turned progressively away from wage issues to deal instead with problems relating to the working conditions, educational opportunities, and so on, of state-employed engineers. No longer did it purport to speak authoritatively for all engineers, but

4 "Förbundsarbetet," *Statsverksingenjören*, Vol. 9, No. 2 (April, 1959), p. 11.

rather sought increasingly to encourage the larger national confederations to press for changes.[5] This explains then its quick reaction to the Televerket May contract offer.

The SI coordinated the efforts of member federations belonging to both TCO and SACO and came forth with an alternative contract proposal, which was promptly rejected by the Televerket as being too favorable to the employees.[6] Then it challenged the legality of the entire procedure by writing to the Ombudsman for Civilian Affairs requesting clarification as to whether a state-run industry could indeed negotiate such a contract at all.[7] Worried by this flurry of activity, the Televerket countered by making a formal petition to the National Board for Employees' Inventions (SNAU) asking whether the Televerket had the power to decide which inventions fell under which section of paragraph three of the 1949 law (that paragraph which established employer rights to employee inventions). If it did, then it planned to issue new contracts stating that henceforth all inventions were to legally belong to the Televerket under clause one of paragraph three, the clause most beneficial to employers. The Televerket also sent along a memorandum to the ombudsman[8] giving its reasons for asking the employees to sign the new contracts.

After the SNAU replied negatively to the Televerket petition and the ombudsman wrote that it was indeed legally questionable whether the Televerket could have its employees sign such contracts, there was only one avenue left: a petition to the Cabinet requesting that a Royal Commission be established to review the 1949 law in the hope of changing it to meet the Televerket's new needs.

By this time the Televerket had alerted other state agencies to its difficulties. From the Office of the Comptroller for the Swedish Armed Forces (Försvarets Civilförvaltning or FCF), it received badly needed support. The agency head in charge of negotiating with employees over compensation for inventions was anxious to see strengthened the claims of state-owned industry to inventions either through the establishment of the right to negotiate contracts or by a change in the law. From the beginning of

---

[5] Interview.

[6] "Dispositionsrätt till uppfinningar vid televerket," *Statsverksingenjören*, Vol. 7, No. 1 (March, 1957), pp. 21–29.

[7] "Rätten att träffa avtal," pp. 5–22. The ombudsman's major function in the Swedish political system is to correct administrative abuses. In this connection his office was a logical target for an appeal of the Televerket's decision to issue contracts to its employees, as the leadership of Televerket is comprised of civil servants.

[8] For more on the role of the ombudsman see Walter Gellhorn, *Ombudsman and Others: Citizen Protectors in Nine Countries* (Cambridge: Harvard University Press, 1966), pp. 194–255.

the conflict officials of the Televerket and the FCF had met to decide strategy, and when all other alternatives had been closed, they met again to draw up the formal petition to the government.[9] At this time the FCF, with the approval of the Televerket, wrote a separate petition to the government also requesting a revision of the law.[10] SAF (the Employers' Association) and in particular the firm of L. M. Ericsson were kept well informed of the activities of the Televerket and the FCF.[11]

TCO learned of the Televerket's difficulties through one of its members, the Federation of Civil Servants (Statstjänstemannaförbundet or ST), which had worked with the SI in its efforts to counter the initial steps taken by the Televerket.

Because of the rivalry between TCO and SACO, TCO could not avoid getting deeply involved in the issue. The two national confederations had been competing heatedly for the loyalty of engineers since SACO's very inception in 1947. Swedish engineers were divided into three categories, depending upon their education: civil engineers (civilingenjör), engineers with a bachelor of science in engineering (läroverksingenjör), and technological institute engineers (institutsingenjör). SACO's original recruiting criteria were based on rigid requirements for university education. Thus civil engineers were a natural target for their efforts, and by 1950 the Swedish Association of Graduate Engineers (Civilingenjörsförbundet or CF) had become and then remained the second largest federation in SACO.

Its strength, however, was based solely in the state sector, as SIF, TCO's largest federation in the private sector, waged a vigorous campaign to prevent the Employers' Association (SAF) from granting wage negotiating rights to the CF. Moreover, federations in the TCO representing both the private and the state sectors were anxious to contain SACO's recruiting efforts, since below the civil engineers lay a large stratum of engineers with a bachelor of science in engineering and below these an

---

[9] Interview.

[10] Interviews. See also the initial requests of the FCF to the government asking that a Royal Commission be established to study the 1949 law with an eye toward making changes. "Försvarets Civilförvaltning PM No. Jb 613/58: Utredning och förslag beträffande viss ändring av lagen om rätten till arbetstagares uppfinning," March 12, 1958, SOU 1964:49 Documents, Riksarkivet, Stockholm, p. 27 (mimeographed). See also Televerket memorandum to the Royal Commission documenting its difficulties in greater detail. "Televerket PM: Erfarenheter i samband med tillämpningen av 1949 års lag om rätten till arbetstagares uppfinningar," October 21, 1959, SOU 1964:49 Documents, Riksarkivet, Stockholm, p. 55 (mimeographed). Interview. "Förslag till ändringar i 1950 års ramavtal mellan SIF och SAF," n.d., SOU 1964:49 Documents, Riksarkivet, Stockholm (mimeographed).

[11] Interview.

even larger layer of technological institute engineers.[12] As SACO progressively began to reduce its entrance requirements during the 1950s, making recruitment from these groups possible, TCO member federations felt seriously threatened. Thus not to act to protect a little band of inventors, all of whom were engineers of one type or another, might eventually prove harmful to TCO.

But TCO's efforts could not be attributed solely to interest in warding off SACO's threat. There was an ideological side to the issue. Both Lennart Geijer, TCO's legal advisor during these years, and Olof Wallerius, chairman of TCO's Special Committee on Inventors' Rights (Uppfinnarkommitté), had long been active in supporting the interests of inventors. Even if the SI had not taken the steps it did, it is very likely that TCO still would have become just as active, albeit at a later date.

Lennart Geijer's interest in the plight of the inventor dated back to the 1940s. As SIF's legal adviser at that time, he had become progressively more disturbed over reports by engineers belonging to SIF that their employers were pressuring them to sign away all rights to any inventions they might make on the job. After receiving permission from SIF's executive board, Geijer contacted SAF in order to negotiate an agreement with them which would regulate the issue.[13] His attempts proved futile at first, but picked up once a Royal Commission was appointed to consider possible legislation in the area.[14] In 1946 SIF and SAF reached a preliminary agreement. In 1948 the Royal Commission presented its proposal (Geijer was an influential member of that commission), which in 1949 was passed into law. A final agreement between SIF and SAF was reached in 1950 with Geijer as a member of SIF's negotiating team.

During the 1940s in an effort to combat SACO's efforts to organize engineers, TCO created an Advisory Council on Problems Affecting Engineers (Ingenjörsrådet) within its headquarters, which served to bring together the representatives of all the engineering federations belonging to TCO. Geijer played an active role in setting up the group and in guiding its development thereafter. As previously mentioned, during the schism between TCO and SIF stemming from the supplementary pensions dispute,

---

[12] On October 1, 1964, publicly employed engineers at the state level included 2,939 civil engineers, 2,813 bachelor of science engineers, and 3,347 technological institute engineers. "Ingenjörer och ingenjörssammanslutningar," *Statsverksingenjören*, Vol. 10, No. 1 (March, 1960), p. 13.

[13] Interviews.

[14] Lennart Geijer, *Tjänstemannarättens ABC*, SIF skriftserie, No. 6 (3rd ed.; Stockholm: Svenska Industritjänstemannaförbundet, 1964), p. 13.

Geijer left SIF to take up a position within TCO headquarters. He there created a Special Committee on Inventors' Rights to oversee and coordinate all attempts to improve the position of this group.

As a member of the National Board for Employees' Inventions (Statens Nämnd för Arbetstagares Uppfinningar or SNAU), Geijer played a role in shaping board advisory opinions which were often quite favorable to the employee's cause. As a member of the Riksdag from the Social Democratic party, he used his position to make inquiries into the reimbursement procedures used by certain state agencies when employees failed to secure compensation commensurate with their contributions. Finally, as will be shown later, he played a significant role in the 1958 Royal Commission and the events which followed its report.

Geijer's actions sprang partly from a desire to see TCO hold onto its engineer membership. But he also firmly believed that the inventor was justified in demanding more from his employer. Alone an inventor could be exploited, but through trade union representation, Geijer felt his interests could be effectively protected.[15]

This altruistic motivation was expressed more openly by Olof Wallerius, the aggressive champion of the rights of inventors. Wallerius headed the Research Institute of the Swedish National Defense (Försvarets Forskningsanstalt or FOA). While working his way up the ladder within the institute, he had become progressively more and more disillusioned with the treatment accorded inventors by the state agencies, especially within the defense field. He became particularly incensed at what he considered to be the lack of reasonable compensation for inventions. Moreover, he became convinced that if Sweden were to continue to prosper, its economy required a constant supply of new discoveries from an active core of engineers. Thus he had striven to create an environment favorable to inventors, believing that this would stimulate their creative impulses to the benefit of all Swedes.[16]

As chief negotiator for inventors in their relations with the Office of the Comptroller for the Swedish Armed Forces (FCF), Wallerius was directly involved on a day-to-day basis for a number of years in trying to secure reasonable compensation for inventions.[17] In his capacity as repre-

---

[15] Interview.
[16] Interview.
[17] Interview. An example, related by Wallerius, of the difficulties he encountered in such negotiations indicates the intensity of his feelings:
"In the area of defense research, they [the Defense Department] wanted to enter into a cooperative venture with Bofors which would entail a certain sharing of

sentative from the Union of Civilian Salaried Employees in Defense to TCO's Advisory Council on the Problems Affecting Engineers and its Special Committee on Inventors' Rights, Wallerius played an important role in focusing TCO's attention on the plight of inventors as he saw it. Moreover, his tremendous activity on the particular question of whether the law was to be revised or not played a significant part in determining the end result.

Both Geijer and Wallerius were influential (Geijer as official member and Wallerius as ex officio) in the decision by SNAU to reject Televerket's demand for greater control over employee inventions. After the SNAU had stated that such a demand was unjustified, TCO and its member unions in the state sector gave the decision a great deal of publicity in their respective newspapers.

From his contacts with the defense establishment, moreover, Wallerius

---

research. I received word that negotiations were in progress from several colleagues in the Air Force department who also sent me copies of the proposed agreement. Well, a short time later word came from a division head in the Defense Department that we should discuss the matter.

" 'I'd like to see the copies of the proposed agreement,' I said. 'No,' he replied, 'that can't be done. They're secret.' 'Oh really,' I answered. 'What is it you want to discuss?' 'It deals with a possible agreement for sharing research with Bofors.' 'Then I'll have to see the proposed draft in order to say anything.' 'No, that's a secret—I can't let it out.'

"Well, this meeting finally came about anyway and I took copies of the proposed agreement with me that I'd gotten from the Air Force, the Marines and the Army and spread them out on the table opposite the division head. Then we began to talk.

"I asked, 'What is in the agreement?' 'Oh, it says this and that.' 'Yes, but isn't there this and that as well?' 'Yes, you are right there.' 'Well, isn't there more?' 'No, there. . . .' 'Come on now, there must be more than that,' I said.

"Finally I had backed this division head, this administrative chief, into such a corner that he didn't know whether he was coming or going. The only thing I hadn't done was to let him see the papers I had in front of me. But still he refused to let me see the agreement which was stamped 'secret' even though it was openly available in all branches of the armed forces. So, I finally told him, 'I'm not going to continue this god-damned conversation. Call the General Director. I don't want to talk with you any longer.'

"Then this division head sat there and told me how the Ombudsman for Civil Affairs viewed the questions raised by this proposed agreement. After I had been sitting on the National Board for Employees' Inventions for six years where the Ombudsman sits as chairman, and knew what he thought about such matters—this division head was going to tell *me* what the Ombudsman said. Moreover, he tried to tell me that the SNAU had made official reports on such questions, which it had not. To sit there and bluff in such a manner is nothing less than scandalous. But this is what the legal representatives of our agencies do. They want us to go and sign agreements before we know all the facts. You see from this example how they try to cheat us, and how we have to have at least as much knowledge about the area as they do to keep up with them."

learned of the meetings between the Office of the Comptroller for the Swedish Armed Forces (FCF) and officials at the Televerket.[18] In an effort to blunt the impact of the anticipated Televerket petition, it was decided in TCO's Special Committee on Inventors' Rights that TCO should send a petition of its own, also requesting a Royal Commission, but on different grounds. If there was no action by TCO (or another group representing inventors) TCO feared the government's directive for such an investigation would focus solely on the grievances alleged by the Televerket and the FCF. Thus, hoping to secure improvements in the compensatory features of the law (paragraph six), TCO sent a petition to the government.[19] Moreover, by adding its name to the list of critics TCO could lay claim to a place on the Royal Commission if one were established. It was decided that the petition should be presented at a formal meeting with the Minister of Justice.[20]

TCO's special committee had been specifically created because problems involving inventors were taking up too much time in TCO's Advisory Council on Problems Affecting Engineers. In many ways it proved a wise step, as the special committee's activity on these issues grew steadily during the next few years. One of the special committee's strategies sought to broaden the base of support for inventors among groups with a nonpartisan air about them. The Association of Swedish Inventors (Svenska Uppfinnareföreningen or SUF) was one logical target.

This venerable old association of inventors had a history dating back to 1886. Every year its chairman received a personal invitation from the King to attend the Nobel Prize festivities, an indication of the high status the group enjoyed.[21] Its membership included not only employees but also a number of employers, and political party affiliations ran the gamut from Conservative to Social Democratic. It functioned primarily as a social group for airing the problems common to all inventors.

TCO saw in this group a valuable forum for stimulating public opinion in favor of inventors. Moreover, as it always was asked to give *remiss* replies on proposed legislation affecting inventors, it could prove a valuable ally in the coming struggle. Hence the decision was made to encourage members of TCO's committee to join the organization and seek leadership

[18] Interview.
[19] TCO's Uppfinnarkommitté, Minutes of meetings of TCO's Uppfinnarkommitté, March 4, 1958, TCO Archive, Stockholm (mimeographed). See also TCO's petition. "TCO petition," April 22, 1958, TCO Archive, Stockholm (mimeographed).
[20] Interviews. TCO's Uppfinnarkommitté, Minutes of meetings of TCO's Uppfinnarkommitté, May 13, 1958, TCO Archive, Stockholm (mimeographed).
[21] Interview.

posts in order to gain some influence over its policies. By October, 1958, the secretary to TCO's advisory committee noted that all its members had become members of the association.[22] And by 1965 the chairman of the organization was Olof Wallerius (and the association's *remiss* reply opposing any change in the law was later to be written by him).[23]

A secondary strategy was aimed at securing support from SACO and the LO. Wallerius was delegated the task of making contact with SACO's CF (Swedish Association of Graduate Engineers) to examine possibilities for common action on this question.[24] Geijer handled the job of bringing the LO into the picture. While TCO organized the largest number of engineers and therefore inventors, SACO's cooperation could be important, since it organized all the remaining engineers. Moreover, SACO would have to cooperate or risk facing the charge that they were "selling out" interests of inventors. The support of the LO was important for two reasons. First of all the LO's close relationship with the ruling Social Democratic party could be counted on to strengthen TCO's hand. Second, the LO's contacts in other Scandinavian countries could (and did) prove valuable to TCO's efforts to prevent changes in their laws. The LO saw such cooperation as advantageous not only from the viewpoint of helping a fellow trade union confederation, but also as a chance to gain some expertise in an area of legal dispute which might eventually prove important for its own organizational activities. Thus TCO's special committee had gained three valuable allies.

Finally, an additional strategy, this one of a long-term nature, was agreed upon: members of TCO's special committee would strive to increase the public's knowledge of the problems facing inventors through an active campaign of article writing for various journals and newspapers.[25]

While all these developments were taking place, with the SI attempting to block the Televerket's efforts to have its employees sign new contracts and the government deciding to set up a Royal Commission, two hitherto unmentioned groups were also active.

First, the Swedish Association of Graduate Engineers (CF) announced that it supported as did TCO the association's petition to the Ombudsman

[22] TCO's Ingenjörsråd, Minutes of Ingenjörsrådets årssammanträde, October 25–26, 1958, TCO Archive, Stockholm, p. 3 (mimeographed).
[23] Interview.
[24] TCO's Uppfinnarkommitté, Minutes of TCO's Uppfinnarkommitté, January 21, 1959, TCO Archive, Stockholm (mimeographed).
[25] TCO's Uppfinnarkommitté, Minutes of TCO's Uppfinnarkommitté, May 6, 1958, TCO Archive, Stockholm (mimeographed).

for Civilian Affairs, questioning the legality of the Televerket's proposed contract. Their views were outlined in a letter sent to the ombudsman. Moreover, after TCO had contacted the CF regarding cooperation on the issue (by then it had become clear that a Royal Commission would indeed be set up), it decided to create a special coordinating committee just for this issue. S. E. Angert, who was later to become SACO's expert to the Royal Commission, was named as secretary to the group.[26]

Private industry's keen interest in these kinds of questions led the Swedish Employers' Association (SAF) to become active and to create a special committee in its headquarters to follow developments. It kept in close touch with the Televerket and the FCF, and when the Televerket's only remaining alternative was to request a Royal Commission, SAF's special committee wrote the government requesting a seat on such a commission.[27]

Policy Deliberation

On October 24, 1958, a Royal Commission was formally established to review the entire 1949 law. Instead of appointing interest group representatives as full-fledged members, as the interest groups had of course hoped,[28] the instructions established a one-man commission to be assisted by experts.[29] The role of experts on Royal Commissions is identical to that of members except that they lack the right to vote. Moreover, as a general rule, if they disagree with the findings, expert status does not allow them to attach their opinions to the final report as reservations, as members can. However, in this case the government decided that because feelings ran so high on the issue, the usual procedure would be waived and experts could, if they wished, append reservations to the final report.

Supreme Court Justice Sven Edling was named as the commissioner. He was to have the full-time services of Einar Mogård from the Ministry of Justice, who would serve as his secretary. Lennart Geijer from the TCO, S. E. Angert from SACO, I. Grundin from SI, C. H. Jacobeus from L. M. Ericsson, C. Nilsson from FCF, W. Persson representing the Televerket, and H. Romanus from the Swedish Inventions Bureau (Svenska Uppfinnarkontoret) were to serve as experts.

---

[26] "Förbundsnytt," *Civilingenjörsförbundets Tidskrift*, No. 8 (1958), p. 128.
[27] "SAF petition," March 30, 1958, SAF Archive, Stockholm (mimeographed).
[28] Interviews.
[29] Sweden, Justitiedepartementet, *Rätten till arbetstagares uppfinningar*, pp. 26–27.

Interest group leaders had anticipated full-fledged membership on the commission instead of expert status, and, moreover, they were not particularly happy about the government's choice of Sven Edling as commissioner.[30] Edling and for that matter his secretary, Mogård, had no familiarity with the problem area, which meant that much time would be needed to "educate" them. From the government's point of view the structure and personnel of the commission were not so strange. The issue was so charged that in many ways it was reasonable to appoint only a single "judge" who was not involved in any way and could impartially listen to both sides before giving an opinion. Moreover, Justice Edling's legal training would help him thread his way through the maze of legal questions surrounding the issue.

Edling's first exposure to the complexities of the question he was to investigate and the passions it aroused came during two meetings held by the Association of Swedish Inventors. On January 22 and 29, 1959, Edling had the opportunity to hear some of the foremost legal experts in Sweden express their views on the problems connected with drawing the line between employer and employee rights to inventions. In addition ample time was also allotted to the protagonists to defend their respective positions. Jan Neumüller from TCO's Special Committee on Inventors' Rights lashed into state agencies and their compensation policies, and the FCF's representative countered by asserting that such problems were greatly overemphasized. He sought, moreover, to shift the discussion to the law's third paragraph (defining employer rights to inventions) which had caused him and the Televerket officers such difficulties, an action provoking a sharp reply from Neumüller.[31]

The views aired at these meetings were in essence those which eventually came to dominate the discussions in the Royal Commission. Representatives to the commission from state agencies wanted to expand employer rights to inventions so that they would include not only section one of paragraph three but also section two, that is, not just inventions relating directly to a specific research job but also those unrelated to the research purpose of the position. They were less concerned with compensation questions (paragraph six), and the FCF in particular was opposed to codifying the procedure for establishing compensation for any invention by making SNAU into a court of final appeals.[32]

[30] Interviews.

[31] *Rätten till arbetstagares uppfinningar 1959* (Stockholm: Svenska Uppfinnareföreningen, 1960), pp. 40–50, 52–57, 60–61, 73–75, 79.

[32] Interview. Minutes of Meetings of SOU 1964:49, November 9, 1959, SOU 1964:49 Documents, Riksarkivet, Stockholm, pp. 1–7 (typewritten).

In the early months of 1959, the advisory group on inventor questions in the Employers' Association (SAF) drew up a list of major questions of concern with which it hoped the commission would deal. Jacobeaus, as a member of SAF's advisory group and an expert to the commission, was to lobby for such views. Regarding paragraph three, that paragraph which defined employer rights to employee inventions, the group agreed completely with the FCF's position that employers were entitled to more comprehensive rights to their employees' inventions. As far as paragraph six was concerned, that paragraph entitling an employee to reasonable compensation for an invention, it held no objection to the statement but would oppose any attempt to spell out amounts of compensation for different kinds of inventions. Moreover, it would oppose any attempt to make the law operative in all cases, as this would thereby prevent employers from privately negotiating agreements establishing guidelines different from those specified in paragraph three.[33]

TCO's position was less clearly formulated. It opposed giving even more power to employers through paragraph three, yet it saw that state agencies were in a difficult position and that some adjustments were probably needed. Thus TCO was willing to compromise, giving up some rights under paragraph three in return for compensatory procedures in paragraph six. Within TCO's special committee the idea of making SNAU more than just an advisory body had strong support, especially from Wallerius.[34]

From the very first meeting Edling found employer and employee group representatives far apart. His efforts during the first year and a half to reach agreement on a wording for paragraph three which would broaden the rights of employers to include sections one and two were consistently opposed by Geijer, Grundin, and Angert. Additional support for the employee position came from H. Romanus of the Swedish Inventions Bureau. On the employer side Edling met equally intransigent positions supporting a change in paragraph three which would insure employer rights to inventions and opposing any detailing of procedures for setting compensation.

To some degree the difficulty Edling encountered stemmed from his desire to concentrate on paragraph three (governing employer rights to employee inventions) instead of attacking both this paragraph and the compensation question (paragraph six) simultaneously. He chose this path because he honestly felt that compensation procedures could not be

[33] SAF's Referensgrupp, "SAF PM: Revision av lagen om rätten till arbetstagares uppfinningar," March 12, 1959, SAF Archive, Stockholm (mimeographed).
[34] Interview.

spelled out more clearly. While he expressed privately his concern to the employee representatives regarding the difficulties inventors faced in gaining reasonable compensation, he felt the commission should work to reach agreement on that section which, in his opinion, lent itself to further specification. This decision stiffened the backs of the employee groups, as they now had no position from which to bargain.

Resistance from the employee representatives and Romanus to Edling's proposed changes in paragraph three also stemmed from strategy discussions held outside the commission meetings. In contrast to the employer side, where communications were infrequent and uncoordinated, the employee representatives, plus Romanus of the Swedish Inventions Bureau, were members of an informal organization created specifically for the purpose of protecting the rights of inventors. In 1959 Olof Wallerius, with the approval of TCO's executive board, had approached members of the Swedish Association of Engineers, the Association of State-Employed Engineers of Sweden, the Swedish Foremen and Supervisors' Association (SALF), the Union of Technical and Clerical Employees in Industry (SIF), and the LO in an effort to formalize cooperation on this issue. The result was a group, informally labeled the ad hoc Employee Organizations Committee on Inventor Problems, which had some thirty representatives, including the three pro-employee experts on the Royal Commission plus H. Romanus.

Because it was not identified formally with any particular group (even though TCO had taken the initiative in setting it up), and because it was dealing with a problem area affecting all the groups, the committee was able to a surprising degree to avoid the tensions normally present among groups which seek to organize the same clientele. Wallerius emphasized the nonpartisan aspect of the organization by choosing to use only stationery with no letterhead to announce meetings.[35] At each of these meetings, which occurred three to five times a year, the experts would report on the situation in the commission and a general policy discussion would follow. From such discussions emerged the common front of opposition among the employee representatives: if no concessions regarding compensation could be expected, they were to display little interest in any changes in paragraph three.

The stiff resistance Edling met at the hands of the employee group representatives was caused not only by his decision to deal only with paragraph three, but also by the rivalry between SACO and TCO, which made itself felt behind the scenes in the commission. Cooperation in the

[35] Interview.

ad hoc group did not prevent each representative from looking for additional ways to improve exclusively the position of his own group. Thus Angert from the CF of SACO and Geijer from TCO indicated privately to the commission's secretary, Mogård, that each felt some sympathy for Edling's proposed changes in paragraph three but would not risk supporting them if his group could not be assured of gaining something in return.[36] Thus Mogård and Edling knew that if they could come up with something that would benefit one or the other, the alliance might be broken. As will be shown later, just such an attempt was made by Edling, but with unintended results.

By January, 1961, it was clear to Edling that an impasse had been reached. From this time until the end of 1962 Edling placed his hopes for achieving a united commission on the possibility that Scandinavian unity on the issue might force the employee representatives to reconsider their stand. In making this point in a memorandum to the other commissions in Norway, Denmark, and Finland, he urged a step-up in efforts to achieve a pan-Scandinavian solution to the problem.[37]

Initial discussions with the commissions in other Scandinavian countries had actually begun as early as June, 1959. In its directive to the commission the government encouraged Edling to search out possibilities for Scandinavian cooperation on the issue. Since the laws in both Finland and Denmark, especially Finland, were more favorable to the employer viewpoint regarding their rights to employee inventions, Mogård believed that any cooperation would result in support for Edling's position on paragraph three. As the first few meetings of the Swedish commission had shown that deadlock might not be far away, both Edling and Mogård saw in Scandinavian cooperation a potential lever to use to secure unanimity within the Swedish commission. If Edling's position were in fact to receive support from Finland, Denmark, and Norway, then the employee representatives would be isolated in their resistance to change and their opposition given the tint of obstructionism. Such a position, Mogård and Edling believed, would be untenable.[38]

The crucial unknown was Norway. The existing laws in Finland and Denmark showed clearly that these two countries were favorably disposed toward Edling's position; in Norway, however, only age-old customs and laws governed the relationship between inventors and their employers. In

---

[36] Interview.

[37] "PM angående nordiska överläggningar rörande lagstiftning om arbetstagares uppfinningar," SOU 1964:49 Documents, Riksarkivet, Stockholm (mimeographed).

[38] *Ibid.* Interviews.

June Mogård had a lengthy discussion with a high-ranking member of Norway's Ministry of Industry which apparently paid off. Word reached Edling in October that the Norwegians had appointed a Royal Commission and that initial discussions showed a positive attitude toward Edling's interpretation of paragraph three.[39] Thus when progress finally did grind to a halt within the Swedish commission and the lines became more firmly drawn, Edling turned the emphasis during 1961 and 1962 to Scandinavian cooperation in an effort to promote agreement within his own commission.

When Geijer learned that Edling was now going to put pressure on the Swedish employee representatives to fall into line with their counterparts in the other Scandinavian countries, he realized he had to make a counter move. This he did through a compromise attempt which would have required that each side give a little, this being preferable to the demand for complete employee capitulation which he knew was to be forthcoming from Edling.

The 1958 agreement between SIF and SAF, it will be remembered, had resulted in a deterioration in the relationship between employer and employee, at least from the latter's point of view. Employers were given rights to inventions stemming from not only sections one and two of paragraph three but also section three. This meant that the employer owned rights to inventions resulting from (1) the efforts of those hired to research a particular project, (2) the efforts of those hired to research a particular project who in the process discovered something unrelated to the specific project but which could still be used by the firm, and (3) the efforts of anyone who worked in the plant, no matter what their original terms of employment. For TCO the agreement had proven to be a considerable headache as it sought to stop the shift of its engineers from SIF to CF.

Geijer approached Mogård with the proposal that he would accept Edling's changes in paragraph three if in return SAF agreed to make such provisions binding, that is to give up its right to negotiate provisions different from those which the new paragraph three would stipulate. As Edling's proposal would have essentially meant a return to the pre-1958 relationship between SAF and SIF, an acceptance by SAF of this point would in effect have meant a revision of the 1958 SIF-SAF agreement. Neither Angert from the CF nor Grundin from the SI were informed of this discussion.[40]

Mogård arranged a meeting for Edling with SAF's Inventor Committee on May 25, 1962, to discuss Geijer's proposed compromise. At that meet-

[39] Interviews.
[40] Interviews.

ing even Jacobeaus, L. M. Ericsson's expert to the commission and a member of SAF's group, argued forcefully for acceptance. Still the effort met with total failure. SAF was unwilling to give up the right to reach negotiated agreements regarding paragraph three even though such a move might benefit its sister industries under state management.[41]

With the collapse of this effort, Geijer and Wallerius decided to deal directly with the pressure which they feared would soon be forthcoming from Edling. They knew that once he began to point to united stands in other Scandinavian countries it would be nearly impossible to continue to hold out in favor of employee interests in Sweden. Employee representatives in other countries had to be alerted to the new urgency of the issue and the justification for TCO's position. Thus Geijer and Wallerius redoubled their own efforts in the field of Scandinavian cooperation.

As early as 1959 the two had sought to broaden TCO's contacts with other Scandinavian countries. In this effort the LO had proved especially helpful. Nowhere in Scandinavia are white-collar workers so well organized as they are in Sweden. In Norway and Denmark, in fact, a large percentage of white-collar workers are actually organized in blue-collar federations, if they are members of any union at all. Through the LO's good offices, then, contacts were established with these blue-collar groups in both Norway and Denmark. Moreover, as Geijer and Wallerius traveled from country to country during 1961 and 1962, they also succeeded in contacting a number of organizations which included engineers.[42]

With the new urgency they now conveyed, these efforts at last proved fruitful. Shortly after the compromise attempt in June, 1962, the Norwegian commission chairman, Hammel, reported to Edling that the employee position, led by the LO's representative, had changed and that he now expected them to make a reservation on his findings.[43] Within a short time unity within the Finnish commission had also broken down.[44] Thus Scandinavian cooperation had indeed encouraged TCO's representative in the Royal Commission to act, but the results were a far cry from what Edling had hoped they would be.

[41] Letter, Forstadius to Edling, June 4, 1962. SAF Referensgrupp angående revision av lagen om rätten till arbetstagares uppfinningar, SAF Archive, Stockholm (typewritten).

[42] Interviews. TCO's Uppfinnarkommitté, Minutes of TCO's Uppfinnarkommitté, February 11, 1959, September, 1959, November 2, 1961, February 13, 1962, TCO Archive, Stockholm (mimeographed).

[43] Letter, Hammel to Edling, May 11, 1962; also letter, Hammel to Edling, September 4, 1962, SOU 1964:49 Documents, Riksarkivet, Stockholm (typewritten).

[44] Interview.

During this same period, 1961 to 1962, the hand of the employee groups was strengthened by developments in yet another area: the thorny problem of collective bargaining rights for state employees was moving toward resolution.

The findings of two Royal Commissions meeting on the question of public employees' strike rights between 1949 and 1960 had resulted in a reduction of the difference between private and state employees on this point. According to the 1960 commission, for example, it was proposed that such rights be extended to all state employees not enjoying civil service status.

The interest groups involved in attempting to secure a change in this field of labor management relations, however, reacted strongly against the refusal of the 1960 commission to propose changes which would allow collective bargaining rights, including the right to strike, to all state and local employees, regardless of the security of their jobs.

In 1961 the Minister for Civilian Affairs, Sigurd Lindholm, took an unconventional initiative. He invited the representatives from TCO, SACO, SR (The National Federation of Civil Servants), and the State Employees Union (SF) of the LO, the advocates of change, to a series of informal "seminars" to see if agreement could at last be reached on this sensitive area of policy. The discussions led to the desired result, as all parties agreed in 1963 to sign an agreement setting out rules and procedures for the conduct of labor relations, including possible strike action, modeled after the famous 1937 Saltsjöbaden agreement between industry and labor in the private sector.

For Edling's commission the direction in which labor relations were heading, and especially the decision by Lindholm to begin seminar discussions with the various interest groups involved, meant that employees would soon have access to an important avenue for regulating their employment conditions in the state sector. As was already the case in the private sector, it was quite apparent that employees in state service would soon be able to negotiate contracts with their employers, including such areas as inventor rights. Thus one of the major reasons for creating the commission in the first place, the Televerket's inability to make legal contract agreements with its employees regulating its rights to the fruits of their efforts, would soon be solved. From the employees' standpoint, moreover, the compensation situation could be improved, as labor unions would then be able to bargain for better procedures.

These changes led to a certain amount of feeling within Edling's Royal Commission, especially by the employee representatives, that a final report was now unnecessary and the commission ought to disband. From the employers, however, came a strong push to continue and finish the job, as they desired to see the law changed to incorporate the advantages they had obtained by the SAF-SIF agreement of 1958. Moreover, as Edling had encouraged other Scandinavian countries to cooperate in this area, he felt he could hardly back out at this late date.

Thus from May, 1962, until the commission presented its report in June, 1964, all attempts to reach agreement within the Swedish Commission had failed. The lines were firmly drawn and the members spent all their time thereafter meeting with other Scandinavian commissions to work out the wording of the majority and minority reports.

Employee groups in Sweden now concentrated on preparing for an all-out offensive to be launched against the report once its contents were made public. As a first step, Geijer, Grundin, and Angert collaborated to write a searching critique of Edling's findings which supported the employers' point of view; this was to be published in the report as a reservation. They were aided in these efforts by Romanus, who, although he felt that his neutral position precluded his joining in on their critique, did write his own reservation.[45]

The next step was an attempt to coordinate *remiss* replies among a wide range of interest groups and state agencies. The main avenue for achieving this proved to be the ad hoc Employee Organizations Committee on Inventor Problems.

Once a ministry in Sweden receives a commission's report, it sends it out to a large number of interest groups and agencies for their comments. Such a process insures that the minister responsible for the eventual proposition has at hand two crucial sources of information necessary to create any workable policy: first of all additional expert testimony from groups affected by the commission's recommendations; and second, the expression of the intensity for and against the proposals by different segments of society.

TCO's strategy was to try to create a united front among interest groups and friendly state agencies against Edling's report. If successful, such efforts might discourage the Minister of Justice from presenting any legislation at all. A second possible result, viewed with less favor than the first, might be the appointment of a new commission, an act which would at least postpone changes in the law.[46]

[45] Interviews. Sweden, Justitiedepartementet, *Rätten till arbetstagares uppfinningar*, pp. 54–78.
[46] Interviews.

A meeting of the ad hoc organization was called for the specific purpose of coordinating the members' *remiss* replies. After a few miscellaneous points had been raised, Wallerius rose to read a complete proposed reply that TCO's special committee had worked out. A general discussion followed, resulting in a consensus that copies would be sent to each group to provide inspiration for the individual replies.[47]

TCO then moved to activate as many neutral groups as possible to insure that their *remiss* replies reflected the ad hoc group's critique. As chairman of the Executive Board of the Association of Swedish Inventors, Wallerius succeeded in gaining its approval for a reply which mirrored the one read by him at the meeting of the ad hoc group. Through Geijer's contacts with Angert, the CF exerted pressure on the Royal Academy of Sciences (Vetenskapsakademien) to come out against Edling's report. Geijer was able to use his own position in securing support for TCO's position from the National Board for Employees' Inventions (SNAU).

As several interest groups and state agencies which could be expected to support the employees' position had been omitted from the government's list of *remiss* requests, TCO sought through informal contacts to encourage these bodies to write to the department asking permission to send *remiss* replies. Such actions were taken by SALF and SIF, both with the desired result.

TCO thus succeeded in achieving a united front. Fifty-four state agencies and eighteen interest groups received the proposal on *remiss*. Half the replies were sharply critical of Edling's report while the remaining half either expressed approval or had no official comments.[48] The main points of criticism reflected those proposed by Wallerius, often with the same phrasing. In summary form the opponents felt:

1. The change in negotiating rights for state employees obviated any need for a change in the law.
2. The law had not been in effect long enough to warrant a revision.
3. Four experts in the commission were opposed to the proposal. With the opposition, especially of labor, to the proposed changes, the Government ought not pursue the matter further.
4. Efforts to achieve Scandinavian unity deserved praise, but should not be made at the price of a decline in status for one group. Moreover, as paragraph three of the law could be set aside through negotiated agreements there would in fact be no common law in any event.

[47] Interviews.
[48] "Sammanställning av remissyttranden över det av justitierådet S. Edling framlagda förslag till ny lag om rätten till arbetstagares uppfinningar (SOU 1964:49) June 6, 1966," TCO Archive, Stockholm (mimeographed).

5. The proposed expansion of paragraph three was unjustified and unnecessary. If employers were willing to institute procedures for reasonable compensation, they could always gain access to the inventions of their employees without any change in the law.
6. No thorough investigation of the problems surrounding compensation and the approval of procedures had been taken up in the hearings. Thus the Commission had not completed its assignment and its results could not be approved.

Seldom were all the above points made in any one *remiss* reply. It was common, however, to find four or five points in each of the statements.[49]

TCO's special committee was not content to simply coordinate the *remiss* replies. Several of its members sought out political party representatives in an effort to prevent the issue from becoming embroiled in partisan controversy. At meetings of the Association of Swedish Inventors Wallerius was able to discuss his reasons for desiring no change in the law with employers who had close ties to the bourgeois parties. On the Social Democratic side, Geijer's contacts with LO representative Husberg from the Federation of Swedish Metal Workers led to the neutralization of an official who was potentially one of the greatest supporters of a change in the law, Member of Parliament Hans Hagnell.[50]

Hagnell had built his reputation in the Social Democratic party through a steady stream of criticism of the management of state-owned industries. Arguing vigorously for reorganization measures which would enable these bodies to compete more effectively with private industry, he had raised the hackles of the party's leadership more than once. Thus in an effort to prevent Hagnell from jumping to support a measure which, although it would have helped state industries, would also have had a detrimental effect on state-employed inventors, fellow trade union member Husberg had several long talks with him. Hagnell agreed not to speak out on the issue.[51]

Within TCO's special committee pressure was brought to bear on SIF to end its agreement with SAF when it came up for review in the spring of 1964. It would be difficult for the employer groups to argue that the law should be changed to make it more like the agreement in the private sector if that agreement no longer existed. This action SIF was willing to take.[52]

---

[49] *Ibid.* See also the individual *remiss* replies.
[50] Interview.
[51] Interview.
[52] TCO's Ingenjörsråd, Minutes from TCO's Ingenjörsråd, February 12, 1964, TCO Archive, Stockholm, p. 3 (mimeographed).

TCO's special committee also sought to increase publicity regarding the positions taken by different employee groups. Stories about *remiss* positions appeared in the trade union papers of TCO and of the several TCO-affiliated federations active in this issue (FCTF, SIF, SALF, and so on). Moreover, informal contacts assured publicity through SACO's and LO's press. Even the organ of the Association of Swedish Inventors, *Industriell Teknik*, featured several articles on the reactions of employee groups to the Edling commission.[53] The strategy was not so much to create the impression of a ground swell of protest against the measure as it was to convince those in the Ministry of Justice that the groups most directly concerned with the issue were strongly against any change in the law.

That such a change was deemed likely is clearly evident in the reports Geijer gave to TCO's special committee. In fact the minutes of one committee meeting quote him as saying that a proposition could be expected in the spring of 1965. Operating on this assumption the special committee tentatively approved a resolution to hold a large public debate on the entire issue at that time to increase publicity on the problems of inventors.[54]

But such a conference never came to be. Geijer's position as a Member of Parliament from the Social Democratic party gave him special access to the Minister of Justice, Herman Kling. He discussed the matter with him once in the corridors of the Riksdag and once again in greater detail at the Ministry of Justice.[55] This political pressure apparently intensified the distaste Kling had felt toward recommending a change which was opposed by so many of the labor groups in Swedish society. At a third meeting in the fall of 1965, Kling informed Geijer that he planned not to present a proposition on the matter. The issue was closed.

TCO's Influence and the Problem of Political Controversy

In assessing the reasons for the defeat of the attempted revision of the 1949 law on inventors' rights, it is clear that SAF's intransigence at a crucial point contributed significantly to preventing a victory on an important issue for its sister industries in the state sector. Moreover, the

---

[53] For *Industriell Teknik* see the series which began in 1965: K. Göran, "Utredningen rörande lagöversynen för rätten till arbetstagares uppfinningar," *Industriell Teknik*, No. 2 (1965), pp. 25–26; "Sex års tankemödor," *Industriell Teknik*, No. 4 (1965), p. 65; Lennart Sjöö, "Utredningen rörande lagöversynen för rätt till arbetstagares uppfinningar—ett genmäle," *Industriell Teknik*, No. 7 (1965), p. 140.

[54] TCO's Uppfinnarkommitté, Minutes from TCO's Uppfinnarkommitté, August 25, 1965, TCO Archive, Stockholm (mimeographed).

[55] Interview.

events surrounding the right to negotiate and to strike certainly made it easier for the government to postpone indefinitely any action on revising the law. But the most important determinant for the case's outcome was TCO's action to prevent change in the law, especially paragraph three, when it saw it was to receive nothing in return. Certainly the attempted compromise by Geijer, the efforts of Geijer and Wallerius to activate their fellow unions throughout Scandinavia, their success in creating a united front in the *remiss* stage of the decision-making process, and finally Geijer's important political connections spelled the difference between victory and defeat on the issue. Of the groups involved, TCO had at its disposal the greatest number of resources for influencing the final decision and it used what it had with greater skill than did the other groups.

Two examples suffice to bring this point home. While SAF's group met regularly during the years the commission was at work, and even had briefings by Edling, there is nothing in the minutes of their meetings to indicate that they sought to coordinate *remiss* replies. On the other hand it will be remembered that TCO provided a model *remiss* reply which all pro-employee respondents followed.[56] Second, the CF's informal group created specifically to follow this issue met only occasionally, and its secretary readily admitted that they followed TCO's lead in all matters. In sum, TCO enjoyed considerable influence on this matter.

Most important, however, the Case of the Uncommon Man suggests that TCO's influence may be greatest when political partisanship is least. As the preceding analysis of TCO's involvement in the supplementary pensions dispute indicated, when an issue moves from a discussion between the major economic groups in society and the government to include the opposition political parties, TCO's cohesion and thus its influence decrease as the temperature of the political debate rises. In this case TCO consciously sought to avoid having the issue become a political football. As the next section will demonstrate, it is in fact within the bureaucratic realm of politics that TCO enjoys its strongest position and is able to use its resources most effectively to influence policy outcomes.

[56] Interviews. SAF's Referensgrupp, Minutes from SAF Referensgrupp angående revision av lagen om rätten till arbetstagares uppfinningar, SAF Archive, Stockholm (mimeographed).

Chapter Eight

TCO and the National Board of Education

Interest groups are represented on four different kinds of administrative organs in the Swedish bureaucracy: the labor court of Sweden and other administrative courts, the executive boards of certain central administrative boards (hereafter called agencies), advisory groups to ministries and agencies, and finally a number of joint consulting commissions.[1]

This section will focus on an in-depth study of TCO's activities in the policy-making process of the National Board of Education (Skolöverstyrelsen or SÖ), where it sits as a member of the agency's executive board.[2] A study of this kind has been chosen for a number of reasons. First of all, interest group representation on the executive boards of agencies represents the furthest advance yet by groups into the heart of the policy-making process in the administration. As voting members, and often in the majority, they hold a power position unequalled by advisory groups or joint consulting commissions. Moreover, policy is more directly formulated by agencies than is the case with the labor court of Sweden and other administrative courts.

Second, TCO considers such representation on the SÖ (National Board of Education) to be of particular importance. TCO organizes 90 percent of the teachers at the primary and lower secondary levels. During the early 1960s stepped-up reform activities affecting these grade levels led

[1] Nils Elvander, *Intresseorganisationerna i dagens Sverige* (2nd ed.; Lund: Gleerup, 1969), p. 233.

[2] The National Board of Education is only one of several important access points through which TCO can attempt to influence educational policy. Additional points include Royal Commission representation, informal discussions with ministry officials, and representation on the ministry's Planning Council. The choice of the National Board of Education for this study is justified in the text.

to pressure from these federations for greater TCO involvement to protect their interests. Moreover, renewed jurisdictional disputes between TCO and the Swedish Confederation of Professional Organizations (SACO) encouraged TCO to be more active at the level of the National Board of Education. During the 1960s, SACO, which organizes teachers at the university and gymnasium levels, progressively lowered its admission requirements in an effort to lure a large number of teachers away from TCO. TCO, of course, took up the challenge by upgrading its efforts to protect its members' interests.[3]

Third, conclusions regarding TCO's activity in the SÖ lend themselves to comparison with materials available regarding group representation on the labor market board (another central administrative board, or agency, with interest group representation on its executive board).

Within the policy-making process of the National Board of Education, TCO's influence in three arenas of policy-making will be examined. These are: agency commission studies, agency budgeting requests, and agency *remiss* replies in response to Royal Commission reports. I shall attempt to establish that TCO effectively influences educational policy through its representative on the executive board in all three of these arenas.

In particular, I shall attempt to establish that it is in SÖ-sponsored commission studies that TCO exercises its greatest influence over public proposals, for when and if consensus is reached at this stage of the decision-making process, the results of such commissions stand a good chance of becoming law.

This is so for two reasons. First of all, groups participating in a commission which is able to reach a consensus and submit a unanimous report are unlikely to encourage the political parties with which they may have

---

[3] While these factors must be considered as paramount in TCO's efforts to influence educational policy at the level of the National Board of Education, they do not entirely explain TCO's general willingness to concentrate a great deal of time, money, and manpower resources on efforts to influence educational policy from pre-school through adult levels at many different points of access in the decision-making process. In this context four reasons stand out, in addition to those cited above:

1. White-collar employees have traditionally attached great importance to education as a means for career advancement.
2. Given the highly advanced nature of the Swedish economy, education has increased in importance as a production factor. This has led to greater interest in expanding opportunities for education, particularly at the adult level.
3. Education can help citizens use their increased leisure time to ends which they deem more satisfactory.
4. Citizenship demands skills learned through education.

close connections to take up the issue. As will be shown below, group representatives often feel morally bound to support a compromise reached at this point. Moreover, they believe on pragmatic grounds that concessions gained at the commission stage may be the best which can be achieved.

The second reason commission recommendations tend to become law is that if political parties choose to become actively involved, they enter the picture at a very late stage. In the short time they have to counter the agency commission's proposals, the political parties are not usually able to reconstruct the tremendous amount of information available to the commission. This disadvantage, of course, is particularly great in the case of the opposition political parties. For at least these reasons, then, access to agency commission studies, in which consensus is reached, provides considerable influence over eventual policy outcomes.

Agencies

Agencies occupy a curious position in the administrative chain of command from the perspective of other West European parliamentary systems. Article 47 of the Swedish Constitution reads: "The administrative boards. . . . shall obey the King's orders and commands."[4] In theory this means that Sweden does not have the usual form of ministerial government, in which department heads serve also as heads of administrative agencies. Instead, administrative agencies take orders only from the King-in-Council (Cabinet). In fact, however, close coordination of policy between departments and agencies has been made possible through the use of the budget (which the ministry proposes), re-staffing during the long tenure by the Social Democrats, and constant informal discussion between ministry officials and agency personnel regarding the wishes of the ministry. Until recently Swedish ministries have acted almost exclusively as policy-making staffs, while the administrative agencies have been responsible for routine administration.[5] As will be shown later, this relationship is undergoing a change, with the agencies asserting new independence from ministerial direction by assuming increased leadership in planning.

The National Board of Education (SÖ) is such an administrative agency. It is responsible for administering all forms of education from the

---

[4] Robert Malmgren, Halvar G. F. Sundberg, and Gustaf Petrén, *Sveriges grundlagar och tillhörande författningar* (11th ed.; Stockholm: Norstedt, 1971), p. 60.

[5] Dankwart Rustow, *The Politics of Compromise: A Study of Parties and Cabinet Government in Sweden* (Princeton: Princeton University Press, 1955), p. 176.

first grade through the gymnasium.[6] While formally responsible only to the Cabinet, its ties to the Ministry of Education, at least until recently, have been close. The tools discussed above (ministerial approval of budget requests, re-staffing policies, and constant informal discussion) have been the chief means by which policy coordination has been achieved.

In an effort to broaden the basis for settling questions of educational policy, the government decided in 1964 that the SÖ should be reformed to include on its executive board representatives from nine important interest groups and administrative agencies. Three employee organizations thus came to occupy seats: TCO, the Swedish Confederation of Professional Associations (SACO), and the Swedish Confederation of Trade Unions (LO). Employer organizations have one representative from the Swedish Employers' Association (SAF), one from the Swedish Association of Commercial Employers (Handelns Arbetsgivareorganisation or HAO) representing the field of commerce and clerical occupations, and one from the Association of Swedish County Councils (Landstingsförbundet) representing the health care area. The Labor Market Board has one representative, as do the Communes[7] and the office of the chancellor of the Swedish universities. From the agency itself there are two representatives: the general director and the deputy director. In all then there is a total of eleven members on the executive board. Important changes in the responsibilities of the SÖ as a result of the 1964 reform are discussed in greater detail below.

Resources for Influence

The decision-making structure of the National Board of Education (SÖ) creates certain opportunities for influence by interest groups. One aspect of this is the privileged position interest groups enjoy as voting members of the executive board. As permanent representatives on a decision-making body convened at regular intervals (monthly) and governed by majority rule, their views must be listened to. This is especially true since only two

---

[6] Educational reforms have transformed the gymnasium into a gymnasieskola, which includes vocational as well as academic tracks.

[7] The representative from the Communes wears two hats on the board. The organization he represents, the Confederation of Communes (Kommunförbundet), cooperates on many issues with the Association of Swedish County Councils (Landstingsförbundet) in their respective capacities as employers. This cooperation carries over on occasion to the National Board of Education, particularly on issues concerning the employment conditions of teachers. Thus the representative of the Communes must in some cases be seen as a representative of employer interests.

of the eleven members of the executive board are agency officials from the National Board of Education itself.[8] Moreover, agency-sponsored commission studies rely heavily on interest group cooperation.

The legitimacy by which interest group activity is viewed in Sweden has affected the decision-making process in the SÖ. For example, it is seen as legitimate, particularly in the arena of agency commission studies, for a group to contact agency officials in an effort to modify the agency's policy proposal to the board before an issue is taken up for decision in the executive board.[9] It is, in fact, a standing rule for agency commission studies that if it wishes a group should be able to get information on agency views or to present its own ideas to agency officials. This often means considerable time spent telephoning and traveling to the head-quarters of various interest groups.[10] To a man, group representatives on the executive board felt that they had a fair chance to present their views to the agency. Each felt that the lines of communication to those working on agency commission studies were open and free of bias against any par-ticular group, a significant fact in light of comparative attitudes in France and Italy and their negative implications for interest group access.[11]

The comprehensiveness of each of the organizations is another factor increasing the power of their positions on the executive board. TCO repre-sents some 90 percent of the teachers in the Comprehensive School, SACO the remaining 10 percent plus virtually all at the gymnasium and univer-sity levels.[12] The LO represents 95 percent of all the blue-collar workers, while in the field of heavy industry, SAF represents almost 100 percent of the manufacturing concerns.[13]

The strong position of groups on the executive board, moreover, has led to an operating system of "anticipated reactions" by both agency of-ficials and group representatives. While this may operate on the one hand to limit extreme proposals by some groups, it serves on the other hand to ensure that the officials in the SÖ take seriously the reactions they anticipate from the interest groups. As one high-ranking official put it:

[8] Representatives from other agencies (the labor market board and the office of the chancellor of the Swedish universities) can usually be counted upon to support the agency officials from the SÖ.

[9] Interviews.

[10] Interviews.

[11] Interviews. See Joseph LaPalombara, *Interest Groups in Italian Politics* (Prince-ton: Princeton University Press, 1964), pp. 289–296.

[12] Two groups not organized by SACO include vocational school teachers (yrkes-lärarna) and extra-subject teachers (övningslärarna).

[13] *TCO's Utbildningsdagar 1965* (Stockholm: Tjänstemännens Centralorganisa-tion, 1965), p. 25. Elvander, *Intresseorganisationerna*, pp. 48–50.

"We have pretty good intuition. We don't propose crazy ideas to the Executive Board which will only be voted down. We're able to say in the discussion within the agency which precedes a meeting of the Executive Board whether groups will or won't accept a proposal."[14]

Confirmation that such was indeed the practice came from an interest group representative on the executive board: "Politics is the art of the possible. We from our organization must make a judgment as to where the other groups in the Executive Board and the agency officials stand when we draw up our proposals. The agency must do the same. They know if they write a proposal this way or that, they are very likely to have this or that group in opposition. They may accept that; but they will never go so far as to risk a situation where the agency's proposal will be voted down."[15] As these statements imply, successful application of Friedrich's well-known "law of anticipated reaction" depends on an intimate knowledge of where the other members of the board are likely to stand on any given issue. The acquisition of the knowledge is facilitated by the considerable overlap of membership posts in other governmental bodies by those who sit in the executive board of the SÖ. Thus, for example, during the time field research was carried out for this study, TCO, SACO, and LO's educational representatives and the general director and deputy director of the agency sat together on the Ministry of Education's Planning Council. TCO, LO, and SAF's representatives in the planning council sat together on the Royal Commission dealing with major education reforms. Often a high-ranking member from the SÖ sat on these commissions as chairman or secretary. LO and SAF's education representatives sat together on the labor market board.[16] As one participant put it: "As you surely have been able to see since you have been in Sweden, it is really a small circle of people who deal with practically everything."[17] The result was a thorough knowledge of where each person stood on any given issue. Moreover, these frequent contacts provided an opportunity for the participants to informally work to modify one another's views.

> By meeting continuously, by continually keeping a debate going, we come to understand one another's positions very well, and thus each stand we eventually take is supported by the belief that we know what the others think.[18]

[14] Interview.
[15] Interview.
[16] Until 1967 SACO's representative to the labor market board also sat on the National Board of Education.
[17] Interview.
[18] Interview.

The more organs in which we have common posts, the better we get to know one another and the better this process of mutual attempts to influence one another works.[19]

A second factor promoting this intimate understanding of views is the recruitment process which has brought these men together. With only one exception the representatives from the major labor market organizations have all been in the same field, that of education, from the time they became active in their respective organizations until they reached the top posts they now occupy; and they have known one another to a greater or lesser degree during this entire period.

Third, and most important, this "law of anticipated reaction" can exist only in an environment where there are no substantial policy differences among the different actors. While two representatives, SACO's and SAF's, are less positive than the others, there is no doubt that all the actors on the executive board accept to greater or lesser degrees the trend of educational reforms which have characterized Swedish life in the postwar period. The same can be said of the entire staff of the SÖ, although in fact a thorough re-staffing at the time of the shake-up of the agency in 1964 was required to accomplish this harmony of views.

The necessity for this re-staffing became evident during the late 1940s and 1950s. Practically all the important decision-making positions (department, division, and section heads), with the exception of the very top position of general director, were held by those who supported the traditional system of education. During the 1950s through the efforts of the general director a number of more progressively minded staff members were hired, particularly at starting positions in the agency. It was still a lonely existence at the top, however, and the general director found himself at odds with his top advisers on many occasions.[20] His most dependable allies in the agency were to be found in those sections responsible for grade and secondary schools. Teachers at the gymnasium level traditionally enjoyed greater status and thus clung more strongly to the age-old student recruitment patterns opposed by the general director. The division between the two groups was so deep, it is reported, that even the lunchroom was affected. Two long tables, one for each of the warring factions, divided staff members into two uncompromisingly distinct camps, making it virtually impossible for them to avoid being identified with one side or the other. Legend has it that, much like the American President at Army-Navy games, the general director attempted to prevent hard feel-

[19] Interview.
[20] Interview.

ings from focusing directly on him during meal times by judiciously alternating between tables during the noon hour.[21]

The 1964 reorganization not only brought in a new general director, even more progressive than the last, but also resulted in a number of other significant staff changes.[22] The position just under the general director was filled by a leading official in the agency who had been chief secretary to the 1957 Royal Commission which drew up the final guidelines of the Comprehensive School reform. Two of the five department heads were brought in from the outside, while the remaining three were promoted from lesser positions within the agency. At the next level of command, the same pattern emerged: of the seventeen division heads, eight came from outside the agency and three were promotions from lower positions.[23] In the reorganization some ten to twelve leading officials lost their positions, so "the new system could function." [24] They were not fired, merely transferred to other jobs while retaining their titles and salaries.[25] Some retired.[26] The end result, aside from a new lunchroom seating arrangement, was an agency of "progressively minded" officials, that is, officials committed to the philosophy behind the new reform.[27]

While attitudes and institutional arrangements create certain opportunities for interest group access, the pattern of policy in the field of education creates others. The wave of educational reform which got started in 1962[28] with the creation of the nine-year basic school was meant to be only the start of a comprehensive overhaul of the entire Swedish educational system from the bottom up. Successive reforms have revamped the gymnasium, the trade schools, the university system, and even the adult educational system. The government left to the various national boards the responsibility of ironing out the rough spots in the initial reforms. Coupled with the expansion of planning resources for the SÖ and the placement of the major groups in society on its executive board, these trends mean the decision-making power of the SÖ is significantly strength-

[21] Interview.

[22] The reorganization also meant the merger of the old Board of Education with the previously existing National Board of Vocational Education—KÖY—a merger which strengthened the forces critical of the academic emphasis of the school system.

[23] Interview.

[24] Interview.

[25] Interview.

[26] Interview.

[27] Interviews.

[28] The basic decision on principle was taken in 1950. Thereafter followed a number of pilot projects. Then in 1962 came the decision to carry out changes on a national scale.

ened. In brief, membership on the executive board means that one is at the right place at the right time.

If the institutions, attitudes, and policies create access channels through which interest groups can influence the character of educational policy emanating from the SÖ, certain specific attributes possessed by each group are also important It is here that TCO, especially, stands out in comparison with the other groups represented on the executive board.

Prior to 1963, TCO's headquarters had only a small educational advisory group consisting of representatives from its various teacher organizations. This Advisory Council of Teachers (Lärarråd) met seldom (at best six times a year), had only a part-time secretary, and dealt for the most part with *remiss* replies.

In the late 1950s pressure from a number of federations led TCO to upgrade considerably its efforts in the educational field. Then in 1962 passage of the Comprehensive School reform opened the floodgates for a revamping of the entire educational system. If TCO was to hope to influence these changes, it needed an even more high-powered educational program.

By appointing Åke Isling in 1963 as educational representative, TCO took a long step toward fulfilling such a need. The first thing Isling did was to create a new research group to deal specifically with long-range educational programs. This educational research group (Utbildningskommitté) had considerable membership carry-over from the old advisory council but included in addition representatives from other unions which did not organize teachers. This was done primarily to broaden the base of viewpoints from which educational proposals would be developed.[29]

The results of this educational research group were impressive. Organized into subcommittees and meeting regularly, in the space of three and a half years it produced two lengthy studies on the state of education in Sweden. One dealt with education from the preschool up through the gymnasium and adult levels, and the other centered specifically on higher education at the university level. As will be shown later, reform proposals from these works have not gone unheeded.

The creation of this educational research group did not mean an abandonment of the advisory council, however. Instead its activities became confined to discussing specific problems concerning working conditions for teachers. Moreover, this body came to play a major role in organizing conferences sponsored by TCO each year on educational problems.

Isling also started an upswing in the propaganda given out by TCO on

[29] Interview.

educational questions. Thus studies by the educational committee were published both in their entirety and by chapters (the latter in more popular format complete with spritely colors and illustrations). *Remiss* replies by TCO on major educational questions were also printed and distributed on a wide scale.[30]

A final innovation was the establishment of yearly conferences on contemporary educational problems, to which teachers, administrators, and governmental officials were invited. Those responsible for administering educational policy were always active participants (for example, in panel discussions or in giving keynote addresses). And not least in importance from TCO's view, there was always a session where TCO presented in an official manner some aspect of its educational program.

It is clear, thus, that in terms of staff and research facilities, TCO was well equipped. What about the other interest groups on the executive board? None was in such a good position for influencing policy. For example, not one group had a full-time educational representative. Instead each group's representative had important duties to perform in other fields of policy and thus could not devote as much time to educational questions as TCO's representative.

The research facilities of the other groups were not so extensive as TCO's. While SAF and SACO did have special educational sections, in terms of manpower, finances, and output, these sections ranked significantly behind TCO's. The LO on the other hand did set up special study groups to deal with specific issues. On the whole, however, TCO enjoyed a clear advantage here.

One resource, moreover, was available only to TCO. This was the close relationship between Isling and the LO's representative, Tore Karlson. This relationship was based on two factors. First of all, the LO organizes those who have generally had no more than a Comprehensive School education, and TCO organizes the Comprehensive School teachers. Thus any reform which improved the quality of this level of education created the preconditions for a coalition between the two men. For the LO such a coalition meant potentially that its members would gain improved skills which in turn would lead to better paying jobs and higher status. For TCO such a coalition meant potentially better working conditions for its members, more pay, and higher status. Second, the two men shared a common value structure. Both were Social Democrats. Both had been prevented from pursuing advanced studies by the elitist system of education prevailing in Sweden until the Comprehensive School reform of 1962. Both had

[30] See, for example, the five reports of TCO's Utbildningskommitté.

gone out on their own to educate themselves. It was not surprising then that the two spoke the same language on a wide range of issues.[31]

Such a coalition was important for TCO because of the political position of the LO. As one agency employee put it, "On some politically sensitive questions we (the agency officials) feel the close relationship which exists between the LO and the Government and are inclined to see that the LO does not vote against the final proposal."[32] One high-ranking official in the agency spelled out such an area: "Clearly we pay attention to what the LO says on educational questions, especially questions with labor market implications. For example, job retraining."[33] Employer representatives as well believed that the LO's views on certain educational questions often get extra consideration.[34] Thus for TCO an alliance with the LO could clearly increase its bargaining weight in the executive board.

All of these formidable resources did not guarantee that any single group or constellation of groups would have influence over a specific policy issue. Rather it meant that the opportunities were there and, depending on how the resources were used, group influence was at least possible.

But does this mean that the SÖ was the helpless captive of the groups which sat on its executive board, particularly of TCO? For several reasons the answer is no. First of all, although the agency had only two of the eleven representatives that made up the executive board, it never started with zero allies. For example, on questions dealing with the working conditions of teachers, the agency could count on support from either the employer representatives or the teacher unions, depending on the position it wanted to take.[35] Hence the agency was never likely to be voted down. Moreover, as will be demonstrated below in the section on *remiss* replies, the agency could at times take a hard-nosed position on the degree of group influence it would tolerate.

However, the most important resource insuring agency independence from group domination was the wealth of governmental expertise available to its staff, for example, that of the Central Board of Statistics. Within the walls of its gigantic building are housed statistics on everything in

[31] Interview.
[32] Interview.
[33] Interview.
[34] Interviews.
[35] Moreover, as mentioned earlier, the representatives from the labor market board and the office of the chancellor of the Swedish universities usually support agency officials from the SÖ. Thus it might be more realistic to see the agency as starting off with four votes.

Sweden that can be quantified. Moreover, the data run back for hundreds of years. But for the purposes of the SÖ, and other agencies as well, the statistics available through such an agency are not its most valuable service. The Central Board of Statistics is empowered to carry out special studies for other governmental agencies upon request, which greatly reduces the likelihood of an agency becoming dependent on a source outside the government, such as an interest group, for information.

In fact, however, the SÖ did not rely on the Board of Statistics for as much help as other agencies, primarily because of the quality of its own information-gathering devices for specific issues. For example, the planning division of the SÖ had such complete data on school districts that interest groups came to them for facts.[36] Thus when requests came in for a new school in a district, the SÖ could critically analyze their merits through its own predictions of future school enrollment, likely population expansion in the area, building plans of other agencies in the area, and so on. Moreover, the SÖ could set up special study groups. For example, in 1963 the SÖ had created eighteen study groups throughout the entire country to pursue developments in the actual application of the curriculum of the new Comprehensive School. Made up of "progressively minded"[37] teachers, these groups began gathering information and making proposals to the SÖ as to needed changes. Later when the SÖ established its commission to review the curriculum a large number of participants in the study groups came to present testimony or to themselves sit on commission subcommittees and advisory groups.[38]

Within the agency itself the SÖ had strengthened its ability to deal with specific issues at two levels. At the middle level it brought in experts in different areas of policy for the specific purpose of following developments in their particular fields. Thus when the wheels of reform started to turn in any given area, the SÖ was likely to already have its own watchdog specialist. Lektor Bengt Cullert, who acted as secretary for the agency's commission on the curriculum review of the Comprehensive School, is an example of just such an official.

At the upper levels of policy-making, the SÖ often succeeded in getting one of its top men appointed as chairman or chief secretary to a Royal Commission dealing with a major reform of educational policy. This not only ensured privileged access for the SÖ views, but also provided valuable political information when the time came for it to draw up its *remiss*

[36] Interview.
[37] Interview.
[38] Interview.

reply over the results of the commission's work. The chairman and the chief secretary, better than anyone else on the Royal Commission,[39] knew where the other members of the commission stood on issues and the degree of intensity with which they held their views. Thus the agency could argue in advance against certain ideas which were likely to be forthcoming in the *remiss* replies of some members of the commission as well as defend those with which it agreed. A knowledge of the intensity with which groups held their views enabled the top leaders of the board to predict which groups would in all likelihood be discontented enough to not only write a *remiss* reply but also contact the Ministry of Education in an effort to secure additional changes. The agency could then seek to counter this action through contacts of its own.

TCO Influence in Three Arenas of Policy-Making: Agency Commission Studies, Budget Proposals, and Remiss Replies

In the following analysis of the decision-making process within the National Board of Education, or the SÖ, three arenas of policy-making are examined. The first and most important is that of agency commission studies. Here the SÖ is delegated the task of studying some problem within its area of responsibility and coming up with proposals for change. One such commission dealing with the revision of the Comprehensive School curriculum will be the subject of detailed investigation. The other areas of policy-making are budgetary requests for the agency and agency *remiss* replies in response to Royal Commission reports.

The Revision of the Curriculum of the Comprehensive School

Until 1962 the Swedish school system followed traditional European lines: a tiered system based on selection of the "most gifted" with the first separation coming at age eleven. The "Americanization" of the school system, as it was called by the opponents of the reform, began to take effect after 1962 with the scrapping of the folkskola-realskola organization and the substitution of a comprehensive school system. All students ages seven to sixteen years were to attend the same school, after which they would choose further study at the gymnasium (which now included not only

[39] Hans Meijer, *Kommittépolitik och kommittéarbete: det statliga kommittéväsendets utvecklingslinjer 1905–1954 samt nuvarande funktion och arbetsformer* (Lund: Gleerup, 1956), pp. 236–238.

academic but also vocational tracks) or direct entrance into the working world.

From the point of view of increasing educational opportunities for groups slighted by the old system, this reform has been a dramatic success. In the 1930s only 10 percent of a graduating class from the six-year folkskola went on to further study at the realskola. Of this original class, only 2.5 percent made it as far as the gymnasium, while a meager 1 percent reached the universities.[40] By 1967 about 65 percent remained in school after the nine-year Comprehensive School and by some time in the 1970s the figures are expected to reach between 80 and 85 percent.[41] For the universities and other schools at the university level the percentage is already over 17 and it is predicted that it will soon reach 25.[42]

The reform that made such change possible originally aroused intense debate and led to sharp party differences. At one point some 11,000 teachers marched on the Riksdag in protest against the proposed reform, an action of considerable significance given the usually staid milieu in which political battles are fought in Sweden.

Passage of the reform was eventually insured during the work of a Royal Commission in July of 1960 by a political compromise between the ruling Social Democratic party and the three opposition parties. This was the so-called Visby Compromise, named after the town where the agreement was reached. The most controversial points which the Visby Compromise settled were the timing and the extent of differentiation of students according to ability.

The old system had differentiated students at an early age and had provided for separate development along academic ("theoretical") and vocational ("practical") lines from then on. The new system provided for common classes until the last year (the ninth) whereupon a broad differentiation into tracks emphasizing either vocational or academic subjects would occur. Electives were allowed during the seventh and eighth years, totaling five and seven hours per week, respectively, out of a schedule of thirty-five hours per week.[43] The five academically oriented tracks in the

[40] Fred Fleisher, *The New Sweden* (New York: David McKay, 1967), p. 319.

[41] *Utbildningspolitiskt program för tjänstemannarörelsen,* TCO's Utbildningskommitté's Report No. 1 (Stockholm: Tjänstemännens Centralorganisation, 1964), p. 127.

[42] Fleisher, *The New Sweden,* p. 319.

[43] *Utbildningspolitiskt program,* p. 61. See also Sweden, Skolöverstyrelsen, *Läroplan för grundskolan,* Kungl. Skolöverstyrelsens skriftserie 60 (Stockholm: Kungl. Skolöverstyrelsen, 1962), p. 117.

ninth year could lead to the gymnasium, whereas the four vocational tracks could lead only to advanced vocational training or the labor market.

Conservative opinion was strongly opposed to diluting the academic rigor of the educational system, and so many practical or vocational subjects (metalwork, textile weaving, and so on) were eliminated in order to make more time for the purely academic subjects. But even these concessions were not enough. By 1961 opposition to the new curriculum had grown to such proportions among the upper echelon of the teacher corps that the Conservative party, under its new leader, Professor Gunnar Heckscher, felt compelled to disavow the Visby Compromise and argue instead for a two-year postponement to test more thoroughly the proposals of the 1957 Royal Commission which had engineered the Visby Compromise.

Heckscher's protestations came to naught as the government, holding closely to the Visby Compromise and enjoying Liberal and Center party support, passed the reform bill in 1962. A revolutionary change had come about in Swedish compulsory education.

Moreover, in the space of five short years the SÖ was to present a further thorough reform of the Comprehensive School curriculum. Among the major changes were the complete elimination of tracks in the ninth year, considerable reduction in differentiation during the seventh and eighth years by reducing hours available for electives, a marked upswing in the number of practical subjects required for graduation, and a considerable increase in practical elements in existing courses. In short, in many ways the Visby Compromise was undone and redone through the activities of the SÖ. A study of how this new package of proposals emerged shows much about the scope and limits of group influence in the policy-making process of the SÖ.

Policy Implementation

TCO started things off. While the rank-and-file of the teacher unions organized in TCO (elementary teachers and some[44] secondary school teachers) had, in contrast to their colleagues in the higher grades of the secondary school and the gymnasium, enthusiastically backed the reform, their representatives in TCO's Advisory Council for Education Questions had as early as 1961 questioned some of the likely consequences of

[44] For example technical school teachers (facklärare) and vocational school teachers (yrkeslärare).

the Visby Compromise.[45] Concern was expressed about the general reduction in practical and fine arts subjects. The suggested organization of practical subjects into home-oriented and job-oriented groupings seemed to promote continued choice by sex rather than interest. But especially worrisome from their point of view was one particular aspect of the elective choice posed for students in the seventh and eighth years. The choice offered in the seventh year was between a second foreign language (English was required of all students from the fourth year) or a course such as vocational mathematics, typing, or metalwork. Because several years of study of a second foreign language were required for admission to the gymnasium after grade nine, a student who did not choose such an elective in grade seven might significantly reduce his chances for further academic education unless he made heroic efforts to catch up. Moreover, one could always get into a vocational training school from an academic track. Thus to TCO, the Visby Compromise raised the spector of parents and pupils choosing a second language over practical subjects not because they were genuinely interested in such an elective, but rather as a part of an effort to postpone as long as possible a decision as to whether to continue academic education beyond the ninth year.

These and other concerns can be summarized in five major kinds of changes TCO wanted to see made in the curriculum devised by the Visby Compromise:

1. Commonality should be increased, especially during the last three years.
2. Optional subjects should be arranged so that they restrict the later choice of subjects as little as possible.
3. All students should study more fine arts and practical subjects.
4. Different subject areas ought to be more coordinated and integrated.
5. Practical and theoretical subjects should not be set up in an either/or choice situation as presently done in the seventh and eighth years.[46]

Policy Initiation

Before it could bring about these changes, however, TCO had to overcome several stumbling blocks. First of all leading officials in the Ministry of Education and the SÖ had to be convinced of the need for reform. While it

[45] TCO's Lärarråd, Minutes from TCO Lärarråd, meetings during 1961, TCO Archive, Stockholm (mimeographed).

[46] *Utbildningspolitiskt program*, pp. 75–76.

is no doubt a political truism that every bureaucratic structure resists pro-
grammatic changes, in this case new reform would be doubly difficult
precisely because of the political nature of the Visby Compromise on
which the original reform rested. Ragnar Edenman, the Minister of Education in 1963 and former chairman of the 1957 Royal Commission,
reportedly was adamant in his opposition to any reform in the immediate
future when he replied to an informal TCO overture in 1963 as to the
possibilities for such a revision.[47] He believed that it was important to let
the new system operate a number of years in order to demonstrate that
the Social Democrats had entered into the compromise in good faith. Also
he felt that a solid period of trial was needed in order to point the way
toward needed revisions.[48]

Second, TCO could not allow standard procedure in the investigation
of the problem. A Royal Commission with political party representation
(including opposition party representation) and interest group membership held out few hopes for tangible gains. That was, after all, the make-up
of the commission which had come up with the Visby Compromise. A second alternative, a commission established by the SÖ, seemed a better
avenue for likely influence, especially since the reform of the SÖ in 1964
guaranteed a place on the executive board for TCO. It was not clear, however, which direction the government would take. The basis for hope of
governmental cooperation was to be found in the proposition presented by
the government to the Riksdag in 1964, which, when passed, charged the
agency to: follow developments which might require changes in the
Comprehensive School; gather documentary information on the practical
workings of the Comprehensive School program; and develop new methods for improving pedagogical effectiveness.[49]

In the final instructions to the agency after approval of the reform by
the Riksdag, the government went even further: "It is the responsibility of
the SÖ . . . to see that the contents and methods of education are continually brought up to date, developed and improved in step with advancements in research, developments in public and private administration,
industry, labor relations and other sectors of society."[50] In any event, the
question of where the investigation was to go could be settled only after

[47] Interview.
[48] Interview.
[49] Sweden, Skolöverstyrelsen, *Läroplansöversyn grundskolan: förslag till Kungl.
Maj:t angående översyn av läroplan för grundskolan*, O nr. 5131/67 U (Stockholm:
SÖ-förlaget/Skolöverstyrelsen, 1967), p. 4.
[50] *Ibid.*

the question of whether it was to take place at all. TCO's first victory came in getting the investigation underway. One of Isling's first steps as TCO's full-time educational representative was to set his new educational committee to work in 1963 drawing up a program for reform. The result a year later was a scholarly criticism of the results of the first years of the Comprehensive School complete with proposed revisions. The suggestions in this report were first made public at TCO's Congress in June, 1964, and later published in book and pamphlet form. By coming out with a critique and a set of reform proposals TCO prodded the agency into action.

The agency, like the Ministry of Education, was reluctant to embark on revisions only two years after the reform had been instituted. Yet in contrast to the ministry, it recognized that reform at some point would be needed. Responsibility for following developments for the SÖ in this area fell to a new man in the agency, Lektor Bengt Cullert, who had been the 1957 Royal Commission's expert on course programs and had played an important role in drawing up the curriculum of the new Comprehensive School.

High officials within the SÖ expressed dismay at TCO's public criticism of the Comprehensive School. Raising the issue of possible reform was politically dangerous, since reform had so recently been the subject for a delicately balanced compromise among the political parties, the so-called Visby Compromise. Officials in the agency feared the LO would jump to support many of the recommendations in the program presented by TCO, thereby reopening the issue to party politics and making the board's task of administration more difficult. In this respect TCO had touched an especially sensitive nerve, for the LO in its *remiss* reply to the 1957 Royal Commission report had called for considerably greater commonality than had finally been agreed to in the "Visby Compromise"—a stand of which both Isling and agency officials were well aware.[51] Moreover interviews with agency personnel on this point suggest that several at least had felt somewhat hurt by TCO's criticisms. In any event the SÖ felt the need to regain the initiative and if possible keep the issue within its domain of influence.[52]

In the fall of 1964, TCO's leaders invited the top leadership of the SÖ to Gällöfsta, one of TCO's schools for the advanced education of white-collar employees, for discussions concerning its educational program, by

---

[51] Interviews. Landsorganisationen, *Verksamhetsberättelse 1961* (Stockholm: Tiden, 1962), pp. 309–325, esp. 320–322.

[52] Interview.

then in published form. In this atmosphere neither side had to worry about prestige, and informality was the watchword.[53] A thorough and frank discussion developed regarding the possibilities of an early reform of the curriculum along the lines TCO proposed. It was at this time that the new general director of the SÖ made it clear to TCO that he was impressed by the evidence and the conclusions they had come to in support of their case and that they could expect the wheels of reform to pick up speed soon.[54]

And soon they did. By April, 1965, just six months later, the general director and his closest working associates came to an informal agreement regarding the major lines a reform should take. Although no decision had been reached regarding the choice offered in the seventh year of a second language, it had been agreed there should be a reduction in differentiation in the ninth year coupled with an increase in practical and fine arts subjects in the seventh and eighth years.[55]

Meanwhile, TCO had established contact with the ministry regarding the need for a review of the curriculum. In June, 1965, TCO presented the Ministry of Education with an official petition requesting a review of the curriculum to be held under the sponsorship of the SÖ. This official channel of communication was supplemented by a more important unofficial meeting held at TCO headquarters with the minister and his chief assistants on the same day. At this meeting Edenman agreed that the difficulties of the system seemed to be of such magnitude that a commission was indeed justified.[56] TCO's efforts had thus significantly contributed to having a commission set up.

The problem over where the study should take place, a SÖ-sponsored commission or a larger Royal Commission, was comparatively easy to solve. Both SÖ officials and ministry leaders wished to avoid giving the impression of yet another major school reform.[57] Hence if a parliamentary-based Royal Commission could be avoided, it was all to the good. Since earlier provisions in the proposition and the instructions provided statutory justification for creating an agency commission, this course was decided upon. TCO's petition to the ministry requesting such a solution, moreover, gave the decision additional legitimacy, as the ministry and the SÖ could point to a group outside themselves which advocated such an arrangement.

As part of its campaign to influence the contents of the reform, TCO

---

[53] Interview.
[54] Interviews.
[55] Interviews.
[56] Interviews.
[57] Interviews.

had scheduled a major conference for October, 1965, to deal with the theme: *"The Comprehensive School: Plans and Reality."* Here, in the presence of teachers, administrators, the press, and high-ranking officials from the ministry and the SÖ, TCO planned to present in expanded form its proposals for change. Moreover, by prior agreement, the SÖ was to announce at this time plans for the establishment of a commission.[58] Unknown to Isling, however, the SÖ's representative also had hopes of recapturing the initiative through his speech.[59] In this he proved highly successful.

After indicating that a reform was in the offing and that it was very likely that the SÖ would carry out the task, Deputy Director Orring sought to demonstrate that the agency was indeed on top of the matter by presenting a detailed examination of the problem complex. Tables and charts served to show where the bottlenecks were. Reform proposals abounded, many dealing specifically with TCO's criticisms and a number of others entirely new. Finally all this was coated with glowing praise for the efforts of the teachers in the field who, in Orring's view, had made such fine contributions in their work with the new Comprehensive School and in their proposals for constructive change.[60]

From TCO's point of view the speech was especially important for it indicated the lengths to which the agency was prepared to go in reforming the curriculum. Indeed, the similarity between many of Orring's points and TCO's educational program were striking, as Chart 1 indicates. Now the problem for TCO's Isling would be to press the agency's commisssion into accepting these new ideas.

Policy Deliberation

The commission to review the curriculum of the Comprehensive School was officially established in January, 1966, by a decision of the executive board of the SÖ.[61] The members of the commission were all high-ranking officials within the agency, Skolrådet Maj Bosson-Nordbö became its chairman, and Lektor Bengt Cullert, one of the SÖ experts from the 1957 Royal Commission, was to be its secretary.

The organizational arrangement within which the commission operated insured close coordination with the Executive Board where TCO's Isling

[58] Interview.
[59] Interview.
[60] *TCO's Utbildningsdagar 1965*, pp. 28–46.
[61] Skolöverstyrelsen, Minutes from Skolöverstyrelsen's Executive Board, January, 1966, Skolöverstyrelsen Archive, Stockholm (mimeographed).

CHART I

A COMPARISON BETWEEN ORRING'S PROPOSALS AND TCO'S EDUCATIONAL PROGRAM

Orring's Proposals	TCO's Educational Program
1. Greater emphasis on practical and esthetic elements in subjects such as math, physics, chemistry, Swedish, and history.	1. All pupils should receive a greater portion of practical and esthetic elements in their heavily "theoretical" subjects.
2. More practical and esthetic courses must be forthcoming and obligatory. For example, music and handicrafts should be obligatory from the seventh year, at least.	2. Beginning in the seventh and continuing on in the eighth years, courses such as music and handicraft should be obligatory.
3. An obligatory second foreign language ought to be possible from the seventh year and perhaps earlier.	3. In order to avoid a choice between practical and theoretical tracks a student ought to take a course from each during his seventh and eighth years, thus keeping open later choice options.
4. Greater attention must be paid to disciplinary questions and to improvement of the environment of the school in order to contribute to better order. Courses must also become more relevant for the students.	4. A better school milieu is a first step in meeting disciplinary problems. Greater application in such subjects as shop or home economics is one solution. Smaller classes, special tutoring, and greater relevance in course materials are other means.
5. Differentiation from the seventh through the ninth year should be reduced through this schedule: Seventh year—obligatory second foreign language and a choice of a practical subject. Eighth year—the same. Ninth year—do away with the tracks, offer the same as seven and eight.	5. Reduce differentiation throughout the last three years. Do away with tracks in the ninth year.
6. Simplify and integrate to a greater degree "orientation" subjects such as social and natural sciences.	6. Orientation subjects should be integrated to a greater degree. Block subjects are a possibility. Instead of history, geography, and political science, a course in social studies can be offered.

SOURCE: Orring's speech:
  1. *TCO's Utbildningsdagar 1965*, p. 39.
  2. *Ibid.*, p. 40.
  3. *Ibid.*, p. 41.
  4. *Ibid.*, p. 39.
  5. *Ibid.*, pp. 41–42.
  6. *Ibid.*, p. 42.

TCO's program:
  1. *Utbildningspolitiskt program för tjänstemannarörelsen*, p. 72.
  2. *Ibid.*, pp. 76, 70.
  3. *Ibid.*, p. 76.
  4. *Ibid.*, pp. 71–72.
  5. *Ibid.*, pp. 75–78.
  6. *Ibid.*, p. 76.

sat. The executive board drew up the general guidelines of reform for each of the three levels of the nine-year school: the lower form, middle form, and upper form. The commission's job was to work out the practical implications of these reforms. This it did in cooperation with a number of subject groups which drew heavily from the membership of agency-sponsored study groups. Occasionally, where conflict developed between the wishes of some of the members of the executive board and the commission, a special advisory group was established with representatives from the relevant subject group, the complaining executive board member, and one or more commission members. Here final compromises were hammered out.[62] The results of the commission's efforts were then sent to the executive board for final approval before investigation of the next three-year period was begun.

During the entire process the commission had the power to set up studies of its own to research a specific point at issue and was instructed to keep in close contact with all the affected interest groups, particularly teachers' organizations.[63]

The list appended to the final report of meetings various members of the commission had with different interest groups attested to the openness of the lines of communications. Some 129 official contacts were made with different national trade union confederations, individual federations, and even single unions during the commission's two-year life span.[64] This list, it should be noted, does not include the many telephone discussions, coffee chats, and corridor meetings at conferences, which were an integral part of the making of the reform.[65]

Members of the SÖ were interested not only in the expertise such groups could offer, but also in the support they could provide for the final package. It is an unwritten law of Swedish politics that a commission's findings weigh more heavily as they run the decision-making gauntlet toward final approval by the Riksdag if the commission comes forward with a report which is supported unanimously by its members.[66] The SÖ leaders, then, had a real interest in involving groups deeply in the reform.[67]

The tempo of the reform went smoothly during the initial stages when

---

[62] Interviews.
[63] Interviews.
[64] *Läroplansöversyn grundskolan*, pp. 152–153.
[65] Interviews.
[66] Hans Meijer, *Byråkrati och policyformulering* (Stockholm: Statsvetenskapliga Institutionen vid Stockholms Universitet, 1969), p. 16.
[67] Interviews.

the lower and middle forms of the Comprehensive School were the subject of revision. Progress slowed considerably, however, when the question of electives, particularly a second foreign language, came up for discussion. It will be remembered that TCO was especially critical of the choice offered seventh-year students between a second foreign language and one of a number of more practically oriented subjects. They argued that many students chose a second foreign language at this point not out of interest but because it was the only way to keep options open for further academic education at a later date. TCO's proposal called for all pupils to both begin a second foreign language in the seventh year and choose a more practically oriented subject.[68] Moreover, as witnessed by Deputy Director Orring's speech at TCO's Conference on the Comprehensive School, the SÖ was not strongly opposed to such a modification. Yet the commission's final recommendation on this point, which was approved unanimously by the executive board, did not go as far as TCO wished. What was the agency's alternative? And why did it come about?

The commission's proposal, put in diagram form, follows below.

	Alternative 1	Alternative 2		
Seventh yr. 4hr./wk.	2nd foreign lang.	Art	Design	Business & economics
Eighth yr. 5hr./wk.	"	"	"	"
Ninth yr. 5hr./wk.	"	"	"	"

Beginning with the seventh year, students were to choose either a second foreign language or one of three practically oriented subjects. Hence the division between the two was maintained. However, two provisions significantly altered the likely impact of such a model from TCO's point of view. First of all, there was to be an increase in theory in each of the practical subjects, thereby reducing the stereotyped difference between the two choices. Second, and even more important, it was stipulated that any of the electives would qualify for admission to the gymnasium.[69] To ensure that those who opted for the practically oriented electives and then decided to pursue study at the gymnasium would not be penalized, special provision was made for such students, during their first year at

[68] *TCO's Utbildningspolitiska program*, p. 76.
[69] *Läroplansöversyn grundskolan*, p. 30.

the gymnasium, to begin study of a second foreign language and to receive from the state the necessary special tutoring.[70]

The reasons why the commission came up with this proposal can be understood after an examination of the activities of two other groups represented on the executive board. Prior to this point actions of groups other than TCO have not been discussed, primarily because there was not much activity on their part. The simple fact is that no groups on the executive board apart from TCO had come up with any reform proposals until very late in the game. In a real sense other national trade union confederations and their member federations were continually reacting to proposals initiated by TCO's educational program, complemented and expanded by the research of the SÖ's commission. Yet this does not mean that other groups were without influence as they began to react, as indicated by this proposal.

Representatives from two groups (SACO and SAF) on the executive board played particularly important roles in preventing the adoption of TCO's alternative on this point. Each came forward with its own proposal for the elective system.[71] Since both felt the academic rigor of the educational program was in danger, their two proposals had basically the same thrust: a desire to maintain the division between a second language and the practically oriented subjects. Moreover, each representative indicated that he would make a reservation if TCO's proposal succeeded in becoming the commission's. Hence the only avenue open to the commission and the top echelon of the SÖ was to pursue a compromise solution which would maintain unanimity within the executive board. What led these three groups, TCO, SACO, and SAF, to accept the compromise proposal?

From TCO's point of view the compromise could be accepted simply because it was the best they could get, for only the LO's representative could be counted on to vote for TCO's proposal. Moreover, the compromise construction appeared to be significantly better than the present arrangement and certainly better than any of the alternatives offered by either SACO or SAF. Furthermore TCO had gotten so much of what it wanted in other areas (see below for further discussion of this point) that it seemed foolhardy to risk jeopardizing the entire package at this point. Finally, there would always be the opportunity to lobby the Ministry of Education as it drew up the final proposition in hopes of modifying the commission's report on this point.[72]

---

[70] *Ibid.*

[71] See *ibid.*, pp. 28–30, for a fuller discussion of these alternatives. Interviews.

[72] Interview.

SACO's representative, Håkansson, could accept the compromise construction for several reasons. First and foremost his heart was not entirely
in the alternative proposal he had presented for consideration.[73] The largest teacher federation in SACO, the Association of Secondary Teachers
(Lärarnas Riksförbund or LR), had been quite upset about the direction
the reform was taking and had taken the initiative of drawing up an official communication (skrivelse) for SACO to present to the commission.
The communication outlined several alternatives to TCO's proposal and
suggested a three-year trial period to determine the implications of each,
with an eventual final reform in perhaps five year's time. The LR had
pieced together its proposal in the summer of 1967, a scant four months
before the commission was to make public its findings. But as the entire
subject had been the target of extensive debate in the executive board
during all of 1967, Håkansson had simply come to the conclusion that
this proposal ought not to be adopted by the board. He said so in the executive board, and in fact did not even argue for "his" alternative.[74] At the
same time his responsibilities to SACO and to the LR prevented him
from accepting TCO's construction. Moreover, the commission's sug-
gestion, while it would in all likelihood result in greater opportunities for
students to take practical subjects and yet enter the gymnasium, still had
the effect of separating theoretical from practical, a key demand of
the LR.[75]

SAF's representative, Director Matts Larsson, had been a member of
the 1957 Royal Commission and thereby a signatory of the Visby Compromise. Thus he had sincere personal motivations for not wishing to go
as far as TCO and the SÖ were apparently prepared to go. In fact he
might well have made a reservation if he had not been scheduled to make
a two-week business trip to the United States during the final discussion
on this question. When he returned he had very little time to get the lay
of the land. He came to rely heavily on the SACO representative, calling
often to the board to find out whether SACO had made any reservations.
When the answers came back continually negative, he also decided to refrain from making any himself.[76] He did so almost regretfully as he knew
the political implications of such an action: namely, that later in the decision-making process when the Riksdag considered the government's
proposition there would be no reservation from the executive board to

73 Interview.
74 Interview.
75 Interview.
76 Interview.

which some or all of the opposition parties could point as they criticized the construction, a distinct disadvantage when attempting to influence popular opinion on an issue.[77] Thus each group representative, for his own reasons, came to see the compromise construction as acceptable. In so doing, moreover, all believed they had increased the probabilities of this being the final settlement.[78]

If TCO did not succeed completely in getting its proposal adopted on this point, there were a number of other areas where success had been greater. One of its demands had been that commonality be increased during the last three years.[79] The commission's proposal ended tracks in the ninth year, simplified considerably the electives offered during the seventh and eighth years,[80] and increased the number of class hours students were to be together in one group from seventy-one hours out of 105 to ninety-one.[81]

A second interest had been for all students to study more practical and fine arts subjects.[82] The commission's approved report made classes in handicrafts (textiles, wood, and metalwork) obligatory for all students from the third year through the sixth (a specific TCO demand).[83] Home economics was made obligatory from the sixth year (another specific TCO request). Throughout the seventh, eighth, and ninth years all students were to participate in courses such as physical education, music, mechanical arts, handicrafts, and typing. In one instance the commission went into territory untouched by TCO's educational program when it made child care a requirement in the ninth year.

Third, TCO had wanted to ensure that the arrangement of the elective subjects which remained would influence the student's later choice of subjects as little as possible. The reduction in the number of electives open for choice coupled with the elimination of tracks in the ninth year went far in meeting this demand. Moreover, as discussed above, the compromise construction reduced the barrier between practical and theoretical electives by injecting more theory into the practical courses. A student could now also change electives after the seventh year. And finally, no matter which set of electives a student chose, the provision that all would permit

[77] Interview.
[78] Interviews.
[79] *TCO's Utbildningspolitiska program*, p. 75.
[80] *Läroplansöversyn grundskolan*, pp. 30–31.
[81] "Fria ämnen för eleverna: Engelska i första klass," *Dagens Nyheter*, June 14, 1968, p. 9.
[82] *TCO's Utbildningspolitiska program*, p. 76.
[83] *Läroplansöversyn grundskolan*, p. 50.

entrance to the gymnasium further reduced the likelihood that an early choice would influence irrevocably the course of a student's education.

Fourth, TCO had sought greater coordination and integration among different subject areas.[84] The course descriptions prepared by the SÖ as part of the commission's report bear out the results of this interest to a considerable degree. Progress along these lines would have been even greater if the commission's members had not run into teacher resistance, primarily from those teaching in the last three years of the basic school. This will be discussed in greater detail below.

Finally, TCO had striven to end the choice between practical and theoretical subjects beginning in the seventh year, making some of both mandatory. As related above, TCO did not succeed in this, gaining only concessions which would make it easier for students electing practically oriented electives to go on to the gymnasium.

In sum, access to the agency commission provided TCO with an opportunity to realize a considerable number of its policy goals during the revision of the Comprehensive School curriculum. Once the commission's report, complete with unanimous support from the executive board, left the agency for the Ministry of Education, it was free game for criticism through *remiss* replies and through informal contacts with government officials.

Policy Decision

The Conservative party led the opposition attack on the proposals. Claiming that the reform would undermine what remained of the academic excellence of the Comprehensive School, they announced their intention to vote against it. The Liberal and Center parties were more moderate in their criticism in part for reasons which are discussed below.

Criticism from the opposition press centered on the considerable increase in practically oriented material. Courses with a heavy dose of theory which did not necessarily lead to some direct application were in themselves good, it was written, as such courses created an outlet for the speculative mind.[85] The SACO-affiliated Association of Secondary School Teachers (the LR) also took the opportunity to present its critique of the entire construction of the last three years, urging greater experimentation and a postponement of reform.[86] Moreover, from many various

---

[84] *TCO's Utbildningspolitiska program*, p. 76.
[85] Editorial, "Läroplanens Mål," *Dagens Nyheter*, February 14, 1968, p. 2.
[86] Olle Anderberg, "LR och högstadiet," *Dagens Nyheter*, March 4, 1968, p. 2.

groups which were not opposed to the reform as a whole but which felt their own special subject areas had been shortchanged, there came a plethora of articles urging that additional time be given for their specific programs. Swedish had not been given the hours it deserved, religion had been mishandled, more emphasis should be given to the study of the environment (such as pollution problems), the study of mathematics would soon deteriorate.[87]

While debate in the press focused on the need to add an hour here or an hour there, informal discussions were underway in the Ministry of Education between interest group leaders involved in the commission and top-level ministry officials on the central issues involved. For example the Minister of Education Olof Palme (now the Prime Minister) made it clear to TCO's Isling that he supported TCO's critique of the option between a second language or practically oriented courses. His intention was to change the commission's proposal on this point when the final proposition was written.[88]

This never came to be, however, for when Palme discussed the matter with Löwbeer and Orring, the top officials in the SÖ, he met total opposition. In the end, rather than go against the agency responsible for administering the reform, Palme decided to leave the compromise intact on this crucial point.[89]

On June 14, 1968, the government presented its proposition, which departed only slightly from the commission's proposal. While students could still choose during the last three years between a second foreign language and one of three more practically oriented subject areas, the hours available for such electives had been reduced from the number proposed by the commission: four in the seventh, five in the eighth, and five in the ninth, to four/three/four—a reduction thus of three hours per week. Moreover, one hour of music and two hours (one in the seventh and one in the eighth year) of typing were taken away.[90] This was in order to create a number of "free subjects" for students to choose among during the last three years. The six hours collected by the modifications made in the electives and the required subjects were to be nongraded, nonexamination courses of two hours a week per year. In an effort to blunt the criti-

[87] Rune Fröroth, "Reducerad svenska," *Dagens Nyheter*, April 25, 1968, p. 2. David Schwartz, "Religionsfrihet i grundskolan?," *Dagens Nyheter*, May 18, 1968, p. 4. Barbro Soller, "Läroplanen lider av fläcktyfus/torftig miljövårdsundervisning," *Dagens Nyheter*, May 31, 1968, p. 17.
[88] Interview.
[89] Interview.
[90] "Fria ämnen för eleverna."

cisms of the special interests who had felt themselves shortchanged by the commission's proposal, the government was willing to let the local interests decide where the emphasis in these special nonexamination courses should go, and it gave to the local communes the responsibility of developing the subject offerings. It was envisioned by the Ministry of Education that such courses as environmental studies, problems facing developing countries, new trends in drama, or even additional time for language or the study of one of the more practically oriented electives would be made possible through this kind of proposal.

From TCO's point of view the modification meant a loss of some of the practical and esthetic subjects for which it had fought so hard in the board's commission. Yet the reduction in the number of hours for the required electives also meant that they would be less important as a determinant of a student's intellectual abilities. Moreover, students who opted for the second language could use the hours made available by the "free subjects" to take practically oriented subjects. Finally, TCO could gain some encouragement from Palme's announcement that, "Within the not-too-distant future we ought to have the methods and material which will make it possible to require the study of a second foreign language." [91]

Final action by the Riksdag the following December, 1968, proved rather perfunctory. While debate on the government's proposition became heated at points, especially between Palme and several Conservative party MP's, there were no modifications and the bill passed easily. [92]

In summarizing the influence TCO had over the reform, it can be asserted that its greatest achievement lay in getting the SÖ and the Ministry of Education to agree to a review of the curriculum in the first place, the Ministry of Education having been especially reluctant. Once the decision to begin a reform had been made, TCO's constant pressure, largely the result of having a specific set of reform proposals already drawn up, kept the agency's commission working in the direction TCO desired. The agency, as well as other groups on the executive board, were forced by TCO's early entrance into the field to concentrate on reacting to what TCO had proposed.

It is important to emphasize that the distance between TCO and key agency officials was not so great on the major points of the reform as it was on the question of whether a reform should be started at all. TCO, in a sense, acted to provide a structure for policy debates and served to nudge and support the commission's efforts once they were underway. TCO's in-

---

[91] *Ibid.*
[92] *Dagens Nyheter*, December 5, 1968, p. 40.

fluence was less, though still important, when it came to the especially touchy issue of electives and the second foreign language. While SACO and SAF blocked TCO's proposal, it can be argued that TCO's expertise, gained from its earlier investigations and demonstrated during the several executive board meetings where the issue was debated, contributed to winning over SACO's representative to a softer position than he otherwise might have taken. Thus SACO's Håkansson was willing to accept the compromise offered by the commission without offering a reservation. TCO used more of its resources (time—discussions with agency officials; money—conferences and publications of its reform proposals; expertise —research proposals), in part because it had more than other groups to begin with, and it used them more skillfully (the timing of the first critique, for example). In short, it is clear that in the case of the revision of the Comprehensive School curriculum TCO had considerable influence over the contents of the commission's report, more, in fact, than any other group on the executive board.

Budgetary Proposals

The executive board of the SÖ not only directs the type of commission study discussed above, but also approves budgetary proposals and *remiss* replies. Group influence in each of these arenas of policy-making will now be examined.[93]

At the agency level, the process of drawing up budget requests begins in February, sixteen months before the final budget is to go into effect. Discussion at this time centers on a short, usually five-page, memorandum drawn up by the general director and is limited to high-ranking officials in the agency.[94] After overall guidelines have been established, a revised draft is discussed in the executive board, and it is here that interest groups first have an opportunity to be heard. From then until late July or early August when final approval must be given and the weighty tome sent on to the Ministry of Education, agency officials work to fill in the details.[95]

While these particulars are being worked out, groups contact section heads to lobby for particular items. It is reported, for example, that for fiscal year 1968 to 1969, TCO and SACO succeeded in getting the agency to increase projected allocations for audio-visual aids. SAF and the LO

---

[93] An additional area of group influence concerns personnel policies. As this is not directly related to public policy, it is not discussed here.

[94] Interview.

[95] Interviews.

defended several agency research projects that were underway and, according to reports, thereby helped ensure their continuation.[96]

If a group becomes adamant it can even prevent, at least temporarily, the inclusion of a specific point in the final draft of the agency's budget request. An example of this was the agency's unsuccessful attempt to include in the 1968 to 1969 budget request funds for library assistants to organize the audio-visual aids presently available for teacher use. The regular librarians already had too many demands on their time and could not handle adequately film requests, repairs of broken machinery, and the checking in and out of materials. For several years TCO and SACO had pushed unsuccessfully for funds for assistants. Finally in 1967 the ministry indicated to the SÖ that some money might be available for fiscal 1968 to 1969 on a matching basis with local communes. When the representative for the Confederation of Communes heard of the proposal, however, he would have nothing to do with it. "He was so sour, so disagreeable about the matter, that we finally had to take out the whole section," related an agency official.[97]

The last stage in drawing up budget requests is a meeting of the executive board to approve the finished proposal. At least three weeks prior to this meeting, members have received drafts and are encouraged by the agency to send in their written comments.[98]

The picture which emerges is one of open channels of communication used by interest groups to secure the budget changes which promote their interests. The agency leadership is anxious to have unanimous group support for its final proposal and so is disposed to listen and to modify. The issues are of minor importance primarily because it is through major policy changes (such as the revision of the Comprehensive School curriculum) that significant new directions are taken, not through the moving here or there of some small sums of money on a line budget.

Remiss Replies

"We sharpen one point, tone down another and even succeed in removing factual errors."[99] This assessment by one group representative on the executive board of the National Board of Education (SÖ) accurately re-

[96] Interview.
[97] Interview.
[98] Interview.
[99] Interview.

flects the extent of influence groups have over agency *remiss* replies, a third means of access to educational policy.

In the Swedish political system after a Royal Commission has presented its report, the relevant ministry sends copies to all organizations likely to be affected—agencies, interest groups, and so on—for comments prior to drawing up the final proposal. It is the responsibility of the SÖ's executive board to pass final judgment on the SÖ's reply to proposals received by the agency on *remiss*. These replies are then sent by the agency to the relevant ministry.

Interest groups have only editorial influence over SÖ *remiss* replies for the simple reason that this is all its officials will allow. Since each interest group on the executive board also receives the same proposal on *remiss*, the agency leaders feel strongly that the reply should be as "pure" as possible, reflecting basically only agency views on the issue under consideration. Through the *remiss* system, the agency leaders feel the government ought to be able to gather in as much information from as many diverse sources as possible, for to water down the SÖ's view through elaborate compromises at the executive board level would deny valuable information to the government as to how the civil servants within the SÖ feel about an issue. Thus if the executive board can agree unanimously on the contents of a *remiss* reply, fine; if not, the SÖ's leadership is prepared to accept reservations on points of difference.[100]

This resistance to group influence over *remiss* replies affects the lines of communication between group representatives and agency officials prior to discussions in the executive board. As a general rule agency contacts with group representatives are kept to a minimum. Officials may call (after approval from the very top leaders in the agency) to request specific information of a factual nature but rarely are they allowed to enter into discussions regarding the pros and cons of commission proposals. Only if a group representative has been especially active on an issue and has achieved some special expertise through participation on a Royal Commission, for example, is he likely to have any success in getting the ear of an agency official regarding the substantive issues. This happens so seldom, according to the participants on both sides, and the results are so meager, that the effort is made only when some draft proposal is far out of line with what the group can accept.[101]

The same holds true in the process whereby a *remiss* reply is drafted.

[100] Interviews.
[101] Interviews.

No advisory committees are set up with groups from the outside. Instead the division chiefly responsible for the area of policy within the SÖ begins to piece together a proposal by using experts from within the agency. Simultaneously the commission's report is sent to the county school boards and to a number of local school boards for their opinions as well. When these replies are in, there is an agency meeting of division heads and the top leaders to revise and approve a proposal for a draft, and this draft is then sent to the members of the executive board. From beginning to end, thus, agency officialdom plays a predominate role in the shaping of agency *remiss* replies.

Interest groups, however, can submit their own *remiss* replies.[102] Accordingly, while they see the potential advantage of using their positions on the executive board to get their views adopted in agency proposals, they do not resent the lack of flexibility shown by agency officials in this arena of policy-making.[103] The pervasive atmosphere is one of agreement to disagree, which does not affect relations in other policy-making areas.

An example of the process at work is provided by the agency's *remiss* reply to the report of the Royal Commission on Working Hours in the School, submitted on October 4, 1965.[104] The Royal Commission sought to bring greater uniformity to the school system by regulating lecture periods, breaks, amounts of homework, and the timing of holidays.[105]

Members of the commission had disagreed substantially on only one point: the length of the school term for the different school levels. A majority in the Royal Commission had supported the proposal that compensation for the loss of teaching time owing to the elimination of Saturday classes should come in the form of fewer holidays and an extra week of classes. Experts on the commission representing employee groups (LO, TCO, and SACO) protested and wrote a reservation on this point. When the SÖ got the commission's report on *remiss* it was clear where each side stood. The agency supported the extra week (in fact, it went the commission one better by proposing an additional two weeks for vocational schools), while the employee representatives voiced their disagreement through reservations.[106]

---

[102] Interviews.

[103] Interviews.

[104] Sweden, Ecklesiastikdepartementet, *Skolans arbetstider*, Statens Offentliga Utredningar 1967:14 (Stockholm: Ecklesiastikdepartementet, 1967).

[105] *Ibid.*, pp. 205–216.

[106] "Yttrande över skolarbetstidsutredningens betänkande *Skolans arbetstider*, SOU 1967:14 (*remiss* 13.4.69.67) d nr 1892/67 U," Skolöverstyrelsen's Archive, Stockholm (mimeographed). Skolöverstyrelsen, Minutes from Skolöverstyrelsens

In sum, while *remiss* replies by the SÖ are important, group influence over agency drafts is negligible; but because groups make their own replies, they are not overly concerned about their lack of influence in this area.

Conclusions

In every arena of policy-making involving the executive board, examples of TCO success could be found. Thus it can be said that TCO effectively influences educational policy through its representation on the executive board of the SÖ.

Moreover, the foregoing suggests that the SÖ-sponsored commission studies seem to be the most important means of access in the agency for a group, more important than either the budgetary or *remiss* arenas. It is precisely here that TCO has enjoyed its greatest influence over policy, outweighing all other groups represented on the executive board of the SÖ. That it does so can be attributed to the amount of resources it has, the amount it uses on any particular occasion, and its skill in using what resources it possesses.

TCO's ability to determine the final outcome of educational issues subjected to agency commission study is directly related to whether or not the commission is able to reach a common consensus on the reforms it wishes to advocate. Where consensus is achieved the likelihood of partisan activity by the political parties later in the decision-making process is reduced.

Does the significant amount of group influence in the arena of SÖ-sponsored commission studies mean that groups run agency policy? In advanced industrialized democratic political systems he who controls *expertise*, that is information or knowledge, often controls policy. While in many West European societies it is possible to talk of the "colonization" of agency policy by interest groups precisely because of the latter's control over technical information needed for intelligent policy formation,[107] the case of the revision of the Comprehensive School's curriculum indicates such a one-sided balance does not exist in Sweden.

The study groups established by the agency in 1963 had already pro-

---

Executive Board, October 4, 1967, Skolöverstyrelsen's Archive, Stockholm (mimeographed).

[107] See, for example, LaPalombara, *Interest Groups in Italian Politics*; Henry W. Ehrmann, "Interest Groups and the Bureaucracy in Western Democracies," *Revue Française de Science Politique*, XI (September, 1961), pp. 541–568.

vided it with information indicating need for the reforms which TCO later spelled out in its 1964 educational program. During the actual revision, agency officials, including its special experts in the field,[108] headed up the commission. The final package, while taking up TCO's criticisms and in many cases proposing reforms desired by TCO, also included a number of areas omitted by TCO. Moreover, under the skillful leadership of the agency's general director, no single group in the executive board got everything it wanted to the detriment of others, and the agency could fully support the final product as educationally sound from its view of the "public interest." Thus the agency's possession of a considerable store of expertise enabled it to hold its own quite well in the competition to influence policy in the executive board of the SÖ.

[108] For example, Lektor Cullert.

Chapter Nine

TCO, Interest Groups, and the Democratic Process

From the three foregoing case studies, certain conclusions can be drawn regarding TCO's ability to affect public policy outcomes. In the introduction to this essay the thesis was stated that:

> TCO's influence over policy outcomes is greatest when political partisanship is least. TCO's leadership seeks to keep issues from becoming politicized, that is to say from becoming the subject of partisan conflict among the political parties. To the degree its leadership is successful, the influence TCO brings to bear during the early stages of the decision-making process can often be crucial in determining the final outcome. To the degree TCO fails, its leadership may still influence the final outcome but such influence if it occurs at all is dependent on the outcome of a conflict among the political parties during a later stage in the decision-making process. Such a conflict is likely to seriously divide and weaken TCO.

TCO's greatest problem is cohesion. As one of the major established interest groups in Swedish society, it participates in a variety of ways in the policy-making process. Recognizing the heterogeneity of political party sympathies which permeates its membership (a heterogeneity which in turn reflects the economic diversity of its membership), TCO concentrates its efforts on gaining access to the early stages of the decision-making process. As the supplementary pensions dispute indicated, when an issue becomes the subject of partisan conflict among the political parties to the position where elections and the Riksdag become the effective points of decision-making (see pp. 76–81), TCO's cohesion disintegrates and the organization's influence on the final outcome becomes marginal at best (see pp. 85–90).

Of course during any given year politically controversial issues, in which TCO has either participated in the Royal Commission stage or has been asked to give a *remiss* reply, do arise. Hence over the years TCO's leaders have come to accept a certain amount of internal tension as inevitable. TCO, however, does not welcome such developments, for there is always the risk that such an issue may develop into a rallying point for the opposition parties in their attempts to unseat the present Social Democratic government, as did the supplementary pensions dispute.

Thus the real danger lies in the fact that TCO cannot always prevent an issue (or for that matter a cluster of issues) from developing in such a direction. In the final analysis this remains the prerogative of the political parties. TCO, however, can try to prevent this from happening, and one of the best ways of doing this is to keep the issue from ever getting into the hands of the political parties in the first place. Certainly Åman tried his utmost to keep the Social Democrats from opting for legislation in the supplementary pensions dispute (see pp. 84–85, 91). Certainly federations in TCO which had previously negotiated arrangements to their satisfaction (federations which in fact represented a majority of TCO's members) felt they could influence events to a greater degree through the labor market than through the political arena on this issue (see pp. 66, 84–85, 91). Åman's failure and the events which followed (culminating finally in SIF's signing a contract with SAF in violation of TCO's constitution) nearly spelled the end of TCO.

Another example of this strategy of keeping an issue out of the hands of the political parties, one which had a happier ending (at least from TCO's perspective), was provided by the case of inventors' rights. Here TCO's leaders successfully convinced political party representatives not to pursue the issue. Success at this point meant that its influence during the deliberation stage remained undisturbed, and it was in fact in the deliberation stage that the outcome was decided (see pp. 116–117).

But there are other means by which TCO attempts to reduce the likelihood that parties will take up an issue as a means for improving their respective electoral positions. The most important of these is the time, money, and effort TCO puts into the administrative sphere of policy-making, for it is here that many new policies are in fact initiated. As the case of the reform of the Comprehensive School curriculum suggested, when consensus is reached on agency commission proposals the likelihood is increased that important modifications will not be made at later stages of the decision-making process (see pp. 142–143, 151).

Moreover, it comes as no surprise that TCO's efforts in the administrative sphere have steadily increased over the years, for the kinds of policies made in the administrative sphere are increasing in importance, as the case of the revision of the Comprehensive School curriculum indicated. While this revision did not provide a path-breaking structural reform of the scope of the Visby Compromise, it was seen by all the actors involved as an important change.[1] To the degree this trend continues in the field of educational policy and is augmented by similar trends in other policy fields, it is in TCO's interest to maximize access to administrative policy-making.

This is particularly true since TCO is guaranteed a position of strength in the administration, while it is not in the larger political system. As a member of the executive boards of various agencies, the labor court of Sweden, advisory groups to ministries and agencies, and even joint consulting commissions, TCO has automatically achieved access for which it must fight elsewhere. For example, it is never definite that TCO can gain a place on an important Royal Commission. Even if it does, it may only be as an expert, rather than as a full-voting member. *Remiss* replies ensure that TCO's views will be made known in the top councils of government, but they do not ensure that these views will be heeded. Thus continuity of access, important for all interest groups but especially so for one which is often at odds with itself over politically charged issues, is provided by representation in the administrative arena of policy-making.

In a very real sense, then, one of TCO's most important resources is its supply of expertise. In a calm rational discussion where facts and figures are important, TCO is at its best. Not surprisingly TCO's headquarters spends a great deal of time and money developing the documentation needed to support white-collar interests. Not surprisingly TCO's representatives try to be first out with their programs in an effort to influence the future agendas of discussions.

The net result of these factors has implications for the role TCO would like its members to play. One might be tempted to say, "the smaller, the better." But as shall be noted in the next chapter, such a statement is only partially correct. TCO wants membership participation, but only of a certain kind. And in this respect TCO exhibits the same attitudes as other groups in Swedish society.

Moreover, the result of these factors also has implications for Swedish democracy. Democratic theory emphasizes that the politically elected

[1] Interviews.

(and therefore politically responsible) representatives of the people in Parliament are to make the decisions over important policy issues. This emphasis (and success!) by a major interest group in Swedish society on keeping issues out of the hands of the political parties raises important questions regarding the future of Swedish democracy.

In general terms, it can be said that opposition political parties need the support of affected interest groups if they are to effectively mobilize public opinion against government proposals. If groups are silent or support the government's proposal, the cues the public has to follow are at best weak (coming only from the political parties and the press) and at worst confused (when groups align themselves against the parties they usually identify with). In the case of the Comprehensive School reform there were no reservations in the commission's final report by groups which normally supported the opposition parties (see pp. 142–143). This was a particularly hard blow for the Conservative party, which came to lead the attack on the proposals (see pp. 144–146). It will be remembered that Larsson, SAF's representative, thought long and hard about the implications of his refraining from making any reservation (see p. 142). Indeed his fears were borne out: the government was able to point to unanimous approval by the executive board of the SÖ (National Board of Education) and thus undercut the potential impact of Conservative party criticism.

Interest group representatives clearly recognized the dilemma functional representation on the SÖ presented for them on this particular issue. As one important member of the business community put it, "If I've been in the Executive Board one day and cooperated in something, then the next day I can't give a speech criticizing the agreement."[2] Interest groups, however, were out first of all to represent the interests of their members. Thus direct representation in administrative agencies provided an avenue for influence separate from political parties. Given the perpetual inability of the bourgeois opposition to gain power, it is small wonder that interests naturally friendly to these parties were quick to take the bird in the hand when it presented itself.

Second, once a proposal has been drawn up there is little time to gain enough expertise to effectively build an intelligent and persuasive critique. It was not until the very late stages of the commission's work that the opposition parties even became aware of the likely results. In fact it was a full two weeks after the presentation of the final proposal that the Conservative party called the SÖ to request a copy of the commission's report. As one agency official put it, "The Conservatives will indeed be at

[2] Interview.

a disadvantage if they try to criticize this proposal and come up with alternatives."[3]

In short, by participating in a commission where members were able to reach unanimity, TCO contributed to the likelihood that the issue would not become politicized and hence contributed to the final outcome. In so doing, TCO, the other interest groups involved, and agency officials participated in a process of decision-making which made it more difficult for the political parties, especially the opposition political parties, to effectively involve themselves in this issue. Such a subsystem of decision-making, in the author's opinion, weakens the democratic fiber of the Swedish political system.

Not only has the ability of the opposition political parties to present constructive alternatives been affected by the growth in importance of the administrative arena of policy-making, but also the very ability of the government to give direction to the policy-making process has been diminished, as effective decision-making has continued to shift steadily from ministries to agencies.

Prior to the 1960s, while agencies were formally independent of ministries, they in fact only carried out the details of policy which had been planned by the ministries;[4] moreover, agency actions were tightly circumscribed by the ministries.[5]

Parallel with the rapid increase in interest group representation on agency executive boards which characterized the decade of the sixties[6] went an upgrading of agency responsibilities and a considerable increase in the resources available to them for executing new tasks.

The National Board of Education (SÖ) provides one example. Prior to the reform in 1964, the SÖ had only carried out routine adminis-

---

[3] Interview.

[4] Dankwart Rustow, *The Politics of Compromise: A Study of Parties and Cabinet Government in Sweden* (Princeton: Princeton University Press, 1955), p. 76.

[5] Hans Thorelli, "Formation of Economic and Financial Policy: Sweden," *International Social Science Bulletin*, VIII (1956), pp. 262–264.

[6] In 1946 only 28 percent of the administrative agency executive boards had representatives from outside the agency. By 1968 the percentage had risen to 64, of which 35 percent came exclusively from interest groups. Just those agencies responsible for the most important policy areas were the ones to receive interest group representation.

Not only was the scope of the representation greatly expanded, but its depth also was greatly increased. Thus interest groups gained access to regional and local administrative organs which hitherto had remained closed entities.

For both these points, see Björn Molin, Lennart Månsson, and Lars Strömberg, *Offentlig förvaltning: stat och kommunalförvaltningens struktur och funktioner* (Stockholm: Bonniers, 1969), p. 357.

trative work, such as field inspections to check on the enforcement of regulations.[7] After the reform the agency was specifically delegated responsibility for planning future changes in the school system. This wide delegation of authority was reinforced in specific terms by every major reform which the agency came to administer. Thus, as was noted in an earlier context, in the final instructions to the agency after Riksdag approval of the 1962 reform of the Comprehensive School, the government commanded: "[It is the responsibility of the National Board of Education] to see that the contents and methods of education are continually brought up to date, developed and improved in step with advancements in research, developments in public and private administration, industry, labor relations and other sectors of society."[8]

As was discussed earlier,[9] the agency has built up an impressive array of expertise. Moreover, its planning resources match those of any group on the executive board and outdistance many. Certainly in the case of the reform of the Comprehensive School curriculum, its expertise and ability to follow developments in the field stood the agency in good stead. Moreover, its planning function continues to increase in importance. In response to student unrest in the Swedish schools during the spring of 1968, for example, the Ministry of Education authorized the National Board of Education to set in motion a series of short, intensive studies into such areas as the possibilities for increased democracy in the school system, the academic milieu, student-teacher relations, and so on. Because it needed to get the results fast, the ministry elected to go directly to the SÖ instead of doing the job itself.[10]

Clearly this points to a shift in functions between the agency and the Ministry of Education. The ministry increasingly is providing a coordinating rather than a planning function. But even more important are the implications for the balance of power between them, for the agency has become in fact more independent of the ministry. An excellent illustration, of course, was Palme's decision, in the face of opposition from agency officials, to drop his idea of changing the Commission's proposals to make

---

[7] Interview. See also Jonas Orring, *Skolan i Sverige* (Stockholm: SÖ-Förlaget/ Skolöverstyrelsen, 1967), pp. 4, 36, 53.

[8] Sweden, Skolöverstyrelsen, *Läroplansöversyn grundskolan: förslag till Kungl. Maj:t angående översyn av läroplan för grundskolan* O nr. 5131/67 U (Stockholm: SÖ-Förlaget/Skolöverstyrelsen, 1967), p. 4.

[9] See pp. 128–130.

[10] "Punktanalys av elevdemokrati: Palmes recept mot skolkris," *Dagens Nyheter*, May 24, 1968, p. 9.

compulsory a second language for all students during the last three years of the Comprehensive School.

Moreover, leading officials in the agency, interest group representatives on the executive board, and high-ranking officials in the Ministry of Education recognize this growing independency of the agency. And, at least at the agency level, there is a desire for even greater autonomy.

Several leading members of the agency, for example, expressed concern for the quality of educational policy when the ministry "interfered" in what the agency was preparing. One respondent saw the problem as primarily a question of who had the most expertise, the agency or the ministry:

> Those at the Ministry level are the ones who are really supposed to be making the policy, yet all the expertise is down here at the agency level. We are the ones who really know what the policy is all about. After all, we developed it. The problem with sending the proposed policy up to the Department is that they don't have the qualified people to deal with it. It's very hard for them to keep in close contact with the agency. . . . The bulk of the expertise lies in the agency—you have some 600 people in the agency, whereas in the Department you have at the most ninety who are working on various problems.[11]

What can be labeled as a desire to take policy out of the hands of politicians and give it to the experts is common to all bureaucrats wherever they exist. What is important here is that the preconditions exist to a considerable degree for doing so in the field of educational policy.

The thesis that agencies with interest group representation are growing more important in the policy-making process can also be supported by reference to developments in the field of labor market policies. The Labor Market Board, which includes interest group representatives on its executive board, is one of the most powerful agencies in the Swedish bureaucracy. Created in 1948, it has since that time steadily been expanding its actual field of operations. This has been especially true since 1957 when the board began moving into the field of deficit spending by freeing investment funds to spur production in the wake of a recession. Moreover, its active labor retraining program since that time has brought international fame to Sweden. Its position has grown so strong that the general director feels safe in following only directives received from the Cabinet.[12] While the board is formally under the Minister of the Interior (Inrikesdepartementet), its leaders steadfastly refuse to take any orders from the depart-

[11] Interview.
[12] Berndt Öhman, "Den nya arbetsmarknadspolitiken" (unpublished seminar paper, University of Uppsala, 1963), pp. 66–67.

ment and even limit the contacts its employees can make to those approved from on high.[13] In short, it sees itself as free to act in almost any manner it chooses within the general guidelines drawn up by the Cabinet, as long as its executive board approves.[14] Criticism of this independence of the Labor Market Board has in recent years grown to considerable proportions but as yet to no avail.[15]

In this respect some comparisons can be made with the United States, where we have had experience with agencies which have succeeded in reducing the influence of actors with values different from their own. The most common method is to form alliances with clientele interest groups and congressional committees. The classic example of this independent position is of course that of the Army Corps of Engineers, with its ties to the House Committees on Rivers and Harbors and on Flood Control and the Senate Committee on Commerce, and its support from various involved interest groups (navigation companies, construction firms, property owners, and so on).[16] There is little or no review of the corp's program by the Secretary of Defense, and therefore presidential values are seldom influential. In fact, if threatened the corps can even defy presidential authority, as was shown by the King's river project.[17]

While developments in Sweden have not gone this far the evidence suggests that there is at least a definite trend in that direction. Large grants of authority and ample supplies of resources enable agency officials and interest group representatives to follow policy developments of mutual concern and to bargain and compromise their way forward to positions of agreement on significant changes in policy. Consensus at this low level serves to make it less likely that important modifications will be made at later stages of the policy-making process. Administrative agencies, in part as a reflection of the important role interest groups play in the contemporary Swedish political system, have increased their importance in the policy-making process. As a result, the democratic process in Sweden is progressively being affected in a fundamental way.[18]

---

[13] *Ibid.*

[14] *Ibid.*

[15] *Dagens Nyheter* has been a leader in the campaign.

[16] Grant McConnell, *Private Power and American Democracy* (New York: Knopf, 1966), pp. 215–221, 243–245.

[17] Arthur Maass, *Muddy Waters* (Cambridge: Harvard University Press, 1951). For one of the best treatments of the implications of interest group-agency subsystems of decision-making, see Theodore J. Lowi, *The End of Liberalism: Ideology, Policy and the Crisis of Public Authority* (New York: Norton, 1969).

[18] It should be made clear at this point that my findings raise a number of important questions regarding Professor Nils Elvander's interpretation of the signifi-

In the face of such developments, what are the alternative choices of action for Sven Svensson, the average Swede-on-the-street, when he becomes dissatisfied with the course of public policy on some particular issue and wishes to make his voice heard?

---

cance of interest group activity in the Swedish political system. (See his study, *Intresseorganisationerna i dagens Sverige* (2nd ed.; Lund: Gleerup, 1969). As his study is used throughout Sweden as the standard textbook treatment of the subject, it is particularly worthy of discussion. However, as it has to date only appeared in Swedish (and hence is accessible only to a limited number of scholars), I have decided to make the following points in footnote form, rather than as part of the text.

In interviewing a number of interest group leaders, politicians, and administrative heads, Elvander requested evaluative statements from each respondent regarding the importance of groups in the political process. Combining his results with his observation that the negotiating of formal written agreements between the government and interest groups (a pattern common during the crisis situation of World War II) had markedly declined since 1945, Elvander reached the conclusion that interest groups during the postwar years had steadily declined in importance in the Swedish policy-making process. If groups had succeeded anywhere in maintaining or increasing the scope of their influence, he concluded, it was over the purely technical details in the implementation stage of policy-making. (Elvander, *Intresseorganisationerna*, pp. 206, 290–291).

The data presented above on the National Board of Education and the labor market board suggest that Elvander underestimated the important role which administrative agencies are increasingly coming to play in shaping significant policy revisions, an importance which in part can be attributed to the inclusion of interest group representatives as voting members of agency executive boards.

To a large degree Elvander's inability to penetrate to any great depth within the bureaucratic arena of decision-making can be traced to the methodology he used. Rather than discussing specific cases, he chose to have his interview respondents speak in general of how one seeks to influence public policy. From each group leader and politician, moreover, he requested evaluative statements assessing the importance of different points of access as well as the overall importance of groups in the policy process.

While the interview technique may yield reliable information regarding the process of policy formation, the literature on community power studies in the United States shows the weaknesses inherent in any attempt to have a respondent assess his or another actor's importance in the political process. The problems associated with reaching a common understanding between interviewer and respondent regarding the terms "power" and "influence" are certainly among the most obvious. (See, for example, Nelson Polsby, *Community Power and Political Theory* [New Haven: Yale University Press, 1964].) Thus, rather than use the reputational method in gathering data for this study, I have relied on the case study method.

Second, my findings suggest that interest group influence may be greatest when informality rather than formality characterized the prevailing relationship between interest group leaders and governmental officials. Thus in detailing the steps which led to the reform of the Comprehensive School's curriculum, I showed how bargaining in countless meetings, corridor chats, and telephone conversations eventually led to the agreement on the final package.

For particularly difficult points, moreover, negotiations took place in advisory groups created especially for that purpose. In fact in one instance concerning the curriculum in religion, agency officials actually took the initiative in starting negotiations before the issue even came up for formal discussion in the executive board. Religious studies are traditionally an area capable of arousing considerable controversy and had been the subject of much concern within the agency at this time. From an agency official involved in this aspect of the commission's work, I learned: "Sentiment in the agency, supported in fact by TCO's Isling, ran high for a total revision of the study of religion. Because of the political sensitivity of the subject [I mean by this that support for religious instruction, especially for the state religion of Lutheranism, is particularly strong in the Riksdag] we had some real concerns within the Commission as to whether we ought to even try to revise the curriculum on this point. If our proposal resulted in alienating a number of important groups, the chances for getting other, more important parts of the package through the Riksdag intact would be lessened. In order to test the winds, we delegated to Skolkonsulent John Ronnas the task of contacting different religious groups to see where they stood on the issue of reform. His contacts proved excellent and he finally succeeded in negotiating a draft proposal which overwhelmed us by its radicalism. I still can't believe it's real" (Interview).

Thus Elvander's assertion that group influence in the political system has declined because formal written agreements no longer are negotiated between the government and the major groups in society can be questioned on two counts. First of all groups have increased their influence over policy precisely because relationships are more informal. And second, negotiations do in fact still go on; Elvander just did not find them.

For a criticism of the historical time period Elvander chose to study, see Pär-Erik Back, "Organisationen—en papperstiger?," *Dagens Nyheter*, February 10, 1966, p. 4. See also Back's study, "Det svenska partiväsendet," in *Samhälle och riksdag* (5 vols.; Stockholm: Almqvist & Wiksell, 1966), II, pp. 6–12.

Having shown the weakness of Elvander's thesis that group influence in the political system declined between 1945 to 1968 (the period covered by the study), I will show in the next section that since the late 1960s the value structure of the average Swede has been significantly altered, and how as a result a large number of ad hoc groups outside the established group structure have come into being. This development serves to weaken not only interest group representation of citizen views, but also political party representation. Thus Elvander ultimately may be right, albeit for the wrong period of time and for the wrong reasons.

Chapter Ten

Alienation

In May, 1968, a group of students at Stockholm University occupied the student union building for three days in protest over a proposed curriculum reform of the university. By the time the reform eventually passed the Riksdag in 1969, the Ministry of Education had fundamentally altered many provisions in an effort to dampen criticism.[1]

In October, 1968, a group calling itself the Society to Save Brofjorden held its charter meeting. Over the next two years it waged an unsuccessful fight against the government's decision to allow a cooperatively owned oil company to build a new refinery in the natural harbor of Brofjorden on Sweden's west coast, traditionally a recreation area of incomparable beauty.[2]

In December, 1969, workers in the state-owned iron ore mines in the far northern town of Kiruna began a fifty-seven–day sit-down strike in protest over certain provisions of the newly concluded collective wage agreement which they deemed unsatisfactory.[3] Their action touched off over a hundred such wildcat strikes during the next several weeks in virtually every Swedish factory, causing serious damage to the economy as well as to Sweden's international reputation as a "strike-free" economy.

These examples could be supplemented by a number of others.[4] The

[1] Marina Stenius Aschan, ed., *UKAS och samhället: en sammanställning av dokumentationen kring och kritiken av UKAS-förslagets första del*, Tribun-serien (Stockholm: Aldus/Bonniers, 1968).

[2] Ronny Svensson, *Fallet brofjorden: regering på osäkert vatten*, W & W serien (Stockholm: Wahlström & Widstrand, 1971).

[3] Anders Thunberg, ed., *Strejken: röster, dokument, synpunkter från en stor konflikt*, Tema serien (Stockholm: Rabén och Sjögren, 1970).

[4] Sören Häggroth, in his study of the greater Stockholm area, for example, found that twenty-four citizen action groups had sprung up just during 1968 and 1969. Sören Häggroth, "Byalagsrörelsen i Stockholm 1968–1970," *Statsvetenskaplig Tidskrift*, 2 (January, 1971), p. 99. Issues receiving national attention in which ad hoc groups have played an important role include among others: the tennis match be-

point, however, is clear: participation in political and economic affairs by "Sven Svensson"—the average Swede-in-the-street—rose sharply during the late 1960s and has now come to stabilize at an only slightly lower level of frequency.

To anyone acquainted with American politics, the style of reform resulting from such ad hoc group activity has a remarkably familiar ring. These groups tend to be single rather than multi-issue oriented, local rather than national, decentralized rather than centralized, dramatic rather than quiet, short rather than long-lived.[5]

For anyone familiar with Swedish politics, moreover, the hullabaloo surrounding their activities contrasts markedly with the normally calm atmosphere in which highly centralized, well-organized, nationally based interest groups and parties rationally bargain and barter to protect the interests of their members on a wide range of issues.

While no explanation of this development can be attempted through a study of the activities of a single interest group, certain hypotheses for future research can be suggested.[6] One of these is that the rise of such groups might well be traced in part to a reaction against the general style of participation which presently prevails within the institutions and non-governmental groups which make up Swedish representative democracy. A second is that such a development seemingly reflects the manifestation of a tension prevalent in Sweden as well as in other Western industrialized political systems, namely, the tension between participation and effectiveness. To compete effectively with well-organized business associations, mass-based organizations need a certain amount of centralization and expertise. Certainly the benefits "Sven Svensson," the average Swede, has come to enjoy, as well as the influence over events the organization to which he belongs has had, can be traced to a considerable degree to his earlier willingness to follow the cues of his group's leadership. Yet in an

---

tween Sweden and Southern Rhodesia, 1968; the battle of the elms, 1971; the grade policy of the National Board of Education, 1971–1972; rent strikes, 1971–1972; the battle against the Stockholm regional plan, 1971–1972.

[5] These are the major characteristics of such groups. Some survive undergoing a metamorphosis to multi-issue oriented organizations. For a discussion of such changes, see Häggroth, "Byalagsrörelsen," pp. 109–110.

[6] For an international perspective, see R. Inglehart, "The Silent Revolution in Europe: Intergenerational Change in Post-Industrial Societies," *American Political Science Review*, LXV (December, 1971), pp. 991–1017. For Sweden, see Olof Ruin, "Participation, Corporativization and Politicization: Trends in Present-day Sweden" (paper presented at the 62nd Meeting of the Society for the Advancement of Scandinavian Study, New York City, May 5–6, 1972). Ruin presents a convincing case for several political causes of contemporary ad hoc group action in Sweden.

age when Sven feels himself increasingly competent to participate, mass-based organizations in Sweden, if they are not to lose effectiveness, may have to allow greater membership participation in group decisions. It will be the task of further research to establish the validity of these and the other generalizations which follow in this chapter.

A constant theme running throughout the pages preceding this section has been the highly centralized nature of political and economic life in Sweden. Royal Commissions can accommodate only a limited number of members. Groups, in order to make their opinions heard, are encouraged to speak with one voice in the *remiss* stage. Invitations go out to national trade union confederations to sit on administrative agencies and ministry planning councils. While a general pluralization of power has occurred within the government-administrative sector, to the advantage of the administrative agencies, effective decision-making within agencies is still centralized in the hands of the executive board where there sit representatives from highly centralized interest groups.

In this context, Thomas Anton has neatly captured the essence of Swedish political life:

> Policy making in Sweden is accomplished by highly-specialized roles attached to a dual structure of societal power. On one side there is the governmental structure which, in a small nation, with a long tradition of governmental centralization, is highly integrated around a strong central government. At the apex of this structure stands the cabinet, made up of elected political officials, each of whom bears responsibility for policy making—but not administration—in some major area of public responsibility. On the other side stands what may be the best-organized structure of interest groups to be found in any nation in the world. Virtually all social interests of any significance—from industrial workers to tennis enthusiasts—are organized into local, regional, and national associations, and the most important interests (labor and industry) are further centralized by "super" organizations that represent the interest of all of their associated organizations in national negotiations. Because of the high degree of multi-level office holding in the governmental structure (e.g. 70 percent of Swedish Riksdag members hold local office), distinctions between "national," "county," or "local" politics have little practical significance. And because of the extraordinary overlap, at all levels, between governmental and non-governmental positions (major labor, management and other interest group officials are elected members of the Riksdag), the distinction between "private" and "public" policy is all but meaningless.
>
> Any and all important social questions are automatically subject to determination by representatives of this twin policy-making structure, which in a real sense constitutes a cohesive national elite.[7]

[7] Thomas J. Anton, "Policy-Making and Political Culture in Sweden," in *Scandi-*

In the economic arena of decision-making the story is the same. Ten-man delegations from SAF and the LO negotiate wage round agreements for nearly one-half of the working population in Sweden. When an issue gets sticky, authority for reaching an agreement is delegated to two single persons, one from each side of the table.

Support for such a concentration of decision-making authority can be found in the attitudes and values of the Swedish population. The concept of functional representation (which finds the community divided into various strata, regards each of these strata as having a certain corporate unity, and holds that they ought to be represented in government) has enjoyed support not only from Swedish conservative theorists, but from Socialist as well.[8] Even nineteenth-century Swedish liberalism, despite its

---

navian Political Studies, ed. Olof Ruin, Vol. 4 (New York: Columbia University Press, 1969), pp. 92–93.

[8] During the early part of the nineteenth century, Swedish conservatives actively defended the system of estate representation and corporate organization which had pervaded Swedish public life during the previous 200 years. Sten Carlsson, *Bonde— Präst—Ämbetsman: svensk ståndscirkulation från 1680 till våra dagar* (Stockholm: Prisma, 1962), pp. 9–92. For example, such leading conservative theorists as Erik Gustaf Geijer sharply attacked the emerging liberal school on the grounds that it fundamentally misunderstood the organic nature of society. The family, the corporation, the estate were all integral parts of that same living organism, the state. Moreover, each was intimately linked to the other. "[Each] develops one from the other. Each contains the other within itself, giving that entire unity [the state] its own unique image." Gunnar Heckscher, *Svensk konservatism före representationsreformen: den historiska skolans genombrott i Sverige* (2 vols.; Stockholm: Almqvist & Wiksell, 1939), I, p. 147.

One can almost hear the echoes of that phrase so dear to British conservative thought which Beer uses to introduce his work: "Take but degree away, untune that string and hark, what discord follows." See Samuel Beer, *British Politics in the Collectivist Age* (New York: Random House, 1969), p. 3. It was through such a system of representation that the individual was made an effective part of the state. It followed, thus, that the state should use such "mediating institutions" (Geijer's term) as instruments for the exercise of power and administration.

The belief that corporate entities, rather than individuals, possessed political rights was natural to those who held an organic view of the state. C. A. Agarth, to cite a second example from the early nineteenth century, rested his defense on the continuity of such organizations in contrast with the fleeting moments spent here on earth by humans. The consequences of granting political rights to individuals rather than corporations would be disastrous, he argued, as only the latter possessed the sense of tradition and the economic standing from which well-reasoned opinions could emerge. Pär-Erik Back, *Sammanslutningarnas roll i politiken 1870–1910* (Lund: Studentlitteratur, 1967), p. 34.

Socialist thought in the latter part of the nineteenth century also viewed the basic units of representation as social groups rather than individuals. Here, as in England (see Beer, *British Politics*, p. 83), however, it was primarily the two major classes

emphasis on individualism, tolerated and even accepted a corporate expression of group interests. That radical strand of liberalism, which has had such a profound effect on party and group politics in the United States because of its strong hostility toward "special interests,"[9] never gained a foothold in Sweden.[10] These factors have in turn affected the basis for group action in the two countries.

of industrial society which made up the basic units of representation, rather than the many subgroups that underlie the great vocational associations of the modern economy.

However, developments in Swedish Social Democratic ideology during the late 1920s and early 1930s led to moderation of this class concept of representation in favor of a more organic view (called the "People's Home") where all groups could participate in shaping policy.

[9] Beer, *British Politics*, p. 40.

[10] This does not mean that the radical tradition lacked spokesmen in Sweden. The chief representative for the radical wing of liberalism (in Beer's sense of the terms) was Johan Rickert. Writing in the 1820s, he argued that the state, once it had developed firm roots among its people, did not need mediating groups. Through the legal order of society, he maintained, the individual could realize his goals, just as the state, through the legal process, could see that the individual fulfilled his obligations. Gunnar Heckscher, *Staten och organisationerna* (Stockholm: Kooperativa Förbundets Bokförlag, 1946), pp. 14–15, 17.

Erik Gustaf Geijer, after his dramatc conversion to liberalism in 1838, initially championed this view of the individual's role in public life as a consequence of his defense of the theme of free trade. In the face of social developments in the rest of Europe and a thorough study of socialist and communist writings, however, he progressively modified his position. In 1844 in a public lecture, he put forward the thesis that free, unbridled competition in reality led only to the reintroduction into societal life of the principle of "might makes right." In order to check this abuse, the individual's resources must be expanded and increased. Thus the freedom of association became crucially important, as it was through group action that individual rights could be protected. Back, *Sammanslutningarnas roll*, pp. 28–29.

It was ultimately Geijer's liberalism rather than Rickert's proto-radicalism that set the tone for further developments in Swedish liberalism. This particular strand of liberalism showed a remarkable tolerance for functional representation. Between 1840 and 1860 a plethora of trade associations sprang up under liberal leadership. By 1865 a cooperative movement had joined hands with these trade associations, and by the 1870s health insurance plans, religious societies, and temperance associations were all serving the same clientele.

Liberals in Sweden, in other words, came to accept early the view that "the unity of such a stratum is not that of mere voluntary association which stresses common ideas and moral judgments. On the contrary, its integration is seen as arising especially from objective conditions that give its numbers a function and are the ground for deeply rooted, continuing—even final—interests." Beer, *British Politics*, p. 71.

Furthermore, while guilds were officially abolished in 1846, liberals did allow them to surface again, albeit in a different form. In Article III, paragraph one, of the law abolishing guilds, which passed in large measure because of liberal support, we learn that: "The existing form of guild association ends with the promulgation of

As Samuel Beer demonstrates, the individualist bias by which "the people" are said to achieve unity by a series of individual acts of mind on specific issues is integral to the radical variant of the liberal theory of representation.[11] In a society such as the United States, where this type of philosophy has come to dominate, allies are those who find themselves in agreement on a specific issue. The style of reform becomes one in which ad hoc groups, organized around specific issues, bubble up, engage in considerable uproar, and fade as soon as legislation is passed. Seldom are they in evidence during the administration of policy.

As Sweden became fully industrialized, the corporate unity inherent in the concept of functional representation came to be expressed in terms of class as a reflection of one's occupation. Thus as the old four-estate system crumbled, it was replaced by a system of workers, farmers, industrialists, and so on.

The sense of solidarity which stemmed from such a concept of corporate unity simplified the problem of identifying allies, for once the class image was accepted political associates became all those who shared one's class

---

this act. Instead in every city, craftsmen who pay taxes will belong to a craft association dedicated to promoting that craft and protecting the interests of its members." Back, *Sammanslutningarnas roll*, p. 31.

As the Swedish political scientist Pär-Erik Back notes, such a clause in effect reintroduced obligatory membership in the new "voluntary associations." *Ibid.* Even merchants in the various Swedish towns were able to maintain much of their old organization through similar regulations. *Ibid.* Finally, during the latter part of the nineteenth century, groups of both the voluntary and corporate variety participated in municipal and national political life without evoking the slightest reproach from liberal theorists. Back observes: "Few restraining ideological elements are noted, and to the extent that these can be traced to the palmy days of *laissez-faire* liberalism, they quickly lose their power in practice. That it was fully logical and correct for an association to make decisions favorable to itself was practically undisputed. The insignificant amount of hypocrisy met in this connection is amazing. . . . Lines of thought often appeared that can be said to be an embryo of "group theory," an idea that the confrontation between the demands and proposals of various organizations lead to balance and harmony." Back, *Sammanslutningarnas roll*, p. 222.

"In the main, one lacked the feeling of the fundamentally sharp distinction between, on the one hand, officially authorized associations armed with the King's sanctions (corporations), and voluntary associations on the other. The result was also that many associations could operate against the background of fairly widely held views that their activities were profitable to the community and were rational." *Ibid.*, p. 224.

Thus while Swedish liberalism contributed in a basic way toward the dismantling of mercantilism and the establishment of the freedom of association during the nineteenth century, it never posed the challenge to functional representation which characterized liberalism and especially radicalism in the United States. If anything it tolerated, even accepted, such an expression of group interests.

[11] Beer, *British Politics*, p. 43.

status. There was no need to go around looking for other like-minded individuals.

This basis for collective action had important implications for the style of reform which developed in Sweden. Functionally based groups sought to promote the interests of their members in every area of societal life. Thus labor unions in Sweden never hesitated to move into the political arena, as they have in the United States. The leadership of such organized groups could count on long-term instead of conditional support. Such groups, moreover, made it a point to be around to see what happened to legislation once it got to the administrative arena.

The concept of belonging to a group on the basis of class also had important implications for the relationship between the leaders of the group and the led. The sense of permanency which pervaded these groups meant that dues could be collected with regularity. This in turn enabled the leadership to hire the expertise it needed to explain and rationalize its views, once it gained access to the important points of decision-making.

This concept of expertise is very important in the Swedish decision-making process. The Royal Commission system with its origins in the thirteenth century[12] is nothing more than an institutionalized reflection of what amounts to a cult of expertise, a cult which has always played an important role in Sweden's political and social life. If the average British citizen defers to those of higher social status, Sven Svensson defers to those who claim to know more than he does about a particular problem. This "deference toward expertise" gives a wide latitude to the leaders at the top of an organization and their consultant experts for developing policy for the members of the bottom.

Highly centralized political and economic institutions, supported by age-old citizen attitudes of deference toward expertise and a long history of functional representation (expressed most recently in class membership in groups), have created a system of decision-making within groups and parties which is highly dependent on a passive style of participation by constituent members.

The internal communications system within groups and parties in Sweden assumes such a style of membership participation. Interest group and party leaders are constantly out busily shaking the bushes in search of issues to pursue. Once discontent among the membership is located it is studied, refined, and dealt with, all by the leaders at the top. At the bot-

[12] As noted earlier (p. 39), the Royal Commission system can trace its origin to the thirteenth century but became an established part of the political system first in the seventeenth century.

tom, Sven Svensson makes known his views and acts as a sounding board for policy proposals. Thus while he is participating in politics, it is in a strictly passive way. The results of a study of the internal communication process within TCO provide an illuminating example of this style of participation.

Within TCO's headquarters a great deal of time and effort is spent feeling the pulse of the white-collar workers. First there are the indirect methods. TCO's research division carries out continuing studies of the economic position of white-collar workers belonging to TCO, covering such areas as income differentials, the effects of taxes, and incomes of working wives, to name just a few. From the findings TCO's leadership makes judgments as to how its members are likely to react to specific policy proposals.

TCO's leadership also relies on federation representatives for indirect information as to what the rank-and-file is thinking. Executive board meetings, general council meetings, and congresses all provide platforms for the exchange of views. TCO's policy of bringing together at regular intervals during the year its representatives from different provincial (län) and local decision-making bodies provides yet another source of information. When TCO is to present a *remiss* reply on a proposal, individual federations are asked for their views. Each of the raft of special committees within TCO's headquarters includes representatives from different member federations and each of these committees has as its secretary a full-time functionary from TCO headquarters. And finally, the leadership at TCO's headquarters follows closely articles in the newspapers of their member federations. In short, there are many sources of information from which the leadership learns indirectly what the rank-and-file membership is thinking.

These sources are supplemented by direct contact between leaders in TCO's headquarters and the average "Sven Svensson" white-collar worker. Functionaries from the headquarters are constantly traveling throughout the country visiting local TCO committees (TCO-kommittéer). Further direct contact with the rank-and-file is achieved through the many sample survey questionnaires executed by TCO's numerous special committees.

Thus the leadership at TCO has developed an impressive network of communications by which it learns of the views of white-collar workers. Moreover, officials at TCO headquarters work long hours in putting information from these channels to use. But at this point it is important to note the kind of information for which they are looking.

TCO's leadership is interested in learning of discontent in different issue areas, and how in general terms its members are reacting to the proposals it has devised to meet such discontent. In so doing, it seeks a passive form of participation from its membership whereby ideas come from the bottom up and decisions (in the sense of a clear definition of the problem, specific recommendations to remedy the problem, and the choice of the correct strategies to achieve the remedy) go from the top down. Let me illustrate how this process worked in two of the case studies analyzed in detail earlier in this study, inventors' rights and the reform of the Comprehensive School curriculum.

During the late 1940s an ever increasing number of engineers came to see Lennart Geijer, at that time an official of the SIF (the Swedish Union of Clerical and Technical Employees in Industry), one of TCO's member federations, about the problems they were experiencing in getting compensation for their inventions from their employers. Geijer did a study of the issue, then sought and won approval from SIF's executive board to begin negotiations with SAF, the employers' association. When that avenue failed to result in any change, Geijer succeeded in arousing government interest in the problem. This in turn led to a Royal Commission study and eventually to a law in 1951 which substantially improved the position of the inventor.

So that in the future it could keep an eye on problems such as this, TCO created an Advisory Council on Problems Affecting Engineers. In 1956 this committee was moved into action by the attempts of state-owned industries to gain over inventions a power which appeared to conflict with the intentions of the 1951 law. Engineers belonging to federations in the public sector alerted TCO's headquarters by going directly to their trade unions and complaining. A trade-federation-turned-social club, the Association of State-Employed Engineers of Sweden, also took up the issue with the Ombudsman for Civilian Affairs, thus again alerting TCO's top leadership to the problem. Within the Advisory Council on Problems Affecting Engineers a new subcommittee designed especially for inventors was formed. Here information was gathered, policies were developed, and strategies were planned. On this committee sat representatives from different TCO federations who had some previous experience with the problems facing inventors.

Between 1958 and 1964 a Royal Commission studied possible revisions in the 1951 law. When Supreme Court Justice Sven Edling, the commissioner, came out with recommendations for revisions which if approved would have favored the state-owned industries, TCO sought to have Edling's proposals shelved.

The strategies which TCO evolved in this case were complicated and multi-faceted, to say the least. Politicizing neutral groups (for example, the Association of Swedish Inventors), building coalitions with a large number of disparate groups interested in the issue, attempting to reach a compromise solution behind-the-scenes, mobilizing groups throughout Scandinavia to oppose the modifications which were emerging in Royal Commissions at work in Norway and Finland, building within Sweden a common *remiss* reply in opposition to the Edling commission's report, filling key periodicals with articles hostile to the reform proposals to create an impression of widespread opposition, informal lobbying with the minister in charge of the issue, and so on—were some of the major twists and turns the leadership at the top took in their efforts, which in this case proved successful, to defend the interests of their members.

Turning to education, I found a similar pattern. When in the late 1950s the Social Democrats began to take effective steps to fundamentally overhaul the entire system of education in Sweden, those TCO members directly affected by such reforms, for example the teachers, naturally wanted to influence the direction of the new reforms. Moreover, those who had been shut out of opportunities for further education under the old system were also interested in gaining new opportunities to go on. Through its network of communications TCO's leadership soon became aware of this growing interest among its members.

In 1963, TCO appointed Åke Isling to be in charge of its program in the educational field. He began by immediately creating a series of study groups within TCO's educational committee to define the problems TCO needed to tackle. The average teacher belonging to a TCO federation had a number of chances to make his views known on particular problems through questionnaires administered by the various subcommittees. The same held true for the average white-collar worker in industry. Later these studies were published as an appendix to the first of what has since become TCO's continuing series of scholarly reports on the Swedish educational system.

It was while researching this first report that the members of TCO's educational committee began to see the necessity of reforming the curriculum of the Comprehensive School. Their detailed critique of the way the new system was working ultimately helped convince the Minister of Education to create a commission within the National Board of Education to propose revisions for the curriculum. During the entire time the agency's commission was at work, Isling kept in close contact with representatives on TCO's educational committee, always securing their consent before making any compromise and making sure they were aware of the concessions he had succeeded in wringing out of agency officials.

While the reform was in progress, moreover, leaders from TCO headquarters gave numerous talks to local TCO committees where the proposed educational program was presented in detail. TCO representatives to provincial and local educational bodies heard the same presentations during gatherings arranged periodically by TCO headquarters.[13]

In every case the process was the same: TCO officials explained their policy in an effort to get those who were listening to understand and agree that they were right. And in each case they apparently were successful, for the questions asked afterward always aimed at eliciting information rather than challenging the basic program. At the end of these conferences, moreover, each representative took home a mound of printed matter which documented and supported in great detail what the speakers had said.

What unites these two examples, of course, is the absence of participation by the average inventor or teacher in any capacity other than whistle blower, complainer, questionnaire respondent, or sounding board. Once TCO learned of the discontent, it set up a study to further define the problem and to develop solutions. These were tested to see what general reactions they elicited. Sven, when asked for his views, was not invited to propose alternative solutions. Nor was he expected to play an active part in the determination of the final outcome of the issue, for leaders at the top saw this as their responsibility. His role at each step of the way was one of purely passive participation. After he had made known his discontent, the organization took it from there.

This style of participation is common to other interest groups and to political parties as well. For one example: the LO's decision to push for an expansion of adult educational facilities came after its leadership learned of member interest through Congress motions and through informal discussions with trade union delegates.[14] Moreover, it is commonplace to see appended to major reports presented at LO Congresses the results of questionnaire surveys among its membership dealing with the specific reform proposals at hand.[15]

---

[13] I attended three of these, one in the spring of 1966, one in the spring of 1967, and one in the fall of 1967.

[14] Interview.

[15] To cite just a few of such reports built upon questionnaires: Erik Bolinder and Bo Ohlström, *Stress på svenska arbetsplatser: en enkätundersökning bland LO-medlemmarna* (Stockholm: Prisma, 1971); Erik Bolinder, Egon Magnusson, and

The ruling Social Democratic party enjoys an advantage over opposition parties since it controls the Royal Commission system. Impulses channeled up from below many times become the impetus for commission study. The opposition parties have developed their own staffs for such work, however. When they are excluded from a particular Royal Commission, they set up their own study groups in an effort to keep pace with developments.

Moreover, such a style of participation is entirely congruent with the general style of decision-making in the Swedish political system. As Anton notes,

> (Reforms) . . . are typically initiated by the official experts employed by either the government or the interest group organizations, reacting to information that reveals difficulties in realizing current policies or in the accomplishment of newly enacted policies. Since Swedish public statistics are probably the most comprehensive and best-kept in the world, opportunities for such expert initiatives arise quite frequently. Once raised, the issue is further refined by the appropriate governmental ministry, with a view toward determining whether official action is necessary and if so, along what lines. Clearly, governmental review of these issues provides plentiful opportunity to avoid action, particularly if the issue is likely to be embarrassing. If action is taken it is in the form of a commission of experts, created to review the problem and propose alternative solutions for consideration by the government and the Riksdag.
>
> Completed (Commission) reports are submitted to the appropriate national ministry, which immediately circulates copies to all parties and organizations that may have an interest in the matter.
>
> Responses from interested parties are considered by the government, which then determines its position. If legislation is required, a bill is drafted for consideration by the Riksdag, whose committees must report all bills assigned to them and whose two chambers must vote on all bills reported from committees.[16]

Clearly, a highly centralized political system and hierarchical authority structures within groups and parties leave little room for Sven Svensson to participate in political life and a great deal of freedom for the leadership elites to set policy priorities.

Lars Nyren, *Risker i jobbet: LO-enkäten: LO-medlemmarnas uppfattning om arbetsplatsens hälsorisker* (Stockholm: Prisma, 1970); Erik Bolinder and Egon Magnusson, *Risker i jobbet: fabriks—en utredning av fabriksarbetarnas arbetsmiljö* (Stockholm: Prisma, 1971).

[16] Anton, "Policy-Making," pp. 93–94.

The Challenge: Ad Hoc Groups

In a number of important policy areas these priorities are being rejected and ad hoc groups are forming the new organizational basis for the challenge. The urban planning process provides a good example.

Until recently the urban planning process in Sweden allowed municipal politicians, city planners, and builders to set priorities in a vacuum so far as public opinion was concerned. Those days are gone, however, as a growing number of citizens have begun to set up new groups to protest the priorities established by these decision-makers.

Sören Häggroth, a Swedish political scientist, has made a study of this phenomenon in the greater Stockholm region. He found that the most common form of protest group is the citizen action group (byalaget). Shunning political party affiliation, these groups seek to influence directly specific issues. They tend to be organized on a block basis (although a trend toward consolidation into city-wide organizations has been observed in recent years) and have sprung up with remarkable rapidity (in 1967 there were none in the greater Stockholm area; in 1968, four; in 1969, twenty-one). Moreover, they are youth-oriented, with 65.8 percent of the participants in such groups under fifty, 40 percent between twenty and twenty-nine. And finally 65 percent have at least the "studentexamen," while 45 percent hold a university degree. (As the section below on changes in the educational system will show, it is not surprising that the well-educated are participating in such ad hoc group action.)[17]

The most telling influence such groups have had is perhaps best characterized as negative, for they have demonstrated the power to disrupt. And disruption has meant a decision cannot be carried out as quickly as intended, if at all. The most extreme recent example is the now infamous "Battle of the Elms" incident which took place in May, 1971.[18]

In this conflict a number of citizen action groups sought to dissuade authorities from removing a large cluster of ancient elms from a major downtown park in order to construct a subway entrance. Planning authorities took no heed of the detailed alternative construction plans presented by the groups. Local politicians quickly passed the planning authorities' proposal and the national government gave its approval, in spite of the

[17] Häggroth, "Byalagsrörelsen," pp. 102–103.

[18] For a discussion of this case, see Per Magnusson and Jens Beronius, "Debatten om Kungsträdgårdens almar" (unpublished seminar paper, University of Stockholm, 1972).

considerable public opinion which had been mobilized. (For example, a petition with 7,000 names was compiled in one day, which must stand as some sort of record for participation by Swedes. Press and TV coverage of the opponents' cause had been substantial. Phone campaigns and letter campaigns had been organized by groups in an effort to influence politicians.)

It was probably this total disregard, even disdain, for public opinion which made the atmosphere so charged. In any event the authorities announced that construction would begin in the morning on May 13, 1971, and that the elms would be the first to go. On the night of May 12, however, actual work began. Sentries posted by citizen action groups witnessed the arrival of the workers. Immediately an elaborate phone network was activated and within an hour 1,000 supporters were on the scene. Before the first tree could be felled, violence broke out. How much violence actually occurred and by whom is still the subject of much debate. In any event construction was postponed. A year later a review of the decision led to the acceptance of an alternative plan in which the elms were allowed to remain standing.[19]

The urban planning process is not the only policy arena in which ad hoc group action has come to play an important role in shaping outcomes. The labor market system provides a second example.

The LO's economic priorities have become the source of growing tension within the labor movement, particularly the question of the relative importance of wages versus environment in the work place. Heretofore the LO leadership has placed wage increases first on its list of priorities, almost to the exclusion of everything else. By 1969 resentment over deteriorating conditions in the work place had begun to play an important role in creating the wildcat strikes which have continued to erupt to this day.[20]

The work environment has deteriorated in two respects: as it affects the individual's physical health and as it affects his mental well-being. On the physical side, for example, while the frequency of "work accidents," the dominant category of occupational injuries, remained approximately con-

---

[19] *Ibid.*, pp. 2–3.

[20] Edmund Dahlström, *et al.*, *LKAB och demokratin: rapport om en strejk och ett forskningsprojekt*, W & W serien (Stockholm: Wahlström & Widstrand, 1971), pp. 203–209. By the fall of 1972 wildcat strikes were erupting primarily over the issue of environment in the work place, as the strike in Trollhättan, Sweden, in October, 1972, demonstrated. See Rolf Åkerberg, "Arbetarna har slutat anser Trollhättefirman," *Dagens Nyheter*, October 6, 1972, p. 36; "Konflikten bör lösas med fredliga medel," *Dagens Nyheter*, October 7, 1972, p. 3.

stant between 1955 and 1968, cases of severe disability (one-third disability or more) increased from 12.4 percent in 1958 to 16.6 percent in 1968.[21]

As to the deterioration of the worker's mental attitude toward his job, a major reason can be found in the increasing rationalization of plant production. As factories have rationalized, the guiding principle has been to distinguish increasingly between the performance of work operations and their planning and control. These latter tasks have been entrusted to highly skilled employees whose conditions of employment are such that their loyalty can be taken for granted. The performance of work operations has been broken down into the smallest feasible number of components, with the result that the worker has little influence over the tasks he is to perform. Supervisory personnel at different levels coordinate and control all these subfunctions. The result is a pyramidal structure of organization within the firm with a single control authority at the top. To regulate order and discipline, rules and administrative procedures are strictly defined. Incentive wage schemes, such as the piece-rate system, link the individual's interest in good earnings with the firm's interest in productivity.[22]

Technological advance and the development of work practices have proceeded apace with the trend toward larger and larger plants or units of production. One study discusses the pros and cons of increased bureaucratization:

> This increased bureaucratization has conferred certain advantages, for instance as regards security of employment, better job assignment (fewer "square pegs in round holes"), more objective assessment of work performance and greater opportunities for occupational and social advancement. However, the large, bureaucratically ruled enterprise also brings with it greater demands for advance planning and formal channels of communication, greater separation of different functions, etc. In consequence the individual forms a less comprehensive view of the firm as a social system and enjoys less influence over his own job and its design.[23]

Rationalization and increased bureaucratization have thus sharply diminished feelings of work satisfaction. Swedish research has shown that people who perform repetitive and constrained tasks derive less pleasure

[21] Hans Berglind and Anna Lena Lindquist, *Utslagningen på arbetsmarknaden* (Lund: Studentlitteratur, 1972), pp. 70, 78, 127.
[22] Sweden, Royal Ministry for Foreign Affairs and the Royal Ministry of Agriculture, *The Human Work Environment: Swedish Experiences, Trends and Future Problems—A Contribution to the United Nations Conference on the Human Environment* (Stockholm: Royal Ministry for Foreign Affairs and the Royal Ministry of Agriculture, 1971), pp. 45–46.
[23] *Ibid.*, p. 46.

from their work and feel it more stressful than those who have more complex and skilled jobs. Decreased work satisfaction, moreover, correlates
with high rates of absenteeism, lower self-confidence, a general dissatis-
faction with life, and psychosomatic disorders.[24]

For example, owing at least in part to the bad work environment,
Swedish industry suffers high rates of labor turnover, especially in those
firms with a high degree of specialization and batch production. For some
firms the annual turnover rate is presently running over 100 percent.[25]
Illness-caused absences in all branches of industry present another formidable problem. The manufacturing industry, for example, is forced to
overman its labor force by 10 percent to make up for absenteeism.[26]
Swedish firms face great recruitment problems also, especially those which
are large, highly rationalized, and operating in expanding markets. These
plants, it should be noted, are characterized by repetitive, machine-
controlled jobs and/or otherwise inferior work environments with high
noise levels, strenuous working postures, and the like. Many of the jobs
in these firms are paid by the piece rate system.[27]

If they do not quit, ask for transfers, absent themselves, or fall ill,
workers may engage in another, more extreme form of behavior (which
from their point of view is also a rational means of defense against an
unacceptable system): the wildcat strike. It comes as no surprise to learn
that the tremendous wave of wildcat strikes which erupted in 1969 and
1970 occurred in precisely those industries which are most rationalized,
and that complaints over work environment were among the most important causes of such direct action.[28] Moreover, recent studies show that
resentment over working conditions has increased rather than decreased.[29]

Questions of the outer environment form a third area where ad hoc
groups have come to enjoy a lively existence. Whereas the large producer
groups (unions and business associations) operate in a countervailing
manner on many social issues, their common emphasis on securing maximum total economic growth has led them to join hands in a united front
against the conservationists on a host of environmental problems. (The

---

[24] *Ibid.*

[25] *Ibid.*, p. 54.

[26] *Ibid.*

[27] *Ibid.*, p. 47.

[28] Dahlström, *et al.*, *LKAB*, pp. 203–209.

[29] In fact both the LO and SAF's experts are in agreement that the work environment has continued to deteriorate. Kerstin Kall, "Sifo-enkät om arbetsmiljö
vållar ny tvist SAF-LO," *Dagens Nyheter*, March 17, 1972, p. 27; "Miljön på arbetet
blir bara sämre," *Dagens Nyheter*, March 22, 1972, p. 25.

case of Brofjorden mentioned earlier is but one example.)[30] Just as workers have found the priorities of the LO difficult to change from within and have resorted to wildcat strikes, reform-minded citizens in the field of environmental policy have often lacked spokesmen in established groups willing to help them make known their views. For them the only alternative has been the creation of ad hoc groups.

School questions have been a fourth source of continuous ad hoc group action. Curricular reforms, grading policies, and school consolidation efforts all have been the subject for ad hoc group action between 1968 and 1972. As with the urban planning process, the system of decision-making within the field of educational policy until recently has remained closed to those outside the select corps of administrators and interest group representatives who sit on the executive boards of agencies determining policy for the elementary, secondary, and university levels.[31]

Finally, ad hoc group action has also focused on international questions, such as Sweden's relationship to the Common Market and the United States foreign policy in South East Asia. Some of the longest-lived issue-oriented groups, in fact, can trace their heritage back to the massive intensification of the war in Viet Nam which the United States undertook in 1965.

As with the urban planning citizen action groups in the larger cities, participants in these issue-oriented groups also tend to be young and well-educated.[32] Some of the reasons for their preponderance in ad hoc activities will become clear in the section below on changes in the school system.

The strategies generally used by these ad hoc groups and their likely effectiveness have important implications for the policy-making process. Mass-mobilization tactics have a greater inherent risk of violence than does, say, the presentation of a scholarly report to a planning commission.

[30] Svensson, *Fallet Brofjorden.*
[31] For an example of how administrators and interest groups strive to decide issues at the agency level (and often succeed), see Chapter 8.
[32] There are no studies done on membership composition of environmental groups comparable to that done by Häggroth on citizen action groups. This statement is based upon a year's observation of environmental group activity in Sweden, interviews with leading figures in the environment in Sweden, and detailed study of two cases of environmental movement in Sweden, Brofjorden and Vindelälven, in connection with a Beloit College seminar on environmental pollution control.

For data on participants involved in ad hoc group action on international questions, see Svante Lundberg, Sven-Axel Månsson, and Hans Welander, *Demonstranter: en sociologisk studie* (Stockholm: Pan/Norstedts, 1970); Bo Lindblom, ed., *Fallet Båstad*, W & W serien (Stockholm: Wahlström & Widstrand, 1968).

Thus policy-makers can no longer rest assured that their priorities will in fact be peacefully accepted. If nothing else, these groups have demonstrated a sophisticated ability to use every available means to postpone the execution of a decision with which they disagree, thereby reducing the ability of policy-makers to achieve their goals. In short, protest at least represents a negative kind of influence.

But the problem, as I suggested earlier, may go deeper than the mere rejection of established priorities. If it were merely the latter, the organizational leaders might adapt by simply modifying some of their priorities while leaving the basic decision-making apparatus intact.[33] But changes in underlying value orientations, particularly views toward participation in group life, have created a Swede more self-confident in his ability to make decisions about problems which affect him.

Edinger and Verba in their writings on the German political culture and Eckstein in his essay on the elements of stable democracy note the importance of studying authority patterns in nongovernmental groups as a way to explain the stability or instability of a particular system.[34] To take Eckstein as an example, the thesis is that system performance depends on a series of graduated resemblances existing in the authority patterns of governmental and nongovernmental organizations. Thus to take the Weimar Republic, the striking incongruence between a highly democratic legal framework in the political system and a highly undemocratic substructure of authority relationships in nongovernmental groups, for example, interest groups, the family and the school system, served to create a tension within the political system which eventually undermined its performance. In contrast, the congruence of authority patterns within the British system, from the political institutions through nongovernmental organizational life through the school and family systems, helps to explain continued system performance in that country.[35] Certainly the harmonious fit (or congruence) between the passive style of participation demanded by Swedish organizational leadership, as well as by the political system in general, and that given by Sven in his role as group member or citizen

---

[33] Even this would be a difficult task, owing to the considerable freedom to set priorities group leaders have enjoyed.

[34] Lewis Edinger, *Politics in Germany* (Boston: Little, Brown, 1968); Sidney Verba, "Germany: The Remaking of Political Culture," in Lucian Pye and Sidney Verba, eds., *Political Culture and Political Development* (Princeton: Princeton University Press, 1964), pp. 130–170; Harry Eckstein, "Appendix B: A Theory of Stable Democracy," in Harry Eckstein, *Division and Cohesion in Democracy: A Study of Norway* (Princeton: Princeton University Press, 1966), pp. 225–328.

[35] Eckstein, "A Theory," pp. 234–253.

must rank as a significant variable in any attempt to explain system performance in Sweden. It is in this context that developments within the labor movement, the school system, and family structure take on particular importance.

The Decline of Working-Class Solidarity—The Rise of Instrumentalism

No longer can labor's leadership count on deferential acceptance by their rank-and-file of its policy priorities. Increasingly conditional support of organizational policy has come to prevail within the ranks of labor.

Goldthorpe (and others') work on the affluent worker in England is directly relevant to the Swedish case. They describe the solidaristic orientation to work in the following terms:

> Work . . . provide[s] the foundation for an entire way of life. Outside the work place, workmates remain preferred companions; work is a central life interest, constituting a perennial topic of conversation; and, perhaps most significantly, the occupational group is the crucial reference group for all its members, setting standards of behavior, forming opinions, creating social identity.[36]

This contrasts markedly with the instrumental orientation:

> The primary meaning of work is as a means to an end, or ends, external to the work situation; that is, work is regarded as a means of acquiring the income necessary to support a valued way of life of which work itself is not an integral part. Work is therefore experienced as mere "labor" in the sense of an expenditure of effort which is made for extrinsic rather than for intrinsic rewards. Workers act as "economic men," seeking to minimise effort and maximise economic returns; but the latter concern is the dominant one.[37]

In Sweden a number of developments in society itself as well as in the firm have promoted this instrumental orientation among a growing number of workers.[38]

Urban redevelopment programs have destroyed old working-class neighborhoods. Society has assumed responsibility for a number of the services provided earlier by the labor movement for its own kind. Free time is no longer spent in "movement" activities. Trade union function-

[36] John H. Goldthorpe, David Lockwood, Frank Bechhofer, and Jennifer Platt, *The Affluent Worker: Industrial Attitudes and Behavior* (Cambridge: Cambridge University Press, 1968), pp. 40–41.

[37] *Ibid.*, pp. 38–39.

[38] For a further discussion of these changes in Sweden, see Jan Lindhagen and Macke Nilsson, *Hotet mot arbetarrörelsen* (Stockholm: Tiden, 1970).

aries are no longer personal friends, but rather "experts" who manage a large office in some other city. The bartering of services (bruksandan) so characteristic of many working-class communities in an earlier Sweden has given way to the principle of market exchange.

Within the firm the deterioration of the work environment has been a major factor in creating an instrumental orientation toward work. Specialization of labor has broken down teamwork since each man has his own specific task. Assembly-line production has created an almost insufferable boredom. The piece-rate system has created a sense of competition within the ranks of labor destructive to the goals of union solidarity.

At the heart of this instrumental view is a conditional form of support for union leadership: if the leadership does not deliver the results he wants, the worker feels no automatic bond of loyalty. Thus the deteriorating work environment has a doubly negative effect on union cohesion: the worse the work environment, the more dissatisfied the worker is with his union's lack of attention to the question *and* the less likely he is to feel any loyalty to the union. This helps explain the relationship between deteriorating work environments and wildcat strikes. It is thus particularly alarming to note that results of Swedish investigations show that nearly two-thirds of today's industrial workers embrace what can be termed as an instrumental view toward their working life.[39]

Value changes, however, have not been restricted solely to the working class. Changes in the school and in the home have also encouraged the development of a more active style of participation in these sectors of social life.

The Educational System

Until the reforms of the 1960s the authority pattern which prevailed in the classroom demanded deference and passivity. Students rose and greeted the entering teacher with a "Good day, Herr Magister." A strictly organized system of class lectures (katederundervisning) emphasized rote learning. The teacher would "hear the lessons," assign new tasks, and in between would have the students work silently by themselves. His purpose was to transmit knowledge and develop the highest possible degree of competence in the pupils.[40] As I have already noted, the organizational

[39] Ministries of Foreign Affairs and Agriculture, *Human Work Environment*, p. 45.

[40] For a description of the "good old days," see Svenska Institutet för Opinionsundersökningar AB, *Föräldrarna, lärarna och grundskolan* (Stockholm: Skolöverstyrelsen, 1970), p. 64.

structure of the Swedish school system supported this conservative approach to education.[41]

Integral to the Social Democratic party's postwar program was the overhaul of this educational system. In 1950 the Riksdag took the first step by approving a decision which in principle called for scrapping the folkskola-realskola structure and substituting for it a Comprehensive School, which all students were to attend. Moreover, attendance was to be mandatory for nine years instead of the earlier seven. During the 1950s a number of experiments were carried out in nearly half of the municipalities with primary and secondary schools in Sweden in preparation for the final decision which came in 1962. Once that decision was taken an additional ten years were allotted for all schools to make the transition. By 1972 the reform had been completed.[42]

The importance of these structural changes should not be underestimated. Educational opportunities have expanded dramatically. Thus in 1971 85 percent of the Comprehensive School's graduating classes continued their education at the Gymnasieskolan (earlier called gymnasium, now reformed so as to include not only academic but also vocational tracks).[43] Later 25 percent of the Comprehensive School's graduating classes will begin some form of university education.[44]

In addition to opening opportunities, the reforms of the 1960s have had the effect of lowering the "snob appeal" or status of advanced education. Name changes (folkskola-realskola to grundskola, gymnasium to gymnasieskola) are only one expression of a conscious attempt to reduce the elite nature of the educational system. The traditional final exam (studentexamen) and white student hats for gymnasium graduates have been eliminated. With nearly three-quarters of the Comprehensive School population continuing on to the Gymnasieskolan, it is no longer special, and all who go there are formally regarded as equals.

The heart of the reforms, however, has been curricular. In this connection the Comprehensive School is particularly worthy of study, for it is at this level that most attention has been focused. While the school still aims

[41] See pp. 130–132.

[42] Sixten Marklund, *The Role of the Teacher in Educational Innovation in Sweden*, report to the directorate for scientific affairs for the project, "The Changing Role of the Teacher and Its Implications," Paris, France, December 6, 1971 (Paris: Organization for Economic Co-Operation and Development, 1971), p. 7.

[43] Sweden, Skolöverstyrelsen, "Slutrapport från utredningsgruppen för samverkan i skolan—SISK," Maj Bosson-Nordbö, chairman (Stockholm: Skolöverstyrelsen, 1971), p. 3 (mimeographed).

[44] Sweden, Utbildningsdepartementet, *Val av utbildning och yrke*, Statens Offentliga Utredningar 1971:61 (Stockholm: Utbildningsdepartementet, 1971), p. 129.

to develop competence in the students, a second goal, a social one, has
been added. The curriculum guide of the Comprehensive School is illuminating on this point.

> All activity at a school takes place within a social environment. In this
> environment, it should be possible for a feeling of belonging to emerge
> which will play a major role in the development of social attitudes and
> habits. As at all other places of work, the results of activities in a school
> are dependent on a continuous interplay between different people. Even
> if the forms of this interplay vary, the will to cooperate, the attitude, is
> always a factor that in high degree characterises the environment. Co-
> operation in this sense must be developed into a form of relationship, a
> working method, which stamps activities at the school, and the relation-
> ships between different individuals and groups. A good collective sense
> and a will to cooperate are necessary conditions for the school's success-
> ful fulfillment of its task.[45]

A thoroughgoing democratization of the decision-making process within the school is one way to realize this goal:

> The school shall be democratic. Essentially, this is a matter of educat-
> ing pupils in shared influence and co-responsibility. An individual share
> of influence in the society of the school must be accompanied by the
> corresponding individual sense of co-responsibility. This the school must
> inculcate in its pupils. A necessary condition for an increased involve-
> ment and participation by pupils and adults in shaping the school as a
> place of work, is that each and everyone takes a real part in fashioning
> his own working environment. The forms for influence and co-responsibil-
> ity on the part of pupils in choosing teaching matter, materials, working
> methods, rules, etc. must be adapted to the age and potential of the
> pupils concerned. This can present difficulties, but these must not be
> allowed to overshadow the fact that it is an undeniably positive develop-
> ment for increased attention to be paid to joint influence and responsibil-
> ity, and that they should be exercised in all situations where it is in any
> way possible.[46]

Competence is not to be neglected, but it is a competence of a particular
sort: "In a democratic society, which is concerned to assign increasing
responsibility to the individual, the schooling of the intellect is of major
importance. The qualities particularly to be borne in mind are clarity
and order of thought. *The ability to think critically and independently*,
the ability to resist tendentious influence, and to analyse, compare, and
summarize."[47] Rather than retention of facts, the process of learning has

---

[45] Sweden, Skolöverstyrelsen, "Curriculum for the Comprehensive School Lgr
69: General Section" (Stockholm: Skolöverstyrelsen, 1969), p. 21 (mimeographed).
[46] *Ibid.*, p. 22.
[47] *Ibid.*, p. 8. My emphasis.

become the important end goal. As one high-ranking official of the National Board of Education put it, "Our emphasis is not so much on what you learn, but rather on how you learn."[48] In this regard the traditional method of lectures is to be supplemented and modified by a number of other pedagogical techniques, such as team teaching and group projects.[49]

All of these changes obviously have important consequences for the role of the teacher. As a report from the research division of the National Board of Education put it, "Teachers must accept [among others] the following principles":

> (a) The students learn by active involvement and not by just being taught by a teacher. As long as a teacher imagines that he is "dealing out" knowledge to his students, he is missing the importance of varying learning situations.
>
> (b) The teacher is not simply a communicator of knowledge and information, but is also partly responsible for his pupils' mental growth and development of attitudes. This involves more behavioral variables in the teacher role than teachers have been accustomed to earlier.[50]

Such fundamental changes in goal orientation have produced a strong reaction among Comprehensive School teachers. While opinion studies show a nearly universal formal acceptance of the goals and methods of the curriculum, teachers express considerable doubt as to whether they can realize such intentions in practice. For example, a survey done in the fall of 1970 showed that 50 percent of the teachers of the first six grades and 75 percent of the teachers of grades seven through nine of the Comprehensive School held negative views regarding their ability to achieve the social goals of the Comprehensive School. For the goal of competence, the figures (again negative) were 33 and 50 percent, respectively.[51] The responses regarding different teaching methods, shown in Table 1, show a definite preference for the classroom lecture method.

The effect of such attitudes has been to retard the speed of change. To cite from one study of Comprehensive Schools in Gothenburg (carried out in 1968):

> Another result which ought to be mentioned in this connection concerns the form and methods of teaching. In the general instructions of the curriculum guide it is viewed as extremely important that the pupils

48 Interview.
49 Skolöverstyrelsen, "Curriculum," pp. 12, 51–53.
50 Marklund, *Role of the Teacher*, p. 5.
51 Lars-Erik Klason, *Insyn i skolan: lärarnas bedömning av arbetssituationen och deras syn på graden av måluppfyllelse i grundskolan* (Stockholm: Sveriges Lärarförbund, 1971), p. 30.

TABLE I

VIEWS REGARDING PRECONDITIONS FOR USING DIFFERENT METHODS OF TEACHING PROSCRIBED BY CURRICULUM GUIDE BY ACADEMIC LEVEL IN COMPREHENSIVE SCHOOL

	Class Instruction				Group Instruction				Indiv. Instruction			
	Academic Level				Academic Level				Academic Level			
Pre-conditions	Low	Mid.	High	Total	Low	Mid.	High	Total	Low	Mid.	High	Total
Very good	21	33	20	25	10	13	5	10	10	9	1	7
Good	46	50	60	51	47	35	33	39	32	28	25	29
Not esp. good	27	14	16	20	35	49	57	45	46	46	61	50
Poor	7	3	5	5	9	4	5	6	12	18	13	15

SOURCE: Lars-Erik Klason, *Insyn i skolan: lärarnas bedömning av arbetssituationen och deras syn på graden av måluppfyllelse i grundskolan* (Stockholm: Sveriges Lärarförbund, 1971), Table 15, p. 31.

participate actively in the learning process. . . . [In] this material we find the teachers appearing as lecturers and the pupils as receivers of information. The information, moreover, does not appear particularly stimulating as it is often of a factual nature on a simple level. . . .

It is also important to note the small amount of attention given to noncognitive goals. This is remarkable given the curriculum guide's emphasis on "placing the pupil in the center," on the "development of personality," etc.[52]

Nevertheless considerable evidence can be marshaled to suggest that important changes in line with the intentions of the curriculum guide have in fact come about.

Revolution from Above

In 1958 a group of teachers at the Communal Girls School (Kommunala Flickskolan) in Malmö devised a program for introducing students to contemporary problems, using an interdisciplinary approach combining history, political science, religion, and geography, among other subjects. Class times were juggled to suit the topic under investigation, study trips were planned, guest speakers were invited, and individual projects were assigned. The consequences of this innovative approach had implications far beyond those originally intended, as the teachers soon began to see,[53]

[52] Gunlög Bredänge and Torbjörn Odhagen, "Didaktisk processanalys: ett studium av lärar- och elevbeteenden i klassrumssituationen," DPA-projektet 2, Report No. 28 (Gothenburg: Lärarhögskolan, 1972), pp. 129–130 (mimeographed).
[53] Bertil Gran, ed., "Försök med växlande gruppstorlek och lagundervisning

for Lloyd Trump's writings had come to Sweden. It is difficult to over-stress the impact of Trump's approach on Sweden's educational system, for his philosophy has formed the very cornerstone of its recent wide-sweeping reforms.

At the risk of oversimplification, Trump's method can be summarized as including the following major elements: team teaching, flexible group-ing of students (including large group instruction, small group discussion, and independent study), and flexible instruction periods.[54] Team teaching maximizes teacher competence, flexible grouping of students provides a balance between the communication of information (large group instruc-tion) and the discovery of relationships (independent study), and flexible instruction periods create the framework under which this learning process can function. Small wonder that the teachers in Malmö immediately grasped the significance of what they had been trying out on an ad hoc basis and of what Trump was proposing for a national system of education.

Even more important, officials at the National Board of Education realized the implications of Trump's ideas for what they were seeking to achieve in Sweden. Critical powers could be sharpened through group dis-cussion and independent study; an understanding of the relationships among disciplines could be fostered through team teaching; and social training and responsibility could be developed through group work, stu-dent initiated projects, and greater student participation in curriculum planning.

An official Trump committee formed within the National Board of Education and took the initiative of launching additional experiments in cooperation with teachers in the Malmö region. When the committee was dissolved in 1964, its operations were transferred to a new group within the board responsible for curricular experiments. Another administrative reorganization led to placing Trump experiments under the project "Flexi-ble Grouping and Team Teaching" (Växlande Gruppstorlek och Lagun-dervisning or VGL).[55] In the Malmö region alone ten different projects using the Trump approach have been underway since 1964.[56]

Drawing on the results of the Malmö program the National Board of Education in 1967 began a new set of experiments in the city of Skellefteå,

---

(VGL) i Malmö," "Pedagogiska-psykologiska problem," Report No. 98 (Malmö: Lärarhögskolan, 1969), p. 5 (mimeographed).

[54] *Ibid.*, pp. 9–11.

[55] *Ibid.*, p. 6.

[56] Marklund, *Role of the Teacher*, p. 19.

in the north of Sweden. The major distinguishing mark of the Skellefteå plan was its comprehensiveness which in turn reflected a further development of thought among reform-minded teachers in the field and officials at the National Board of Education.

Reform adherents had come to view the educational system as a complex of working units including (1) the school, (2) the class, (3) the lesson, (4) the subject, (5) the teacher, and (6) the textbook.[57] Rather than allowing them to continue to function as solid blocks, reformers argued that they all must undergo modification and be recombined in new ways, if real change was to be achieved.

In Skellefteå this was done through flexible pupil grouping, team teaching, extended teaching periods, independent study, and student participation in curricular matters. The traditional system of progression from one grade to the next was replaced by a system of hours for subject areas, allowing students to work at their own pace in each individual area. Even the structure of the school was affected, with rooms and corridors being divided and subdivided to suit the new demands of individual and group work.[58]

The Malmö and Skellefteå experiments have been evaluated by a battery of different tests.[59] The results have consistently proved heartening to reformers.[60] Student and teacher attitudes toward group work, individual projects, and team teaching have been overwhelmingly positive. Students believe that their study habits have improved, they have learned how to gather information, and they can evaluate and report their findings. Most important for our purposes here, students in these experiments show a much greater willingness to express their views and take stands than do students in the control groups tested.[61] These students feel competent to do in their own way what others previously have told them to do. New

[57] *Ibid.*, p. 24.

[58] Ruth Andersson, "Pedagogiskt-organisatoriskt försöks- och utvecklingsarbete," in *Flexibel Skola*, ed. Göte Rudvall, Pedagogisk Orientering och Debatt, No. 39 (Malmö: Utbildningsförlaget, 1972), pp. 39–40. See also Anders Nilsson, "PEDO-Projektet: ett kombinationsförsök," *Skolhus*, Nos. 4–5 (1972), pp. 6–9.

[59] The difficulties inherent in evaluating such projects are enormous, if for no other reason than they are continually being modified in light of experience. Standardized tests between experimental and control groups, attitude studies of teachers and students, participant observation, taping of classroom activity, and interviews are those methods most often used. No single evaluation has relied on the use of any single method.

[60] Gran, "Försök," p. 83. See also Andersson, "Pedagogiskt-organisatoriskt arbete," pp. 36–40. Both also discuss less favorable results of the experiments.

[61] *Ibid.*

authority patterns have created new confidence which is expressing itself in a new style of participation.

By no means have experiments been limited to Malmö and Skellefteå. Not only are they underway in a large number of other cities in Sweden,[62] but also it is official policy to initiate a new experiment each year in a new city.[63] In this regard it is important to note that such new ventures normally include a number of schools at different levels in the same city. These efforts, of course, do not include the many individual modifications in the approach to education which have sprung up in response to the new curriculum guide.[64] Nor do these include the numerous reforms aimed at democratizing the decision-making process of the school and modifying teacher training programs.[65]

[62] Andersson, "Pedagogiskt-organisatoriskt arbete," pp. 35–44, gives a good introduction to the long list of such experiments underway.

[63] Interview.

[64] Interview.

[65] Regarding democratization efforts, the activities of the study group on cooperation in the school (Samverkar i Skolan, or SISK) are important to note.

Created in 1968 within the National Board of Education, its charge was to review and develop means to encourage all forms of cooperation within the school, including all-school forms of government (samarbetsnämnd).

After an extensive survey of existing forms of all-school government showed the organs to be virtually useless, the committee set about designing a new format. Student representation was expanded, the scope of questions to be discussed broadened, the number of meetings increased. Most important, the authority of the body was changed. Instead of mere advisory functions, it received a modified veto right on certain questions and the power to decide other issues. During a two-year period experiments were carried out in 309 different schools to test the organization in practice. A series of six follow-up survey and interview studies were done with forty-five randomly chosen participating schools. Assessments by students, teachers, and administrators consistently proved positive. This in turn led the committee to draw up a final set of recommendations to serve as guidelines for the activities of all such organs. These were published in 1971. Skolöverstyrelsen, "Slutrapport—SISK," pp. 2–3, 19, 27–38, 47–50.

Teacher training programs have undergone reforms on two levels. Schools producing new teachers now offer training in techniques which will help realize the goals of the new curriculum guide. Many teacher training institutes either have their own laboratory schools which apply the new curriculum guide or feed their students into classes in the local school system where such experiments are underway. Moreover, many of the follow-up studies of experimental efforts are carried out at the teacher training institutes, thus encouraging continual debate within the school on the value of different pedagogical tools.

For teachers already in the field, the National Board of Education has a program every summer which can accommodate 6,000 teachers for retraining, both in pedagogical tools and in specific subject matter. See Anna Lena Wik-Thorsell, "Över 6000 lärare på kurser får nya undervisningsideer," *Svenska Dagbladet*, August 10, 1972, p. 4.

In short, through an alliance between a progressive minority of teachers and the officials at the National Board of Education, a vast network of experimentation leading to results in line with the intentions of the curriculum guide has been undertaken. Every year its impact is deepened.

The change in authority patterns in the school is potentially of major social significance. To go from a system in which students are the passive recipients of "the truth" from their unquestioned teacher to one in which they not only play a major role in designing and executing their own learning program but even take part in the actual running of the school, is nothing short of revolutionary. And given the ultimate aim of the curriculum guide, that the school should "play a major role in the development of social attitudes and habits," there should result some far-reaching effect on how Swedish citizens view their role in the political system. The predominance of the young and well-educated in the ad hoc group activities discussed above might well be attributed in part to this new style of participation fostered in the schools.

Broadening the Reforms

While the attention of reformers on curricular matters has primarily been focused on the Comprehensive School, other levels of education have not been neglected. The Gymnasieskolan's curriculum guide received its first major modification in 1965 and was revised again in 1971. The universities have felt the pressure for reform since the late 1960s. The changes in textbooks, teacher training programs, and school buildings referred to above as well as the experiments in democratic decision-making apply with equal force to these levels of education.

One of the most striking examples of change has come about in the field of adult education. The expansion here has been enormous. In October, 1968, 37,000 participants were registered in various courses sponsored by municipal governments. By 1969 the figures had jumped to 62,000 and by 1970 to 87,000.[66] A similar explosion occurred within the adult educational organizations affiliated with interest groups: 87,060 study circles included 882,771 participants during the academic year 1961 to 1962; by 1970 to 1971 the figures were 205,504 and 1,679,704, respectively.[67]

What is important for our purposes are the pedagogical methods used

[66] LOVUX, *Vuxenutbildning: fakta-erfarenheter-förslag* (Stockholm: Prisma, 1971), pp. 14–15.

[67] Tore Hultqvist, "Folkbildningens uppgifter och villkor" (unpublished paper, Educational Division of TCO, 1972), p. 4 (mimeographed). A person can participate in several courses.

in adult education. For municipal schools, a curriculum guide mirroring that of the Comprehensive School and Gymnasieskola is used. For the study circles, no such guide is needed, for the essence of their activity is group discussion complemented by individual projects.

Reforms have also been extended downward. Thus the curriculum guides for the preschool level also emphasize group activity and social development.[68] Moreover, as will be shown below, the preschool level is presently undergoing rapid expansion, in part to aid mothers who wish to enter the labor market. Given the scope and depth of the reform efforts underway in Swedish education today, it is not surprising that old perceptions as to how one is to participate are giving way to new. That is, after all, the intention of the reforms.

Changes in the Family Structure: Daddy on the Ropes

Just as reforms in the educational system have affected the patterns of authority in that socializing agent, changes in the relationships between man and wife and between parents and children have affected the once dominant position of the father in the family structure.[69] As with changes in education, changes in the family also now serve to encourage the development of individuals (the wife, the children) who see themselves as competent to make judgments about their own well-being and who have had the experience of participating in decision-making—two developments which conflict with the passive style of participation which prevails in the established group structure outside the family.

The trends in Sweden are clear. To quote two Swedish authorities on the subject, Professor Edmund Dahlström and Dr. Rita Liljeström:

> A greater equality between the sexes is apparent in rearing and training practices, in the patterns of association among children and young people in organizations, at workplaces and in the social exchange of adults. Certain of the traditional sex role norms have been expunged. The view of the woman as the weaker sex and the one requiring protection has been greatly modified.
> Relations between husband and wife have changed. Sociologists have

[68] See especially Sweden, Socialdepartementet, *Förskolan Del 1*, Statens Offentliga Utredningar 1972:26 (Stockholm: Socialdepartementet, 1972), pp. 93–232. See also, Tjänstemännens Centralorganisation, *Familj och samhälle* (Stockholm: Prisma, 1970), pp. 60–67.

[69] For a brief historical perspective on the position of the father in the family, see "The Status of Women in Sweden: Report to the United Nations 1968," in *The Changing Roles of Men and Women*, ed. Edmund Dahlström (Boston: Beacon Press, 1967), pp. 222–229.

described the development as one from institutionalized patriarchalism to equality and companionship. Marriage, according to the currently dominant view, is a product of mutual affection and assent; both partners are thought to play an active role in preliminary love play, with both having an equal right to satisfaction and happiness in marriage. Both have the right to consideration and influence in resolving family crises and both are assumed to play an active role in the marriage within the framework of a pattern of role differentiation, which is today in the process of transformation.[70]

Jonsson and Kälvesten's study of 222 boys from the Stockholm area supports these conclusions. In an effort to present a picture of the "average" Stockholm boy, his personality, and his home, the authors probed, among other things, authority relationships within the family.

First they asked the parents—each one separately—whose word was decisive if there were divided opinions on some matter. The usual answer was that both decided equally. Only 21 percent of the men and 26 percent of the women saw the male as predominant. For the boys 43 percent, in response to the question, "At home decisions are made by . . . ," said "daddy," 18 percent, "mommy," and 39 percent, "both equally." The complete figures are listed in Table 2.

TABLE 2
DOMINANCE OF FATHER, MOTHER, OR EQUALITY ACCORDING TO BOYS, FATHERS, AND MOTHERS, BY PERCENT

	Father Dominant	Mother Dominant	Equality
According to boys	43	18	39
According to fathers	21	12	66
According to mothers	26	18	56

SOURCE: Gustav Jonsson and Anna-Lisa Kälvesten, *222 Stockholmspojkar* (Stockholm: Almqvist & Wiksell, 1964), p. 488.

The same question was approached from a different perspective, with the statement, "Within the family the father's work must be followed as an unbroken rule." The majority of both men and women rejected the assertion, often with the laugh, "That was a long time ago." Only a minority (21 percent of the women and 18 percent of the men) agreed.[71]

The woman's greater role in family decision-making can be seen in part as a result of her strengthened economic position. As Table 3 shows, dur-

[70] Edmund Dahlström and Rita Liljeström, "Family and Married Women at Work," in Dahlström, ed., *Changing Roles*, pp. 40–41.
[71] Gustav Jonsson and Anna-Lisa Kälvesten, *222 Stockholmspojkar* (Stockholm: Almqvist & Wiksell, 1964), p. 312.

TABLE 3
NUMBER AND PERCENT OF EMPLOYED WOMEN BETWEEN AGES OF 15–64 FROM
1930 TO 1965 ACCORDING TO CENSUS DATA

	Single	Married	Married Earlier	*Total*
1930				
Number of employed	558,658	89,908	54,854	703,420
Percent	59.1	9.0	47.4	34.1
1940				
Number of employed	542,566	123,543	59,362	725,471
Percent	61.0	10.1	43.6	32.3
1945				
Number of employed	495,957	149,857	66,341	712,155
Percent	63.9	10.9	46.6	31.0
1950				
Number of employed	473,176	233,090	81,194	787,460
Percent	68.1	15.6	52.3	33.6
1960				
Number of employed	418,906	422,556	100,740	942,202
Percent	61.3	26.3	57.4	38.2
1965				
Number of employed	408,431	611,325	111,623	1,131,379
Percent	58.6	36.7	59.3	44.3

SOURCE: Sweden, Socialdepartementet, *Familjestöd*, Statens Offentliga Utredningar 1972:34 (Stockholm: Socialdepartementet, 1972), Table 33, p. 97.

ing the postwar years there has been a dramatic increase in the number of working wives.[72] An outside income means less financial dependency on a husband, a contribution to the entire family's economic well-being, and thus a lever for gaining greater influence over important decisions affecting the family.

During the last few years the figures have continued to rise, especially for mothers with younger children. For example during the fourth quarter of 1971, 47 percent of those mothers whose youngest child was under three were working, 59 percent of those with a child between the ages of three and six, 69 percent with a child between seven and ten, and 75 percent with a child between eleven and sixteen.[73] To assist the women with children under seven (the age at which Swedish children begin public school) the government has undertaken an ambitious program of expand-

[72] "Working-wives" in the table means working at least half-time. Sweden, Socialdepartementet, *Familjestöd*, Statens Offentliga Utredningar 1972:34 (Stockholm: Socialdepartementet, 1972), pp. 97–98.

[73] *Ibid.*, p. 200.

ing preschool centers, as Table 4 indicates. The tax system, too, has been altered to encourage married women to enter the labor market, the Riksdag passing in 1970 legislation which enables married couples to file separate tax returns if they so wish.

TABLE 4
NUMBER OF PLACES AVAILABLE IN KINDERGARTENS (INCLUDING FAMILY DAY NURSERIES) AND NURSERY SCHOOLS IN SWEDEN, 1960–1972

Year	Kindergarten	Nursery School	*Total*
1960	16,700	38,400	55,100
1965	22,900	52,100	75,000
1966	25,500	56,400	81,900
1967	37,000	60,000	97,000
1968	44,300	71,200	115,500
1969	57,700	75,700	133,400
1970	71,500	86,000	157,500
1971	91,000	95,000	186,000
1972[a]	107,000	105,000	212,000

[a] Estimated.
SOURCE: Socialdepartementet, *Familjestöd*, Table 7, p. 70.

Thus, labor market policies, family policies, and tax policies have all been used to assist, even lure, married women back into the job market. As a result, figures suggest that today's typical Swedish family no longer consists of a married man with a wife who stays at home, but rather of a family where both partners normally work and where the mother makes one or more breaks in her career when the children come. Of course this in no sense means that equality between the sexes has been achieved, for it is still the woman who in the overwhelming number of cases must interrupt her career. Women tend to be confined to certain jobs, for the most part in the health care and service sectors—in effect an extension of housewifely duties in the home. Promotion is hard to come by, and even when men and women have identical positions, the woman often receives less pay.[74] "Nevertheless," to quote from the findings of an important Royal Commission on methods of family support, "it is likely that the increase in employment among married women has contributed to a more even distribution of tasks within the home and in general to a changed view of the traditional roles of men and women."[75]

Child-rearing patterns and the position of children within the family authority structure have also changed. It is commonplace now in Sweden

[74] See the articles in Dahlström, ed., *Changing Roles*.
[75] Socialdepartementet, *Familjestöd*, p. 201.

to talk about a "child-friendly (barnvänlig) atmosphere," which implies greater tolerance by adults of children's individuality and childlike behavior patterns. Young people in general are not so strictly controlled as before.[76] Increasingly the Swedish family is moving in a democratic direction: parents take an open view of their children's questions and opinions, and children are allowed to participate in family decisions. Studies from the United States show that children from such environments are less likely to change their behavior as a result of commands from others, a fact which augers ill for deference as it traditionally has functioned in Sweden.[77]

As in the case of the school system, these changes in family authority patterns affect virtually everyone in Sweden and the effects can be expected to be long lasting. If, as I maintain, these changes are at least in part responsible for the increased level of citizen participation in Sweden, this new activism cannot be expected to diminish in the near future. It may have a certain ebb and flow, but the general trend is clear: Sven Svensson is going to insist more and more on expressing his individual opinion, and if no established group will represent his view, he will help create another one which will.

Elite Response and the Challenge of the Future

The rise of ad hoc group action should not be overemphasized, for in fact, as earlier chapters have demonstrated, Sweden is still a country characterized by bargaining among well-organized groups and parties in a highly centralized political system. However, in the future, these ad hoc group activities may increasingly come to effect the Swedish political system.

For interest groups such as TCO, which seek a calm, depoliticized atmosphere in order to maximize cohesion and thereby influence, such developments suggest potentially greater difficulty in realizing policy goals in issue areas affected by ad hoc group action.

But more than the effectiveness of a single interest group may be at stake. As new patterns of authority emphasizing active participation increasingly replace the old passive form of deference toward expertise, the central problem facing all established interest groups and parties becomes how to maintain organizational effectiveness while allowing greater membership participation.

As deference toward expertise steadily yields to a self-confident desire for active participation in the decision-making process, confrontations be-

[76] Tjänstemännens Centralorganisation, *Familj*, p. 43.
[77] *Ibid.*, p. 47.

come increasingly likely. If they are to meet the present challenge, parties and groups might well begin to systematically think through which issues might be suitable for genuine local decision-making and which can effectively be dealt with only by the top leadership. Such a conscious effort to decentralize would in fact necessitate recognition of the desire and competency of "Sven Svensson" to decide policy issues.

Such changes would eliminate one of the major sources (one which otherwise will continue to grow) of ad hoc group action, namely, the individual's sense of hopelessness about having any real voice in established group life. As we know from attitude studies, those who are able to participate in decisions develop a higher effectiveness for the system, be it a group, party, or political system, than those who do not.[78] This is true despite the fact that conflict over issues can often develop. For although in some extreme cases a splinter faction can be prepared to leave the organization over a difference on a particular question, the support among those remaining is still likely to be greater when the remaining consensus has been built on discussion rather than demands for deferential obedience. Of course such cohesion will never be as solid as that which rested on an accepted passivity, but the days of such deference are now on the wane.

To date (1972), however, there are few signs that elites within parties and groups are responding in any meaningful fashion to membership demands for increased participation.

1. EXPLOIT

One response to the desire for greater participation has been exploitive in nature. When I use the word exploit, I mean that these groups officially support the notion of greater participation, while they in fact pursue policies which reduce citizen involvement. The Center party's program in the field of environmental pollution control provides a good example of this response.

The Center party has been a consistent champion of decentralized decision-making, insisting that more people should participate in the policy-making process. In the field of environmental protection, for example, its program is replete with such passages as:

> People who are affected by society's decisions must have increased opportunities to influence them. This is best done if power is decentralized in society. Environmental politics is a part of the policy of solidarity the

[78] Gabriel Almond and Sidney Verba, *The Civic Culture* (Princeton: Princeton University Press, 1962), pp. 253–257.

Center Party pursues both in Sweden and abroad. All people have the right to economic and social security in an environment which has been shaped as much as possible to the individual's wants and needs.[79]

Certain planning tasks now at the national level must be transferred to regional units. Planning with a local emphasis should remain at the municipal level.[80]

In the spring of 1972 interviews were carried out with leading Center party officials responsible for the party's environmental program. Very quickly it became clear that while the party officially supported a decentralization of the decision-making system, its elected representatives supported a system of centralized decision-making in the field of environmental pollution control. For example, when on one occasion two Center party members of Parliament were asked directly which environmental issues were most suitable for local determination, they could not think of one! The conclusion was stated succinctly by one of the two MPs when she said: "I think this [discussion] has been very good for us. We don't often connect our decentralization thoughts with our environmental thoughts. And I don't think it comes as a big surprise if we say that concerning the environment, concerning pollution, we don't believe in decentralization."[81]

2. DISCREDIT

"If you can't ignore them, smear them," seems to be an appropriate description of a second kind of reaction. Most of the time such attacks criticize the single-issue orientation and temporary nature of the ad hoc groups. Prime Minister Olof Palme, in a speech held in the summer of 1971, remarked:

> It would be wrong to denegrate such groups; they can point up shortcomings. They can stimulate people, make them active. They are well-suited to draw attention.

> But their strength is also their weakness. Their lack of long-term goals, their inability to look at the entire picture, as well as their temporary nature, lead them to pass quickly from the scene. Those who suggest that these groups can replace our popular movements (folkrörelser) are being tremendously pretentious. That would lead to anarchy, power for the strong and danger for the weak and downtrodden.[82]

[79] Centerpartiet, *Vår Miljö* (Västerås: Centerpartiet, 1969), p. 5.
[80] *Ibid.*, p. 9.
[81] Interview.
[82] Socialdemokraterna, *Demokrati: rådslag om kommunal demokrati och parti-demokrati* (Stockholm: Tiden, 1971), p. 11.

Sten Andersson, the Social Democratic party secretary, took an even harsher view in the fall of 1971:

> These [groups] cannot possibly achieve a well-rounded view of a problem or balance different interests. Moreover, they have abstained from precisely the problem which is most difficult for politicians, namely consideration of how reforms are to be financed. In so doing they avoid the necessity of balancing one need against another. In other words—such people must belong to parties, for it is within parties that such balancing takes place.[83]

The chairman of the National Tenants Association, Erik Svensson, was totally negative in his assessment of the ad hoc urban renewal groups in his speech before the association's 1972 congress:

> In discussions about urban renewal, voices are heard now—they sound as though they are coming from the grave—to the effect that everything old is precious. Their only wish seems to be to block necessary changes.

> They remind me of the landlords who forty years ago tried to keep the NTA from installing bathrooms in their apartments on the grounds that the working class had neither the means nor the desire for such modern conveniences.[84]

When confronted with ad hoc group opposition on a particular issue, the Social Democrats in particular have been quick to assert that the group represents only a small number of the privileged and that their arguments should thus be dismissed. This has been their argument particularly in the field of environmental policy.[85]

Finally, established organizations have also gone on the offensive. In the fall of 1971 the Social Democrats and the LO launched a major PR campaign to improve the sagging image of organizational functionaries. (It has become commonplace in recent years to refer to such representatives as the "pampar"—the big wigs—which neither the LO nor the party felt did much to foster respect for the decisions of these functionaries.) Speeches were held, much press and TV coverage sought (and given) to praise the hard-working organizational representative.

3. ADVISORY COUNCILS

Far and away the most prevalent response by interest groups and parties has been the creation of an "advisory council." The Social Democrats

---

[83] *Ibid.*

[84] "Angrepp på villaräntorna: hård kritik mot byalagen," *Dagens Nyheter*, May 24, 1972.

[85] See, for example, the treatment by the Minister of Agriculture of the ad hoc group, Rädda Brofjorden, in the case of Brofjorden. Svensson, *Fallet Brofjorden*, pp. 27–28.

have their "Rådslag" meetings, the Liberal party its "Samråd" meetings, the LO its advisory groups, the cooperative movement its "Konsument-kongress," the tenants association its local advisory organs, and so on. A great deal of horn-tooting has accompanied the creation of these organs —all oriented toward demonstrating that organizations are indeed capable of meeting the challenge of greater participation.

All of these bodies share several important characteristics. They are in fact new channels of information and contact. But their basic function is to advise. To greater or lesser degrees (mostly greater), they are not a part but rather an appendage of the decision-making structure of the organization. The leadership determines the questions to be discussed by the advisory group and usually the possible alternative solutions. The role of the participants thus is to react, to indicate preferences, in short, to act as sounding boards—once again the old form of basically passive participation.

Such a strategy is not surprising, for organizational elites could be expected to make small concessions in order to retain power. And in so doing they are still trying to maintain organizational effectiveness as they define the term.

The reaction, too, has not been surprising. Many who participate, often for the first time in group life, leave feeling they have somehow had an influence over policy. Others, a minority, leave feeling frustrated over their inability to do anything except make recommendations, often in response to questions which had obvious answers. The power to decide what to do with the recommendations and when to do it still remains in the hands of the leadership at the top.[86]

[86] Let me give three examples of how these advisory organs operate in practice. The examples are taken from the cooperative movement's "Konsumentkongress," the Social Democratic party's "Rådslag" activity and the Liberal party's "Samråd."

The cooperative movement has undergone considerable centralization. Effective decisions over a number of issues seemingly appropriate for local influence are now made at higher levels. Product assortment, for example, is centrally programmed. The size of each store puts it in a certain class which is automatically given a certain specified assortment of goods. Thus each co-op store of the same size, no matter where in Sweden it is located, has precisely the same assortment.

If a co-op member wishes to make his views known on any given issue, he must act through the decision-making centers within the organization—local district meetings, the association meeting, the congress. But it is not such activity the leadership has sought to encourage, for little attention has been given to activating local districts. Most districts for example meet only once a year and then only for half an hour. Interview.

The leadership decided instead to convene every fourth year a "consumers' congress," which will supplement the two decision-making congresses held each year and will be purely advisory in nature. The first one met in the fall of 1971.

4. DECENTRALIZE

A fourth and last response to demands for increased participation is to truly decentralize. Changes in the school system and the work environment have been such that decision-making authority over some issues has been decentralized to smaller groups within the school and the firm. As

---

The central leadership made careful preparations for this first consumers' congress. Study groups were organized, materials distributed, and motions solicited. The result was over 5,000 motions. The overwhelming number of these tended to be relatively specific requests or questions, for example about local assortments, special products, or new items—but they did indicate how much interest existed about local issues and also how little members knew about ways to achieve change within the movement.

The leadership of the cooperative movement established its control over the direction of the congress at an early stage. A special committee of functionaries from the co-op's central office made up a summary of the motions, complete with background information, questions for discussion, and possible resolutions. This material, plus the complete set of motions, was sent to every representative prior to the congress. Once the congress was underway, experts from the central office sat on every committee which was to prepare resolutions for congress discussions. "En kongress med många engagerade," *Kooperatören*, 10b, p. 8.

This close guidance from above came under sharp attack during the final session of the congress. A number of representatives claimed that the intent of many motions had been lost in the summary, that the experts all too frequently had steered the committee discussion, and that the leadership's preliminary resolutions too often had been accepted as final. *Ibid.*, pp. 57, 59–60.

One group of dissidents went so far as to present a motion detailing these criticisms and recommending that in the future attention be focused instead on activating membership interest in local decision-making bodies: "[It is recommended] . . . that co-op's first Consumer Congress be its last and that instead efforts to activate consumer interest be made at local level organs which have the power of decision." *Ibid.*, p. 57.

The majority of representatives, however, were satisfied. For them, the *feeling* of influence was gratifying (although how long the feeling of influence will suffice remains to be seen). Representative J. V. Lindgren spoke for this group when he said, "We who have come from far away have appreciated this opportunity to meet the experts and to give our opinions on questions; an opportunity which we have not had before." *Ibid.*, p. 58. Shortly after his speech the dissidents' motion was rejected.

At the conclusion of the congress, the executive director of the organization, Harry Hjalmarson, promised that the leadership would seriously examine the resolutions passed by the Congress, a clear indication of the purely advisory nature of the entire proceedings. *Ibid.*, p. 62.

The Social Democratic party's energetic efforts to involve its supporters in policy-making has taken a similar path: channeling increased desire to participate into new purely advisory bodies. One of the architects of the "Rådslag" concept succinctly stated its central purpose: "The leadership [of the Party] in these activities must make sure that it gets the advice *it needs* on the questions *it is interested in*." Interview (my emphasis). To this end it is the executive board of the party which decides the subjects to be discussed, the specific questions to be answered, and the time limit for returning replies. *Ibid.*

"Rådslag" activity has been organized along slightly different lines from the

I have discussed efforts to democratize the school system earlier in this chapter, I will examine here only the interesting and provocative proposals for the field of environment in the workplace put forward by a study group within TCO.[87]

The question of greater membership participation always involves the question of influence—how much and over what kinds of questions. TCO's study group presented in May, 1971, a systematic analysis of the possible kinds of influence workers could expect to achieve. Moreover, models for influence were related to different questions.[88]

Thus, for example, three different kinds of influence were discussed: participation in decisions, consultations, and information. In the first case participation could take the form of negotiations; equal representation in committees which would seek unanimous decisions, or failing that, majority decisions or negotiations; and smaller groups of employees with decision-making authority. In the second case, consultation, it was stipulated that consultations were to be sought before decisions were made.

---

cooperative movement's congresses, however. Rather than holding one big central meeting, the Social Democratic party forms groups throughout the country to discuss suggested questions, the answers to which are then sent in to the party's central headquarters. (It is important to note that the direction may well be toward a congress type of meeting as the 1971 "Rådslag" suggests. *Ibid.*) Participation in these groups has been greater, on the average between 20,000 to 30,000 for each "Rådslag" in contrast to the 13,000 who participated in study groups prior to the "consumers' congress." And the number of meetings held has also been greater, an average of one a year since 1965.

Criticism, however, has run along similar lines. An evaluation report made in 1969 for the party's internal use warned that the all too obvious efforts by the leadership to elicit the answers they wanted to hear was creating a credibility gap regarding their intentions with "Rådslag" activities. [For example, one question cited in this report asked, "Is it right that wage earners and consumers use the public sector to increase their ability to influence societal change?" Bo Elmgren and Inga-Lena Nau, "Skapande Dialog: Utkast" (Stockholm: Socialdemokratiska partiet, 1969), pp. 23–24. (Mimeographed).]

The Liberal party (Folkpartiet) has also instituted a series of advisory discussions on different policy issues (called "Samråd"). As with the "consumers' congress" and the "Rådslag," "Samråd" activities are a means, according to one important member of the party's headquarters, "to make it easier for members to channel their views to the decision-makers." Interview. The power to decide policy, however, still remains at the top.

[87] For specific examples of experiments underway, see Christopher W. Wheeler, "The Decline of Deference in Sweden: The Tension between Participation and Effectiveness in Organized Group Life in Sweden," in Thomas J. Anton., ed., "Myth and the Politics of Change in Modern Sweden" (unpublished manuscript). I also elaborate on the strategies discussed earlier.

[88] TCO's Kommittè för Samarbetsfrågor på Arbetsplatsen (SAMKO), *Demokratisering av arbetslivet* (Stockholm: Tjänstemännens Centralorganisation, 1971), pp. 6–19.

(That the study group needed to be so specific on this point says a lot about the way advisory bodies work in Sweden!) Finally, some questions seemed appropriate for information only.

The degrees of influence were coupled both to the form of decision-making within the firm as well as to the kind of question. Thus the goal was to ensure that all three kinds of employee influence penetrated the major levels of decision-making in any firm: the top level (the executive board or supervisory body), the middle range (departments or sections), and the lowest level (the individual employee or small groups of employees). In general, policy questions were assumed to belong to the top level, program decisions to the middle level, and questions of detail to the lowest level.

The major questions in the firm were: work environment, economy, wage and employment conditions, marketing, organization, personnel administration, and production. Thus, for example, regarding questions of work environment, the executive board might decide how much money to allocate, and a joint committee of employee and employer representatives might decide priorities based on information gathered from smaller groups of employees. The advantage of a systematic analysis of this kind was that it served to shift the emphasis away from a general debate over whether or not to increase employee influence at all, to a specific discussion of how to do it on a particular question. Moreover, as the study group discovered in the process of its work, the number of questions suitable for negotiations could be considerably increased.[89]

Second, such an analysis helped to clarify priorities. Thus TCO could point to questions which definitely ought to be negotiated and others which were more appropriate for consultations and information. Thus, for example, in TCO's model personnel administration and work environment questions were all considered to be of such fundamental importance that employee influence through negotiations had to be accepted as basic. In contrast, questions of economy (such as storage policies or assessments of general economic trends) could be the subject for consultations and information.

Finally, this systematic analysis provided TCO with the opportunity to launch a new concept in Swedish labor market tactics: the veto principle. Some issues decided in a joint committee, for example, might be judged so important to one or the other of the parties that a veto right (temporary or permanent) would be justified. The discovery of a dangerous environ-

[89] Interview.

mental hazard was one type of issue in which employees might refuse to execute tasks until the condition was changed.

The joker in the deck as far as proposals for increased participation through decentralization in the firm are concerned is that the major organizations avidly supporting such changes are in fact supporting decentralization as long as it affects their major opponents, and not their own organizations. Thus neither TCO nor the LO have taken up for serious discussion the logical implications for their own internal authority structures of greater autonomy for groups of employees in the firm: namely, a decentralization of the right to strike, which now can only be decided at the national trade union federation level or higher. Worst yet, both organizations have only considered discussing decentralization in terms of the single issue of environment. No attempt has been made to ask what other issues might better be handled by the locals than by the national union headquarters. As it is the internal system of decision-making within the firm which has been the object of demands for change, it is not surprising to learn of employer resistance.

Of course decentralization of decision-making authority within groups and parties would have important consequences for Swedish political life. For such a strategy to be effective, more policy issues would have to be determined by county council and municipal officials with the result that localities would have to be given greater freedom within the framework of general legislation to implement programs. Greater experimentation at the local level might also create greater inequalities in program results, although careful monitering by the state could keep such developments to a minimum.[90] Such decentralization would affect the political system in yet another way as the prevailing pattern of all-party coalition government would probably have to give way to a parliamentary majority system at the county council and municipal levels.[91] As for the political culture, the Swedes, who shun face-to-face contacts and conflict situations, would certainly have to learn to tolerate a little more noise in their political life. But then a vital democracy is never quiet, and Sweden has been quiet for a long time.

[90] The National Board of Education, for example, applies this policy with its experiments.

[91] Support for a change-over is quite high, judging from the results of the Social Democratic party's "Rådslag" returns on the issue. Nearly 75 percent supported some form of a parliamentary majority government at the communal level, Socialdemokratiska partiet, "Kongressrapport från arbetsgruppen för partidemokrati" (Stockholm: Socialdemokratiska partiet, 1972), p. 12 (mimeographed).

The issue of the 1970s from the point of view of organizational life in Sweden may well focus on whether group leaders can strike a new balance between membership participation and group effectiveness or whether events will pass them by.

From a comparative perspective, Sweden's dilemma is common to other advanced industrial democracies as well, where both the rational and nonrational grounds for compliance have been weakening. In summarizing the results of his coauthors as well as his own research, Samuel Beer notes that, "the connection between burdens and benefits has been obscured by the inherently complex and technical modes of action by the modern polity . . . (which) makes it hard for the individual to connect burden and benefit, to see the immediate sacrifice as a necessary cost of the ultimate outcome." [92]

> Characteristic processes of modernization are also eroding the nonrational grounds. The most interesting change is what appears indubitably to be a decline of class as a factor shaping political behavior. In Britain, the country in which class has been outstandingly important, the behavioral indexes of this decline are striking. In Germany there are indications, such as the growing independence of voters, that suggest a similar trend. In France . . . class is of little significance as a basis of party allegiance. The reasons for this decline inhere in modernization and can be found generally in advanced countries. Affluence, bureaucratization, and corporatist representation all play their familiar parts. Moreover, the rational, pragmatic, calculating spirit undermines not only sentiments of deference and noblesse oblige but also old solidarities of class identification. [93]

The result has been a politics of fragmentation which rejects the corporatistic structures of economic planning and management. Its emphasis is on ad hoc voluntary associations, rather than class-based parties. Participation in decision-making becomes almost as important as the content and effect of the decisions themselves. [94] In the Swedish case, it is such a variant of "radicalism" (in Beer's sense of the term) which in one form or another may make its mark on Swedish society—for better and for worse.

[92] Samuel H. Beer, "Modern Political Development," in *Patterns of Government: The Major Political Systems of Europe*, eds. Samuel H. Beer and Adam B. Ulam (3rd ed.; New York: Random House, 1973), p. 112.

[93] *Ibid.*, p. 113.

[94] *Ibid.*, p. 114.

Index